"Mr. Taxpayer versus
Mr. Tax Spender"

"Mr. Taxpayer versus Mr. Tax Spender"

Taxpayers' Associations, Pocketbook Politics, and the Law during the Great Depression

---

LINDA UPHAM-BORNSTEIN

TEMPLE UNIVERSITY PRESS
Philadelphia • Rome • Tokyo

TEMPLE UNIVERSITY PRESS
Philadelphia, Pennsylvania 19122
tupress.temple.edu

Copyright © 2023 by Temple University—Of The Commonwealth System
    of Higher Education
All rights reserved
Published 2023

Cataloging information is available from the Library of Congress.

978-1-4399-2373-3 (cloth)
978-1-4399-2374-0 (paper)
978-1-4399-2375-7 (ebook)

♾ The paper used in this publication meets the requirements of the
American National Standard for Information Sciences—Permanence
of Paper for Printed Library Materials, ANSI Z39.48-1992

Printed in the United States of America

9 8 7 6 5 4 3 2 1

*For my spouse, Peter,
and my mother, Betty.*

Contents

Acknowledgments		ix
	Introduction	1
1	The Emergence of Taxpayers' Associations in the Nineteenth Century: Self-Interest and Civic Duty	17
2	The Tax Revolt, 1930–1941: The "Taxpayers Are Rising" and "Want to Pay Less for Government"	30
3	Taxpayers' Associations' Legislative and Education Programs: The Pursuit of "Constructive Economy"	54
4	The Populist Politics of Taxpayers' Groups: "*Vox Populi, Vox Dei*"	81
5	The Specter of Tax Strikes: "Shutting Off the Money"	106
6	Taxpayers' Litigation in the Great Depression: Protecting the Taxpayers' "Hard Earned Money"	123
	Conclusion	146
	Notes	165
	Selected Bibliography	193
	Index	201

Acknowledgments

This book has its genesis in the basement of my husband's law office in northern New Hampshire in the late 1990s. While perusing decades-old files and law books, I found bound copies of *The Coos Guardian* from 1934, of which attorney Arthur J. Bergeron, my spouse's senior law partner, had been the editor. The issues of *The Coos Guardian* provided contemporaneous accounts of the efforts of Arthur and the local taxpayers' association to effectuate economic and political change in the community, the region, and ultimately the state. This story is the case study in Chapter 4, and it spurred me to investigate whether this manifestation of organized taxpayer activity was unique to northern New Hampshire or part of a broader movement during the Great Depression. In the ensuing years I identified a plethora of rich, untapped primary sources that documented the emergence of a nationwide taxpayers' association movement in the 1930s and that form the basis of this book.

On this journey I have incurred countless debts from institutions and individuals. In the early years, assistance was provided by the professors and staff in the History Department at the University of New Hampshire, who were always available to answer my questions, offer encouragement, and critique my arguments. I am indebted to many colleagues, past and present, for their advice and support, including Jeffrey Bolster and William J. Harris of the University of New Hampshire and Daniel Ernst from Georgetown Law School. Professor Harris's knowledge of taxpayers' associations in the Reconstruction South reshaped my analysis of that period. He also taught me that a simple and direct approach is more effective than a complex and convoluted analysis. Most significant, and the most difficult to express, is my deep appreciation for the encouragement and critiques provided by my friend and colleague Lucy Salyer of the University of New Hampshire. She was there from my first tentative steps in graduate school, encouraging me to reach outside the proverbial box and break new historical ground. Professor Salyer's keen insights provoked me to consider a significant change of direction in my research and inspired me to pursue this book on taxpayers' activity. I greatly appreciated her continued guidance, encouragement, and friendship throughout this process.

As I moved on in my career, new colleagues joined my efforts to move my research forward. Those at Plymouth State University include Thaddeus Guldbrandsen, Marcia Schmidt Blaine, John Krueckeberg, and, most especially, Rebecca Noel. I am very grateful for their support and willingness to listen and advise during those times when I was stuck. It was Thaddeus Guldbrandsen who suggested that I attend the Organization of American Historians' conference, where I submitted my book proposal to Temple University Press senior editor Aaron Javsicas. Throughout the process from proposal to publication, Aaron has been supportive and encouraging.

The University of New Hampshire History Department also graciously provided generous financial assistance by, first, awarding me the Rutman Family Graduate Fellowship and, the following year, the Doctoral Fellowship. For work on the Berlin Taxpayers' Association and the Berlin Farmer-Labor Party, I was awarded the Wilcox prize for best graduate research paper. Many of my travel expenses were also defrayed by the History Department's Gunst-Wilcox Fund.

Research for the monograph took me to a number of libraries and archives, whose staff I thank for their assistance. Trips to the manuscript collections at Tamiment Library at New York University, the National Archives and Records Administration, the Rare Book and Manuscript Library at Columbia University, the New York Public Library, and University of California, Los Angeles, provided a wealth of information. The New Hampshire Supreme Court librarian Mary Searles graciously located Arthur Bergeron's 1934 Supreme Court brief in storage and retrieved out-of-date law books. I also thank the staff at the California Taxpayers Association for their assistance.

The research for Berlin, New Hampshire activities was gathered from several locations in New Hampshire. The staff at the New Hampshire Historical Society was always ready to assist in locating materials. In particular, I want to thank the society's former editor Donna-Belle Garvin for her editorial skills and enthusiasm regarding the article on the Berlin story. I also received assistance from the staff at Berlin City Hall and the Northern Forest Heritage Park, and from James Wagner, former vice president of Fraser Pulp and Paper in Berlin. Residents of Berlin, New Hampshire, have a passion for preserving their story; to them I owe much and applaud their dedication to the local community.

Early versions of my research were presented at several conferences. The Law and Society Association invited me to participate in their Graduate Student Workshop, and I presented papers at both its annual meeting and regional meetings. I also presented papers at annual meetings of the Organization of American Historians and the American Society for Legal History.

My family warrants special recognition for their patience and their belief in me. My parents always worked hard and expected me to do the same. They instilled in me the values and determination I needed to achieve this goal. My children, Alison and Alexander, were always ready to cheer me on, especially on those dreary days when writer's block impeded my progress. Their telephone calls, IMs, emails, pictures, and cartoons brought smiles after long, fruitless days. None of this, however, would have been possible without the love and support of my best friend and husband, Peter, to whom I dedicate this work. He sacrificed his own time to make this happen for me. No one knows better what was involved in the long journey researching and writing this book. He was there by my side every day, willing to engage in a discussion of taxpayers' actions, explain various aspects of the law, edit each paragraph, and hold my hand when I wanted to give up. I am eternally grateful that he is in my life.

"Mr. Taxpayer versus Mr. Tax Spender"

Introduction

In November 1933, perhaps the bleakest year of the Great Depression, journalist Hal Steed of Atlanta, Georgia, published in the *Saturday Evening Post* a two-part article, "Adventures of a Tax Leaguer," in which he related his experiences in the taxpayers' association movement that was sweeping the United States. Steed, the longtime real estate editor of the *Atlanta Constitution*, described the financial squeeze in which middle-class property taxpayers had found themselves, observing that

> until January, 1932 when I became a civic uplifter, I was just another property owner, paying my steadily mounting tax bill without protest. As early as 1928 I had felt a suspicious calm in the business atmosphere. The banks began to tighten up; mortgagees refused to renew their loans at the old figures. In 1929, when I paid my taxes, I found myself with only a small surplus. In 1930 and 1931, my rentals, thanks to bankrupt tenants, were not enough to pay my taxes. Meanwhile, my assessments were being raised. Taxes, for the first time in my life, became a problem.[1]

Because nearly all other real estate owners were in the same predicament, the local real estate board decided to call a meeting of property owners to discuss the subject of taxes. When Steed arrived at the meeting, he immediately "sensed a different attitude. I was conscious of a certain determination born of desperation." Attendees were frustrated because they had reduced expenses in their own business operations during the past few years in order to remain financially viable, but, in contrast, city and county governments had expanded their staffs and run deficits. The taxpayers decided to form a "Taxpayers League whose members could speak a language at the polls that the politicians would understand."[2]

The tax leaguers adopted a platform "calling for efficient government and lower taxes."[3] By April 1932, the Taxpayers' League of Atlanta and Fulton County had more than three thousand members.[4] The group pursued a variety of tactics and programs but was largely unsuccessful with traditional political activity at the polls. The members discussed the possibility of a tax strike, in which property owners would refuse to pay their property taxes, but did not call for one. The taxpayers' league had its greatest success through what Steed described as a conciliatory approach, in which the organization examined the operations of city and county governments and then pressed local officials for operational and fiscal reforms. Steed expressed satisfaction that "through conferences, agreements, and persuasion, we came into 1933 with a city tax reduction of $3,000,000 and an additional one from the county of $750,000." In Steed's view, such reforms and relief were attainable "when good citizens get together."[5]

Steed's antitax agitation, the "determination born of desperation" that he sensed, and the resulting political efforts of Atlanta taxpayers were hardly isolated phenomena at the time. On the contrary, they were representative of a groundswell of populist taxpayer political activity in the United States in the 1930s. The proliferation of local taxpayers' associations during these years was dramatic and unprecedented. As late as 1927, one examination of taxpayers' groups identified just forty-three local and state taxpayers' leagues.[6] Only six years later, Edward M. Barrows, a frequent contributor to the *National Municipal Review*, wrote that the

> multiplication of these local taxpayers' associations from scores into thousands in the last few years is a fact well known to most students of American civic trends. . . . A study of such sources as are available and authentic indicates that there are not less than three thousand and probably not more than four thousand such local groups now in action, and that their number is rapidly increasing.[7]

In August 1932, Howard P. Jones, the secretary of the National Municipal League's Committee on County Government and later editor of the *National Municipal Review*, warned that "there has gone sweeping across the country like a prairie fire an irresistible demand that the cost of local government be reduced, no matter how that reduction be accomplished." Jones went on to estimate that "county taxpayers' organizations were being formed this spring at the rate of one a day throughout the nation—a fact all the more remarkable when it is realized that these were relatively spontaneous."[8] Milwaukee mayor Daniel W. Hoan, who sardonically characterized taxpayers' associations as "'cut the cost of government' leagues," rued the fact that "taxpayers' leagues have sprung up or grown strong all across the country during the present depression."[9] In the late 1930s, the Tax Policy League conducted a survey in an effort to create a national register of taxpayers' associations and found 1,142 state and local ones.[10] Although precise figures are somewhat elusive, clearly the number of taxpayers' organizations and their memberships grew exponentially between 1930 and 1934.

Taxpayer group growth abated somewhat in the last half of the decade, in part because New Deal policies and spending helped to shore up the finances of many taxpayers and of state and local governments. Moreover, while this taxpayers' association movement was not approaching a saturation point, taxpayers had already established so many organizations that there simply was less room and opportunity for further growth. Although the rate at which taxpayers' leagues proliferated slowed after 1934, taxpayers continued to form new taxpayers' groups, attract new members, and engage in a wide range of tax-resistance activities beyond the end of the decade. Organized taxpayer activity was still sufficiently intense and widespread in the three years before the attack on Pearl Harbor that it garnered the attention of journalists at *Forbes* and *American Magazine*.[11] Historian David Beito has suggested that, "measured in numbers of organizations, the tax revolt of the 1970s and 1980s looks puny by comparison."[12]

This surge in organized taxpayer activity was a direct consequence of, and a response to, the economic crisis of the Great Depression and the expansion of the size and scope of government. As Hal Steed candidly acknowledged, the fiscal crunch caused him and other American taxpayers to think for the first time about the burden of taxes. In a similar vein, in 1933, political scientist Thomas H. Reed observed that "it has been said that the depression made us tax conscious."[13] Steed likewise noted that it "was only when business let down" that the average taxpayer began to question the cost of government and that "it is only in periods of stress that reform is born and thrives. It would have been impossible to organize a Taxpayers League back in 1926."[14] The concurrence of a rise in taxpayers' assessments and a decline in their rental income, farm income, and real wages impelled them to action. Although the taxpayers' organization movement drew on a long-standing American tradition of opposition to taxation and big government, it was the cratering economy that catalyzed and provoked widespread organized taxpayer opposition.[15]

This taxpayers' association movement was a local and state phenomenon, and the taxpayers' groups exhibited little concern with the structures and operations of the federal government, or with federal spending, debt, or taxes.[16] Their focus was on making local and state government more efficient and less expensive and with lightening their state and local tax burdens. The local and state taxes that taxpayers' leagues targeted included various business taxes, gift and inheritance taxes, and taxes on tangible and intangible personal property, but the taxes to which tax resisters devoted most of their time, energy, and resources were taxes on real property.[17] One reason for this emphasis is that a substantial number of taxpayers who participated in organized tax resistance in these years owned real estate. Homeowners, farmers, owners of apartment buildings and commercial rental properties, and business owners comprised the memberships of these groups. Moreover, because real property taxes were due and payable in large (quarterly, semiannual, or annual) installments, they were far more visible and burdensome to owners of real estate than the small sums they paid for sales, tobacco, liquor (after Prohibition ended), and other relatively hidden taxes that were collected at the time of transaction. Last but certainly not least, the real estate levy was the tax that posed the greatest threat to taxpayers: delinquent real estate taxes could at some point result in the loss of the property through tax sale, eviction, and financial ruin.

Although this subnational tax revolt was directed at local and state governments and taxes, it played out in the context of the federal government's response to the economic crisis, and the tax revolt was connected to that response in important ways. During the last two years of the Hoover administration, the president, Congress, and federal officials took a number of actions that exacerbated the downward economic spiral and the "tax problem" of more and more taxpayers and thereby fueled the tax revolt. Among these were the Federal Reserve's decision to reduce the money supply in October 1931, which further dried up business and consumer credit; Hoover's obsession with the federal deficit and balanced budgets and his consequent insistence on "retrenchment in government" and resistance to federal spending for public works, unemployment relief, or farm relief; and the Revenue Act of 1932, which codified huge federal tax increases on a broad swath of taxpayers.[18] New Deal initiatives, in contrast, helped to moderate tax resistance by providing various forms of assistance to distressed taxpayers, especially the agricultural, housing, direct relief, work relief, and public works programs. The intensity and nationwide scope of the tax revolt in turn constrained New Dealers as they fashioned federal tax policy, and it also influenced welfare, agricultural, and social security policy.[19] The taxpayers' association was one of the many local political and civic institutions through which the forces of localism molded New Deal policy.

In the story of the taxpayers' association movement of the 1930s, one sees the interplay of the dynamics of American politics and American law. With respect to the former, the Great Depression transformed organized taxpayer activity in the United States, and taxpayers' associations in turn transformed the nature and forms of state and local governments. Paying taxes has never been popular, and the citizen's tax burden has been a flash point for political rebellion from the American Revolution to the more recent "Tea Party" revolt. During the Great Depression, however, organized taxpayer protest reached a new level of sophistication and organization, with lasting implications as the taxpayers' association became a permanent and potent institution in American politics. Just as many working-class Americans found a new voice in the New Deal labor organizations, middle-class Americans claimed that taxpayers had become the "forgotten Americans" and mobilized to make the political and legal systems more responsive to their concerns. The result was that organized taxpayers revolutionized how state and local governments were organized, operated, and financed. Many of the features of modern public administration that we take for granted today, and for which proponents of the business model of government had advocated since at least 1900, only gained widespread acceptance and adoption when taxpayers' organizations applied concerted pressure on public officials in the 1930s to take such measures. Such reforms included the county and city manager plans of government, transparent and scientific systems of budgeting and accounting, consolidation of government departments and functions, and the increasing professionalization of public administration generally. The emergence of taxpayers' associations in the Great Depression as significant subnational institutions in American politics and the considerable degree to which they shaped state and local government institutions and policies are crucial developments in American political history.

The taxpayers' association movement of the Great Depression is also a key episode in American political history because it brought into sharp focus the conflicting interests and perspectives of taxpayers and tax spenders (whom I define as state and local government units and officials who expend public funds, and those individuals who support greater state and local government spending). The tension between taxpayers and tax spenders was especially palpable during the Great Depression. As a consequence of the huge increase in the number of taxpayers' associations in the early 1930s, Americans debated, with perhaps more urgency and effect than ever before or since, the critical questions regarding the role and funding of government that the nation has confronted for nearly 250 years. How should the operation of federal, state, and local governments be funded? What revenue-raising mechanisms are most fair and equitable? What is the appropriate level of government services, and what services should government provide? How big or small should government be?

In 1933, the National Municipal League attempted to convey the essence of this political-civic contest in the *Mr. Taxpayer versus Mr. Taxspender* radio play, in which Columbia University professor Luther Gulick spoke for the taxpayer and Milwaukee mayor Daniel Hoan spoke on behalf of public officials. Hoan synthesized the problem as follows:

> There is . . . a universal demand . . . for greater and greater governmental functioning and activity. There is, on the other hand, a widespread insistence that government shall reduce its expenses. The average citizen will furnish a list of activities a yard long of what he believes the government should undertake and the same person will bewail the fact that government should raise and spend the money necessary to meet his demands.[20]

Hoan's synthesis encapsulates the same incongruity that political historian Julian Zelitzer observed in the context of federal taxation, the "awkward juxtaposition of an antipathy toward taxes with stronger demands for [government] services."[21] Such conflicts over whether and how to spend tax dollars and between expanded-government sentiment and small-government sentiment have figured prominently in the nation's political history, appearing in contexts ranging from the clashes between Federalists and Jeffersonians on the role of the federal government to the debates about the proper congressional response to the credit-market crisis in 2008.

Organized taxpayer activity opens up fruitful lines of inquiry in the field of what, in 2003, political scientist and historian Ira Katznelson termed the *new analytical political history*, which employs two methodological approaches: the new institutionalism and sociocultural political history. The new institutionalism focuses on the structures of government and how institutional forces inform and constrain political elites, political development, and public policy. It also examines the "political and voluntary institutions through which Americans gained their political standing, and mediating institutions that connected citizens to elected officials." Sociocultural political history takes a grassroots, bottom-up approach to the study of history and emphasizes nonelites, political activism at the local level, and the impact of local actors on state building and public policy at all levels of government. Evolving conceptions of citizenship and associationalism are also salient considerations in sociocultural political history.[22]

The taxpayers' association movement affords the political historian ample opportunity to employ both approaches, as Depression-era organized taxpayer activity embodies many of the driving forces and exhibits many of the features of American political culture with which the new political history is concerned. It is a subject in which historians may examine the importance of taxation in American politics, integrate fiscal constraint and opposition to taxes into their political history accounts, and contend with antistatism as exhibited in tax resistance. It highlights the taxpayers' league as a civic associational institution that mobilized like-minded citizens to oppose taxes, mediated between taxpayers and public officials, reorganized state and local government, and fashioned public policy regarding taxing, government spending, and public administration. Organized taxpayer activity in the 1930s also underscores the integral role of local institutions and of state and local government in American political development, to which, new political historians have argued, scholars have given short shrift. In addition, the taxpayers' association movement was an exceptionally spontaneous affair that offers a bottom-up perspective on political protest, state building, tax resistance, and other expressions of antistatism.[23]

Organized tax resistance in these years highlights the power and durability of the forces of localism in American politics. Much of the action in the taxpayers' association movement occurred at the local level. The majority of the achievements of taxpayers' groups concerned the operation, financing, and fiscal demands of counties and municipalities. New Dealers, who were in the process of implementing the largest expansion of central government authority in the nation's history, were mindful of and constrained by the grassroots tax revolt as they crafted tax and spending measures. The forces of localism not only survived the activist, top-down New Deal state but also shaped the content and execution of some New Deal programs and, in some instances, forced the New Deal state to yield to local interests and stakeholders.[24]

Organized taxpayer activity holds promise not just for scholars of American politics but also for the legal historian. The taxpayers' association movement has meaning for American legal history because it is a sphere of associational activity in which one may apply the perspectives of both the consensus school of thought, which emphasizes how citizens used and impacted the law and legal institutions, and the critical legal studies school, which stresses the flow of influence from the law and legal institutions to the wider society. This two-pronged interpretive strategy allows the legal historian to gain insights from each perspective, explore how and where the two intersect in collective tax resistance, and attempt to synthesize them.

During the Great Depression, ordinary citizens frequently used the law and legal institutions in order to achieve their objectives. Law occupied a central place in the taxpayers' association movement. Organized taxpayers brought taxpayers' lawsuits against local government officials to control government expenditures and lower taxes. Taxpayers' associations helped to persuade legislators to enact numerous constitutional and statutory tax limitation measures during the 1930s. In addition, their legislative programs and research activities convinced state and local legislative bodies throughout the United States to adopt a plethora of reforms relating to public administration and finance. The extent to which taxpayers' groups called on the law and the courts for assistance during the Great Depression reflects the extent to which, by that time, the American legal order was actuated by a "common instrumental belief" that people could use the law to control their environment to their ends.[25]

Conversely, Depression-era organized taxpayer activity evidences the profound influence of the law in the United States. The law and the legal institutions that taxpayers' organizations invoked remade the structures of state and local government across the nation, affected public policy concerning the fiscal and administrative systems of government, determined particular outcomes for government spending and revenue raising, defined taxpayer–tax spender disputes, and constrained the parties to those disputes. In these ways, the programs of taxpayers' leagues confirm the constitutive power of American law.[26]

The Depression-era tax revolt, then, is important both to the history of American politics and to the history of American law. For the political historian, the taxpayers' association movement represents the coming-of-age of a vital institution that reformed and restructured state and local governments. Taxpayers' organizations in the Great Depression illustrate the prominence of local institutions in American public life and what historian Thomas Sugrue calls the "persistence of localism" in American politics.[27] Organized taxpayer activity also provides a vehicle to debate larger questions about the funding, functions, and size of government and the citizens' role as "watchdogs." Disagreements about the amount of government spending and on what matters tax dollars should be spent have been recurring elements of taxpayer–tax spender engagement. The 2008–2009 recession and the 2020 coronavirus pandemic again brought this conversation to the front and center of American politics.

The taxpayers' organizations of the 1930s matter to legal history because the degree to which citizens relied on the law as an instrument of political, institutional, and public policy change to further their interests during these years was extraordinary. Time and again, taxpaying citizens successfully resorted to the law to refashion state and local governments and thereby appreciably shape their environment to their ends. Taxpayers' leagues functioned as conduits of legal influence through which the formative power of American law and legal institutions was channeled and disseminated throughout their communities and states. The taxpayers' association movement of the Great Depression reveals organized taxpayer activity as a sphere of civic life in which the law, conceptions of citizenship, pocketbook politics, political protest, and political reform intersect and stand out.

Notwithstanding its significance, organized taxpayer activity in the 1930s has received little attention from historians. Occasionally, one finds a passing reference to or a short discussion of taxpayers' associations in works on other subjects.[28] The only treatment of taxpayers' organizations in the United States is in David Beito's work on the 1930–1933 Chicago tax strike, but Beito's survey of taxpayers' leagues in this period is, historian Mark Leff notes, "regrettably brief."[29] In contrast, I undertake a more comprehensive investigation of organized taxpayer activity, examining the evolution of taxpayers' associations, their rapid proliferation in the early 1930s and the public discussions regarding this development, the tactics or tools that Depression-era taxpayers employed to advance their interests, how those tactics reflected broader impulses in the nation's history, the conceptual basis for taxpayers' claims, the accomplishments of taxpayers' organizations, and the legacy of the taxpayers' association movement. Looking at organized taxpayer activity both from a national perspective and in particular local contexts provides insights into its salient characteristics and how they played out in specific instances.

Depression-era taxpayers' organizations had four principal tools or weapons in their armory that they employed in their tax resistance efforts. The first and most common was what contemporary political scientists and public administration professionals termed "constructive economy" activities.[30] These consisted of research, public education, and legislative programs in which taxpayers worked together with public officials to promote economy and efficiency in government. Among other things, taxpayers' associations conducted investigations of local and state government operations and finances, made recommendations to public officials, educated the public, sponsored legislation that promoted good and efficient government, and opposed legislation that threatened the public treasury.[31] The collaborative efforts of the Taxpayers' League of Atlanta and Fulton County that Hal Steed described typified this strand of organized taxpayer activity. These constructive economy activities had been the traditional and chief functions of taxpayers' associations prior to the Great Depression, and they continued to predominate in the 1930s.

The crisis of the Great Depression, though, made taxpayers' organizations' programs more multidimensional and adversarial and gave them a sharper edge. This sharper edge took three forms: traditional political activity, tax strikes, and litigation. In the 1910s and 1920s, taxpayers' associations had largely eschewed traditional political action, especially of a partisan nature, but in the early 1930s they began both actively promoting their own candidates for state and local offices, with respectable electoral results, and applying political pressure to public officials to cut government spending. Taxpayers also brought about fundamental structural change at the ballot box by securing the passage in dozens of states of constitutional and statutory amendments limiting the amount of property taxes.[32] The most militant weapon in the taxpayers' association's arsenal was the tax strike, in which taxpayers refused to pay their property taxes unless and until certain demands, usually relating to budget cuts or other government cost-reduction measures, were met. Finally, taxpayers' organizations instituted taxpayers' lawsuits to control state and local government spending and to restrain unlawful acts of public officials. Organized taxpayers had utilized these aggressive tactics, particularly litigation, in the past, but after 1930 they did so more commonly and extensively. The taxpayers' association movement of the 1930s had something of a contrapuntal tenor to it, with cooperative efforts and energies comprising the major key and confrontational ones being the minor, but still important, key.

In examining these efforts, I connect collective tax resistance in the 1930s to the big picture of American history. Each of these four strategies manifests a broader impulse in the history of the United States. Depression-era tax resistance is noteworthy because powerful currents in the nation's historical development percolated to the surface with particular vigor in the taxpayers' association movement.

The constructive economy programs of taxpayers' leagues exhibited Progressivism's good government component. The Progressive model of good government consisted of certain key features: a merit-based civil service system, scientific and open systems of public finance, a functionally departmentalized administrative structure, strong executives and administrators, nonpartisanship, the professionalization of government, and the involvement of policy-generating experts to effectuate that transformation.[33] Beginning in the 1880s, good government Progressives undertook to design and implement structural reforms to state and local governments. Reformers made some progress in this regard in the following decades, but their efforts were directed mainly at large cities. During the Great Depression, however, taxpayers' associations pressed for organizational and operational improvements to state and local governments with considerable success. Organized taxpayers embraced with a vengeance Progressivism's impulse toward the professionalization and rationalization of government and thereby overhauled the structures of government at the municipal, county, and state levels nationwide.

Taxpayers' organizations' political efforts tapped into a long-standing tradition of populist politics in America. The United States had experienced episodes of populist agitation since its inception, from the Whiskey Rebellion in 1794 to Jacksonian populism in the early and mid-nineteenth century to the agrarian revolt in the 1870s and 1880s that culminated in the creation of the People's, or Populist, Party. The Great Depression brought about a resurgence of intense populist sentiment and spawned, among others, the political protest movements spearheaded by Huey Long, Francis Townsend, and Father Charles Coughlin.[34] It likewise impelled taxpayers to organize and engage in a grassroots politics of upheaval with a view toward reducing local and state taxes.

Tax-striking taxpayers in the 1930s were emulating the American labor movement. In the preceding six decades, workers in the United States had unionized in most sectors of the industrial economy and had demonstrated the effectiveness of collective action in industrial relations. During that period American labor engaged in hundreds of strikes. Its history with work stoppages both moderated the labor movement's goals and outlook and taught labor how the American legal order in general, and the injunction in particular, diminished the efficacy of the strike as a tool of industrial relations.[35] A number of Depression-era taxpayers' associations considered, and a few implemented, tax strikes. Organized taxpayers also came to appreciate the limitations that the law, the courts, and public opinion imposed on strikers.

Taxpayers' increased reliance on litigation during the Great Depression is grounded in two features of the American legal order that emerged in the previous century: the taxpayers' lawsuit and Americans' instrumental conception of the law. In the decades following the Civil War, courts in nearly every state came to recognize the right of taxpayers to bring lawsuits to restrain illegal or corrupt acts by local government officials and to force them to perform their duties. In those states where the courts did not afford taxpayers this right, the legislatures, responding to political pressure from taxpaying citizens, authorized such taxpayers' suits. The evolution of the taxpayers' suit, in turn, was but one of many developments that reflected nineteenth-century Americans' growing confidence in the law as an instrument of change with which they could "meet the challenges of [their] environment."[36] Depression-era taxpayers brought taxpayers' suits against local officials to challenge unlawful government spending, enforce good government reforms, and compel public officials' compliance with the law. These lawsuits influenced and often determined the conduct of municipal and county governments across the country regarding taxing, spending, and operations. Taxpayers' frequent use of litigation shows that they too generally espoused an instrumental view of the law and that they regarded the law and the courts as honest brokers in disputes between taxpayers and tax spenders.[37]

Although taxpayers' leagues were few and far between before the 1930s, taxpayers first began organizing in the Civil War era. Chapter 1 examines the origins of taxpayers' associations, the antecedents of Depression-era taxpayers' groups, the reasons taxpayers organized, and the role of Americans' conceptions of citizenship in early organized taxpayer activity. Taxpayers' organizations provided a forum in which taxpayers could associate and collectively assert and advance their rights as citizens to hold public officials accountable for how they raised and expended tax dollars and operated government. The overarching goal of most taxpayers' associations was to reduce taxes, though in many cases taxpayers also had a genuine interest in promoting the public's interest in good and efficient government. Sometimes, however, tax resistance under the guise of good citizenship was merely the means to other, ulterior ends. This was especially true in the Reconstruction South, where taxpayers used collective tax resistance in an effort to weaken government authority, "redeem" state governments from Republican control, reestablish the institutions of white supremacy, and nullify in practice (if not as a matter of law) the post–Civil War amendments to the United States Constitution. For nearly all taxpayers' leagues outside the South, however, lower taxes were the ends, not the means to other ends. In the seventy years before the 1929 stock market crash, taxpayers' groups experimented with various tax resistance strategies, including legislative and public education programs, tried-and-true techniques of applying political pressure to public officials, and litigation. By 1930, taxpayers' associations had at least a rough template for their antitax campaigns.

Chapter 2 provides an overview of the taxpayers' association movement. It explores the political and economic conditions that energized the tax revolt, the seriousness of the tax crisis, the remarkable proliferation and growth of taxpayers' groups in the 1930s in response to the tax crisis, the views of taxpayers and contemporary observers on this development, and the purposes and objectives of taxpayers' organizations. I identify the defining characteristics of organized tax resistance in these years: it was fundamentally an economic phenomenon that was mainly about the taxes themselves; it was a middle-class and largely white male undertaking; and it was a spontaneous, grassroots, local tax revolt. I then place the taxpayers' association movement in the wider context of the politics of the Depression at the national level during the Hoover administration and the New Deal era, focusing on those federal decisions, policies, and programs that most impacted, and were impacted by, the tax revolt. I show that influence flowed both ways between the New Deal and this local, indigenous tax revolt. I also assess organized taxpayer activity through the prism of the conservative strain of American politics and opposition to the New Deal. The chapter concludes with an examination of two recurrent themes in Depression-era tax resistance: how it manifests the interplay between rights and obligations in Americans' notions of citizenship, and how it embodies the contest between statism and antistatism and sheds light on Americans' attitudes toward the role of government and "big government."

In order to understand the tax revolt of the 1930s and its impact, it is essential to understand how taxpayers engaged in organized tax resistance. The next four chapters survey and assess the tools that taxpayers' associations used to reduce local and state taxes. The "four weapons in the Depression-era taxpayers' groups' arsenal" framework serves as an organizing principle in this manuscript. Chapters 3, 4, 5, and 6 each examines one of those weapons or strategies: constructive economy activities, political efforts, tax strikes, and litigation. These four chapters have a common structure: an opening vignette and introduction followed by a discussion of the historical impulse or development to which that strategy is connected, then an examination of how taxpayers' organizations across the United States employed that weapon, including a case study in which I focus on a specific taxpayers' group's execution of that strategy.

Taxpayers' leagues relied heavily on their constructive economy (education, research, and legislative) programs from the start of the tax revolt to 1941. Chapter 3 surveys the form and content of the programs of a wide array of taxpayers' groups in diverse regions, evaluates their effectiveness and their reception by those outside the taxpayers' association movement, and looks at how taxpayers' organizations drew on Progressivism's good government reform agenda. It also highlights what these constructive economy efforts had in common: their goal was to put in place structural and operational reforms in local and state government in order to improve the quality and reduce the cost of government; taxpayers' ability to do so was facilitated by close cooperation between large taxpayers' groups and small, local ones; and taxpayers relied heavily on the law and legal institutions to achieve their objectives. In most states and communities these constructive economy programs resulted in more efficient government and lower taxes. The programs of the California Taxpayers Association (CTA) are typical of the constructive economy activities of taxpayers' associations during the Great Depression, and I examine the CTA to illustrate how taxpayers carried out this strategy.

Taxpayers' organizations turned to political strategies in the 1930s as the tax crisis worsened. These included campaigning to elect officials sympathetic to their tax-reduction agendas, bringing political pressure to bear on public officials to cut expenses and taxes, and pressing for tax limits that capped the amount of property taxes that could be assessed. Chapter 4 looks at the many ways in which taxpayers executed these strategies; how the populist impulse energized and shaped these efforts; and their successes, failures, limitations, and consequences. The case study looks at how organized taxpayer activity in Berlin, New Hampshire, a city with a population of approximately twenty thousand in a heavily forested county north of the White Mountains near the Canadian border, led to the formation of the Berlin Farmer-Labor Party, a progressive, explicitly populist political party that achieved respectable results in the 1934 city election and controlled city government from 1935 to 1938.

The tax strike was the most radical, disruptive, and potentially destructive tool in the taxpayers' league's toolbox. It personified antistatism in the extreme, challenging the very authority of the state to make fiscal demands on its citizens. Drawing on the experiences of organized labor with work stoppages, organized taxpayers sometimes considered, sometimes threatened, and on occasion called for tax strikes when other tax relief avenues proved to be a dead end. In Chapter 5 I look at when, where, why, and how taxpayers' groups deployed the tax strike; the ensuing backlash from the business community, public officials, and good government experts; the methods these stakeholders employed to defeat tax strikes; and their significance. I zero in on the Chicago tax strike, which went on for almost two years and wreaked havoc on the city's finances.

The fourth and final weapon that taxpayers' groups wielded in the tax revolt—the taxpayers' lawsuit—is the subject of Chapter 6. Taxpayers had resorted to litigation against counties and municipalities in their quest for lower local taxes since the earliest days of organized taxpayer activity. By the turn of the twentieth century, most states recognized the right of taxpayers to bring lawsuits to enjoin illegal acts of local officials concerning spending decisions, incurring debt, and entering into contracts, among other things. In the 1930s, taxpayers made considerable use of the taxpayers' lawsuit for three purposes: to compel public officials either to take or refrain from taking some action, to require the return of funds improperly paid out of the public treasury, and to enforce municipal or county causes of action if officeholders unlawfully declined to do so. Taxpayers' groups used litigation as a means of enforcing their legislative programs where good government measures had been put in place, but public officials were ignoring or working around them. The taxpayers' associations' litigation programs reveal the significant degree to which taxpayers invoked the law and judicial processes to advance their interests as taxpaying citizens and, in turn, the powerful influence that the law and the American legal order had not only on the parties to these lawsuits but also on the communities affected by these court decisions. The taxpayers' association in Bell County in rural southeastern Kentucky instituted a number of taxpayers' suits in the execution of a concerted litigation strategy.

In the conclusion I assess the efficacy of the taxpayers' association movement and its importance. I survey how taxpayers' groups, the media, public officials, the business community, and experts in public administration evaluated the achievements and impacts of taxpayers' organizations. I conclude that taxpayers' associations largely succeeded in making state and local government more efficient and less expensive and in lightening their tax burdens. Not all aspects of organized taxpayer activity deserve a positive evaluation: tax strikes were dangerous and destructive, and tax limits adversely affected municipal credit and sometimes went too far in throttling the revenue streams of local and state governments. Even so, the overall impacts of collective tax resistance on state and local governments in the long term were constructive. In part, this was attributable to the fact that most taxpayers acted responsibly in weighing their interest in lower taxes against their duty as citizens to pay for the reasonable level of services that they expected government to provide. In the conclusion I also revisit the themes touched on earlier in the introduction: the durability of a powerful antistatist tradition in the United States, the perpetual conflict between big government and small government attitudes, the importance of subnational institutions and the tenacity of the forces of localism in American political life, the relevance of Americans' notions of citizenship to the taxpayers' association movement and the politics of taxation, the prominence of the law and legal institutions in Depression-era tax resistance, and the vital relationship between law and society in the United States. Next, I briefly survey the work of taxpayers' organizations since World War II. Finally, I compare and contrast the Depression-era tax revolt with modern tax resistance, from the tax revolts beginning in the 1970s that produced tax limitation measures such as Proposition 13 in California to the Tea Party movement, and look at the relationship between modern antitax movements and conservative antistatism of the New Deal era.

The sites of organized taxpayer activity that I investigate are geographically diverse and widespread because the tax revolt was itself geographically diverse and widespread. In 1930, large taxpayers' organizations, numbering at least twenty nationwide with some in every region, along with a smattering of local groups, were already actively advancing the interests of taxpayers. In the following decade, taxpayers formed not only several additional state taxpayers' associations (in Iowa, for example, in 1935) but also a plethora of local ones across the country: in large, midsize, and small cities; in counties; in urban and rural settings; and in large and small states. The taxpayers' groups I selected for in-depth analysis also reflect that geographical and organizational diversity and are highly representative of how taxpayers' leagues executed each of their four strategies. Additional considerations for the selection of these four stories of tax resistance were the wealth of previously untapped primary source material concerning the California, New Hampshire, and Kentucky taxpayers' associations and the fact that the Chicago tax strike, though familiar to scholars of the period, was by far the largest, longest, and most disruptive tax strike in the history of the United States.

Elements of political reform, populist politics, labor history, and legal history all played critical roles in organized taxpayer activity in the 1930s, but the taxpayer–tax spender dynamic was its overarching characteristic. The engagement, and often conflict, between taxpayers and tax spenders is one of the recurring themes in American political history. A tradition of tax resistance harks back to the nation's founding, and there is still a powerful antitax sentiment in the United States. Taxes and spending remain "at the white-hot centre of political debate" in the twenty-first century.[38] During the Great Depression, tax spenders faced a tax resistance campaign of unparalleled scope and intensity. In harnessing Americans' antipathy toward taxes, taxpayers' associations brought to bear "some of the most effective grass-roots political pressure during the Depression."[39]

1

The Emergence of Taxpayers' Associations in the Nineteenth Century

Self-Interest and Civic Duty

While taxpayers' associations came into their own and assumed a prominent role in American life in the 1930s, they did not then suddenly appear, fully developed and ready for battle, like Athena was said to have sprung from the head of Zeus, but trace back to the last half of the nineteenth century. Citizens' frustration with excessive or unequal taxes and with municipal graft and corruption was evidenced by the episodic formation of taxpayers' associations across the United States, starting in the 1850s. Although the organizations varied in purpose and makeup, most were established by taxpaying stakeholders as a tool to lighten their tax burdens by making local government more efficient, more accountable, and less costly. Organized taxpayers characterized themselves as good citizens acting in the public interest and their association's efforts, in the words of the San Jose, California, Taxpayers' League, "as being . . . in the interest of the taxpayers of the entire community, its object being to obtain an economical and business-like administration of the affairs of the city and county."[1] In some instances, however, considerations of class, race, and power motivated taxpayers to organize.[2]

As early as 1858, the *New York Herald* reported that taxpayers in assembly districts across New York City were forming "Citizens and Taxpayer Association[s]" and nominating candidates for alderman. One taxpayers' association proclaimed that its candidates had received support "from the best and most influential citizens . . . [and] they therefore . . . invite every voter who desires to elect honest and reliable men . . . to support the ticket."[3] In 1861, the *Herald* identified another taxpayers' organization in New York City, which urged citizens to "restore capacity and honesty in the administration of the municipal government," based on reports that Fernando Wood, the Democratic mayor and a Confederate sympathizer, had mishandled city funds and allowed "traitors" from the "rebellious States" to seize arms from the New York armory.[4] In California, rapid expansion and development of settlements fueled conflict between local officials and taxpayers' leagues in that state in the early 1860s.[5] Taxpayers continued to organize over the next six decades in response to local conditions and circumstances.

A combination of self-interest and civic duty gave rise to most nineteenth-century taxpayers' associations. The stated objective of taxpayers' groups was tax relief, but taxpayers' leagues also appealed to their members' and prospective members' better angels and sense of social responsibility. At a meeting of a taxpayers' organization in New York City during the Civil War to ratify the association's endorsement of a mayoral candidate, the chairman had urged citizens to "show themselves worthy of republican institutions" by supporting its efforts to elect officials who would clean up municipal government and make it honest, transparent, and efficient. In 1915, the Taxpayers' League of Wilkes-Barre, Pennsylvania, characterized its backers as "unselfish men," declared that its "chief purpose . . . is to equalize the burdens of taxation" by reducing the cost of government, and invited "all citizens interested in good government . . . to become members." Taxpayers' associations often framed their mission in terms of advancing the public interest. The Reading Taxpayers' League called on the public to join in the league's "efforts to secure an honest, faithful, and economic administration of public affairs." In Wisconsin, the Oneida County Taxpayers' Association vowed to advance "the doctrine of Municipal economy" and to teach "the public officials their rights, responsibilities and duties." The Taxpayers' League in San Jose, California, emphasized that it was a nonpartisan organization whose "purposes are to see that the government of the city and county is conducted along lines of economy, and in accordance with the laws" for the good of the community. Commitment to economy in government and the rule of law figured prominently in the worldview of most organized taxpayers. Taxpayers' associations tapped into not only the taxpayers' pecuniary interest but also their notions of public virtue and what it meant to be a solid citizen.[6] The former dynamic, however, predominated in this mix. Taxpayers' organizations were fundamentally interest groups mobilized to control the cost of government and reduce taxes and secondarily associations of individuals motivated by a "beneficent commitment to communal goals" and the public interest.[7]

Taxpayers' declarations of motive grounded in civic virtue must be evaluated critically, in some cases taken with a grain of salt and in some cases disregarded completely. In many instances organized taxpayers were indeed driven by a genuine desire to make local and state government more effective and efficient and to reduce their tax bills. In others, taxpayers' leagues employed the language of good citizenship to mask political, class, and racial motives and to lend them a facade of civic legitimacy. This was especially true of taxpayers' groups in the post–Civil War South, which hoped to engender support among Northerners for winding down Reconstruction and, therefore, did their best to hide their true objectives, which were inextricably intertwined with Southern Democrats' policy of Redemption, through which they sought to "redeem" their states from Northern Reconstruction and restore the antebellum political, legal, and social status quo. Sometimes self-interest and civic-mindedness came together to impel taxpayers to organize. Whatever their reasons, almost all taxpayers' organizations proclaimed they were acting in the public interest and for the benefit of all citizens. The importance of these declarations of motive rests not only in their sincerity or lack thereof but also in the fact that taxpayers' associations broadly considered it necessary, or at least useful, to anchor their claims in the realm of civic duty, clothe them in the language of citizenship, and act under the guise of the public good.

The connections between taxpayers' associations and citizenship are fundamental and vital. Citizenship, as historian Linda Kerber has asserted, "is basic to all other claims which individuals make on the state, or the state makes upon them." Citizenship is a complex and multifaceted concept. In general, it refers to the status or standing of members of a state with respect to the state. It denotes a mixture of obligations, privileges, and rights that stand in various relations to one another. Such "rights and obligations are reciprocal elements of citizenship" and, in that sense, are two sides of the same coin.[8] One of the obligations of citizenship is to pay taxes, but in the mid-nineteenth century taxpayers began to argue that this obligation gave rise to a corresponding right of citizens to hold public officials accountable for how they spent public funds. Since that time, organized taxpayer activity in the United States has been galvanized by that obligation and rooted in that right.

The development and expansion of the taxpaying citizen's right to hold public officials accountable is a hallmark of organized taxpayer activity in the United States. Such a right was not contemplated when the nation was created. When the colonists declared "no taxation without representation," they were merely asserting a general right to have their own elected representatives vote on taxes, not a specific right to oversee how those taxes were spent or to restrain particular expenditures by public officials. In the mid-nineteenth century, the latter right was still incipient. Around 1850, however, taxpaying citizens started to articulate and advance such a right through taxpayers' associations. For the next eighty years, they pressed and expanded that right, mainly through traditional political activity and through taxpayers' lawsuits against local government officials.

By the late 1920s, this aspect of citizenship in America was firmly established but by no means prominent or dominant. Collective action by taxpayers in general, and citizens' assertions of their right to government accountability in particular, remained occasional and sporadic. The economic crisis of the Great Depression precipitated the explosive growth of taxpayers' associations in almost every state. As a consequence, Americans nationwide intensively pursued, enforced, and expanded their right to hold public officials accountable for how they operated government and expended public funds through a broad array of organized taxpayer activities, including research, legislative, legal, and political efforts. The taxpayers' association movement of the 1930s played an indispensable part in the evolution of Americans' conception of citizenship from one based on obligations to one based on rights. It helped spawn a more distinctively "modern" notion of the taxpayer as citizen with the rights to insist that government officials be made to account for how they spent tax dollars and to check specific public expenditures, rights which from that time on were widely recognized and invoked.

Taxpayers' groups also exemplify another critical aspect of citizenship in the United States—the "daily use which [Americans] make of the right of association" that Alexis de Tocqueville had observed in 1830. Such organizations were symptomatic of the propensity and the tradition of "the citizen of the United States . . . to rely upon his own exertions in order to resist the evils and the difficulties of life." Tocqueville argued that liberty of association in America was a principal means by which its citizens engaged in self-help to promote their interests, to resist "the tyranny of the majority," to "prevent the despotism of faction or the arbitrary power" of the state, and otherwise to advance their political objectives.[9] This tradition of self-help explains in part the indigenous and spontaneous character of taxpayers' leagues. The scope of organized taxpayer activity in the United States confirmed Tocqueville's observations that Americans are "freely and constantly forming associations for the purpose of promoting some political principle" and that they also make use of public associations "in civil life, without reference to political objects."[10]

Freedom of association, however, was not only a right but also an obligation of citizenship. Historian Christopher Capozzola has contended that, throughout much of the nineteenth and early twentieth centuries, "being a good citizen meant fulfilling your political obligations and doing so through voluntary associations," and that Americans "preferred voluntary associations as forums for public discussion and the execution of political agendas" to the expansion of central government.[11] The freedom of association that Americans exercised by participating in taxpayers' groups implicated reciprocal components of citizenship in the United States, right and duty.

As the evolution of the taxpaying citizen's right to accountability suggests, the relationship and balance between rights and obligations in Americans' notions of citizenship have not been static. Capozzola has noted that "throughout American history, a citizenship of obligation has always coexisted with one of rights" but that "a rights-based vision of citizenship . . . play[ed] a [more] prominent role in twentieth-century America."[12] Some historians, such as Kerber and Capozzola, have focused on the obligations of citizenship. Others, like Meg Jacobs, have concentrated on the rights side of the citizenship coin. Jacobs has identified an economic aspect of citizenship that emerged during the twentieth century and was "based on participation in the mass consumer economy" and the right to consume. She argued that "in the twentieth century, as the economy and society became increasingly organized around a new national mass consumer market, the means to consume became important . . . as a marker of economic citizenship and full membership in the American polity." Taxpayers, in their status as taxpayers, do not consume goods, but they do pay for and consume government services. Consequently, the extent of their tax burden directly affects the extent to which they are able to "become full economic citizens" and enjoy the "promise of a better, richer life."[13] During the past century, organized taxpayers, like Americans generally, have embraced and advanced modern concepts of citizenship that emphasize the standing of all citizens to claim rights from the state and to have the state secure and enforce those rights.[14] Collective action by American taxpayers has, for the most part, been the product of a culture of citizenship emphasizing rights rather than obligations.

The precursors of Depression-era taxpayers' organizations were founded in the mid-Atlantic states, the Midwest, and New England in the 1860s and 1870s. In a number of cities in the North, taxpayers formed taxpayers' groups in order to confront the "reckless expenditure of the people's money."[15]

In the 1870s, Camden, New Jersey, and its neighbor Philadelphia, Pennsylvania, both had active taxpayers' leagues. In 1875, the Camden Taxpayers' League obtained an injunction to restrain the city treasurer from paying "certain bills allowed by Councils to the former and present supervisors of highways." The league promoted measures to "prevent future excessive rates of taxation," and its members "closely scrutiniz[ed] the expenditure of public funds." The next year it sought an injunction restraining the "city treasurer from paying the additional $3.00 per week to the clerk's messenger," arguing that the messenger's weekly salary had been improperly increased from $12 to $15 by the council.[16] In 1878, on the other side of the river in Philadelphia, citizens who were convinced that the present political parties were incapable of correcting "abuses" in local government formed a taxpayers' association in the Twenty-Seventh Ward in response to a tax increase. The *Philadelphia Inquirer* characterized this action as a "reform movement." Unlike many taxpayers' organizations that purported to be politically independent and nonpartisan, the Philadelphia group aligned itself with the Labor Party. In contrast, in Philadelphia's Eighth Ward a taxpayers' league called on voters, "irrespective of party, to elect none but good men . . . who have . . . at heart the interests of the people."[17]

There was a considerable amount of organized tax resistance in New York, where taxes were relatively high, during the Gilded Age. Taxpayers' associations in Hunters Point, Brooklyn, Long Island, Gravesend, and New Utrecht (a suburb of Brooklyn) utilized political pressure, injunctions, and lawsuits to address municipal mismanagement. In Hunters Point the Citizens' and Taxpayers' Association opposed the "collection of unequal and unjust taxes" and demanded equal property valuation and the economical administration of town affairs. In 1872, the Taxpayers Association of Newtown, Long Island, was formed to investigate "charges against the trustees and constables" and to reform municipal affairs because the "taxes were recklessly and dishonestly squandered." The attorney for the Long Island group asserted that a "public officer can make more money by robbing the people violating his oath of office, than by honestly discharging his duty." The Brooklyn Citizens' and Taxpayers' Association appointed a committee to "collect . . . evidence of fraud . . . in connection with certain public works and submit it to the Attorney General." In 1893, taxpayers in the town of New Utrecht organized the Citizens' League and, joined by the Bensonhurst Taxpayers' Association, brought suit against the town to have declared void a contract into which town officials had entered with a gas company extending the company's monopoly of supplying gas to the town at "a higher price than was just . . . in violation of their trust." The following year, New Utrecht's and Gravesend's taxpayers' associations joined with other local political reform groups to create what the *New York Times* called a "Citizens' Movement" or a "Citizens' League" in an effort to defeat Democratic "ring" politicians and fight corruption in local government.[18]

The same themes of graft, mismanagement, and "ring" politics echo from the pages of the *Baltimore Sun* in the 1870s. Both Washington, D.C., and Baltimore taxpayers organized to fight municipal cronyism and excessive property taxes and to elect honest politicians. Taxpayers in the capital contemplated withholding property tax payments because property assessments made the previous year were from "twenty-five to one hundred percent in excess of the actual cost value." In August 1874, the *Sun* published a "Letter from Washington" that outlined the work and policies of the District of Columbia Taxpayers' Association. In an 1876 editorial, the *Baltimore Sun* commended the Baltimore County Taxpayers' Association for its efforts to "protect taxpayers against waste and extravagance on the part of the county officials." The association added its voice to the call for nonpartisan municipal government to benefit "all the people" who are "citizens and Taxpayers of Baltimore." In 1880, it sent a petition to the state legislature protesting the ability of the wealthy to avoid taxation. The petition declared "that exemption from taxation by contract is inadmissible" and demanded "that all such laws which may be inconsistent with the principles of equal taxation shall be repealed." The association also recommended that Baltimore voters send representatives from each ward to a "citizens' convention." Its avowed objective was to oversee the spending of municipal government independent of any political party.[19] Such pleas to keep municipal government free from partisan politics continued to reverberate among organized taxpayers into the twentieth century.

Not all Northern collective tax resistance was spurred by concerns about honesty and efficiency in, and the cost of, government. In some large cities in the North and the Midwest, business and professional elites embraced the cause of tax resistance in an effort to augment their political influence vis-à-vis the lower-middle and working classes. In the 1870s, for example, upper-class New Yorkers mobilized under the moniker of a "movement of 'tax-payers'" and proposed an amendment to the state constitution that would consolidate important powers of municipal government in New York City in a board of finance elected only by property owners and thereby deprive roughly half of the electorate of any say in these matters. The amendment was defeated in 1878, but New York City elites continued to press for tax relief in the hope that reducing the size and reach of city government would diminish the power of political machines and of their propertyless supporters. Elites in other northern cities, including Boston, Cincinnati, and St. Louis, also advanced the notion that political power, as evidenced by the right to vote, should reside in the class of property-owning taxpayers.[20] This upper-class strain of organized taxpayer activity was not, however, representative of taxpayers' groups outside the former Confederate states. In this era, most taxpayers' organizations and their members were actuated by the cost of government and its impact on their wallets, not elite political consciousness.

Early organized taxpayer activity in the American South was of a very different variety. Taxpayers' groups in the South diverged from those in the North in both ends and means. For Southern taxpayers, tax reduction was not an end in itself; instead, tax resistance was a cause they harnessed to achieve broader political and ideological objectives. Their methods included extrajudicial violence, which was absent from tax protests outside the former Confederacy. This distinctively Southern form of tax resistance was the product of two things: a peculiarly Southern antistatist and antitax worldview that was linked to what John C. Calhoun referred to as the "peculiar institution" and that slaveholding elites had developed over the course of the previous century, and a political agenda that Southerners embraced in response to Republican Reconstruction.

The institution of slavery guided and defined Southerners' views of government and taxation in the antebellum South. Slaveholders recognized that the power of taxation in the hands of strong, democratic governments endangered the slaveholding system. Slaveholder elites saw the relationship between taxation and slavery through the prism of Chief Justice John Marshall's dictum that "the power to tax involves the power to destroy." Because the "peculiar institution" was especially vulnerable to taxation, slaveholders preferred and promoted weak, undemocratic governments and excluded nonslaveholding majorities from decision-making concerning taxation. This antistatist, antimajoritarian belief system in which the property rights and political rights of slaveholding elites reigned supreme predominated among Southern Democratic Party leaders and slaveholders by 1860.[21]

The advent of Reconstruction intensified Southern elites' deep-rooted hostility toward taxation and vigorous, democratic governments. In the South, the Democratic Party's response to Republicans' efforts to reorder Southern society was to pursue a so-called politics of Redemption. The Redeemers' agenda, in historian Eric Foner's formulation, was "dismantling the Reconstruction state, reducing the political power of blacks, and reshaping the South's legal system in the interests of labor control and racial subordination."[22] What the Redeemers ultimately desired was a return to a de facto antebellum South in which the political structures, race relations, and class relations were unaffected by the Fourteenth and Fifteenth Amendments. After Democrats regained control of state government of Georgia in 1871, the state's governor expected that Georgia "could hold inviolate every law of the United States and still so legislate upon our labor system as to regain our old plantation system." In 1875, a Southern newspaper promised to render the Fourteenth and Fifteenth Amendments "dead letters on the statute book."[23]

Organized tax resistance was one vehicle that Southern Democrats appropriated in order to realize these goals. Former Confederate states witnessed a surge in the number of taxpayers' associations, sometimes denominated "taxpayers' conventions." These groups accused Republican governments of malfeasance and wasteful spending and called for substantial spending and tax cuts. Taxpayers' leagues charged that Republican officials levied property taxes that many people, especially farmers, were unable to pay. In Mississippi, for example, one newspaper described state and county taxation as "enormously excessive" and "oppressive."[24] As such, they professed to be motivated by the same economic concerns as other taxpayers' groups throughout the nation. The "unnecessary" spending to which white taxpayers mainly objected, however, was for anything that would make state and local governments stronger and more efficient and any expenditure that would facilitate Republican reconstruction of the Southern social order, especially funding for public education for the children of former slaves.[25] The concerns that taxpayers' organizations in the South regularly expressed—"the tyranny of a majority," "rights of property," "taxation without representation," and the "right of revolution," among others—belie their claims that their focus was pecuniary, apolitical, and nonideological.[26]

Taxpayers' leagues proliferated throughout the South in the decade following the Civil War. In 1868, taxpayers in Nashville, Tennessee, organized to protest against "unwise and wicked legislation" in municipal affairs and to prevent "burdensome and unjust taxation." The association proclaimed it would take steps to correct the injustices in municipal administration and "bring the guilty parties to justice." An article in a Memphis daily newspaper called on local taxpayers to look to Nashville's example and form their own organization because

> no city in the world so badly needs an organization of this character as Memphis. . . . In view of the numerous rings and their nefarious plans and interlacing schemes, to make private fortunes out of public misfortunes, crushed as the property holders and tax-payers are generally in Memphis, the necessity of such an association is obvious.[27]

The villainous rings to which the writer referred were the Republican administration of the Reconstruction government and its allies.

Contemporary news accounts throughout the South identified several influential taxpayers' associations emerging in South Carolina and Alabama. They attributed this phenomenon to the current political and military circumstances that, according to local opponents of Reconstruction, allowed "thieves and miscreants" to control municipal governments. The *Macon Weekly Telegraph* complained about the "number of blacks who occupy seats in the Legislature," as a result of which that body was "made up almost exclusively of degraded and venal paupers. . . . Not one representative in ten stands for a tax-paying or property-holding constituency." It further argued that the conditions that existed in South Carolina would never be tolerated in "any Northern State without a tax-payers' league being organized to resist the payment of taxes imposed for fraudulent purposes."[28] Two years later, in 1874, the same newspaper commended the taxpayers in two counties in Alabama who had "united to resist in every lawful and legitimate manner, the thieving of their Radical and carpet-bag officials." The Alabama taxpayers vowed that if they could not effectuate change in municipal administration through "the strictest scrutiny," then, "as a last resort, [they would] appeal to the courts for justice against [the carpetbaggers'] knavery." True to their word, in May 1874, the Montgomery County Taxpayers' League successfully pushed for the prosecution and conviction of the tax collector and the filing of indictments against several other officials. The *Telegraph* showered praise on the Alabama taxpayers' group and called for such action by taxpayers in all Southern communities in "hopes that the law may yet have its course, but at present the carpetbagger's star is in the ascendant, and he bids defiance to all legal process."[29]

Frustration about Northern interference with Southern property owners' individual rights and local control spawned taxpayers' associations in other states in the former Confederacy. In 1873, in Smith County, Tennessee, a taxpayers' group sought to enjoin the county from expending $300,000 to purchase stock in the Tennessee and Pacific Railroad Company, arguing that the 1869 election authorizing that expense did not include the taxpayers in the Eighth District of Smith County and that, therefore, the election and the expenditure of public funds pursuant to that vote were illegal. The Supreme Court of Tennessee ruled in favor of the taxpayers and granted the injunction. Why the taxpayers in the Eighth District did not participate in the election is unclear. What is significant was the taxpayers' decision to organize promptly and bring a taxpayers' lawsuit in order to assert their claims and protect their rights as taxpaying citizens.[30]

What distinguished the methods of taxpayers' associations in the South was their members' willingness to use violence to achieve their goals.[31] When political, bureaucratic, and legislative efforts were ineffective, it was not uncommon for Southern white taxpayers to threaten and engage in violence and even to murder black officeholders. The central role that violence played in taxpayers' organizations in the South was all too evident in Vicksburg, Mississippi, where in 1873 taxpayers formed a taxpayers' league numbering six hundred following a large property tax increase, which they claimed was the result of "reckless extravagance." The league launched an investigation of city officials and found evidence to suggest that the city clerk had forged stock certificates in a municipal corporation and practiced "other rascalities." The taxpayers' goal was "to examine the books of the Chancery Clerk," but the clerk had refused to cooperate, stating, "I don't represent you or any of your crowd." The league responded that since its members paid 90 percent of the taxes, they had a right to ensure that the clerk was "competent and honest." This episode exposed the deep rift between white Southerners and Reconstruction government officials, whom leaguers asserted were robbing white property owners. A violent backlash resulted against local black residents, who, according to white Southerners, were in cahoots with the Reconstruction administration. Northern news accounts of the events in Vicksburg suggest that the taxpayers' league and one of the White League groups that Democrats had established to help them regain control of state governments were one and the same and were affiliated with the Ku Klux Klan. Members of the Vicksburg taxpayers' group defended their actions, claiming that "there was nothing political in [their organization]; colored men, if taxpayers, could join it."[32] There is, however, no evidence that any former slave or free black person belonged to a white taxpayers' association in the South, which is unsurprising given the fact that the promotion of the supremacy of the white race was basic to these groups' missions. Such denials of racial exclusivity may be treated with "the taxpayer doth protest too much" skepticism.

Collective opposition to taxation in the states of the former Confederacy was fueled largely by the political, racial, and social divisions in the South during Reconstruction. Property rights and minority (meaning elite) rights were as central to organized taxpayer activity in the South as they were to Southerners' antebellum philosophy of government and taxation. Invectives about the influence of propertyless (meaning black) public officials and their propertyless constituents abound in the publications and pronouncements of taxpayers' leagues. Southern elites regularly employed the language and the cause of tax resistance for purposes of defending the property rights of the propertied classes and diluting the political power of the propertyless, Northern carpetbaggers, and former slaves.[33] The members of the Vicksburg Taxpayers' League likely went out of their way to disavow political and racial motivations for their actions in order to obscure the class, racial, and political issues at play. Taxpayers' associations provided white Southerners a facade of legitimacy, a forum for civic protest that was neutral on its face but behind which boiled profound societal tensions. In many Southern states during Reconstruction, the enmity between white taxpaying Southerners and Republican political leaders, black or white, was exhibited in some cases by political activity and taxpayers' lawsuits and in others by violence, as seen in Vicksburg. Though some organized taxpayer activity in the South in this period was spurred by taxpayers' genuine desire to reduce their taxes, for the most part taxpayers' associations served as fronts for white supremacists determined to undermine or oust Republican regimes by any means necessary, including terrorism.

The organized tax resistance that appeared in the former Confederate states was sui generis: in its broad ideological objectives that related only indirectly to tax reduction, in the methods Southern taxpayers' groups employed, and in its disconnection from Americans' developing understanding of citizenship. Except for the small number of taxpayers' organizations that Northern elites founded in hope of enhancing their political power at the expense of the working classes, it was the taxes that spurred taxpayers in the North to organize. Their target was tax reduction, their motivation was mainly financial, and organized tax resistance was the means to that financial end. For taxpayers' leagues in the South, the destination was the "redemption" of state governments from Republican control and the restoration of the antebellum social and racial orders, and slashing taxes was a vehicle to get them there. The readiness of Southern taxpayers to resort to violence also set them apart from organized taxpayers in the North, who eschewed the use of force in their antitax efforts. Finally, tax resistance in the former Confederacy was untethered to the evolving notions of civic responsibility and good citizenship that broadly animated Northern tax resistance. Most taxpayers' groups outside the South were interested in, and worked for, better and more efficient government. Southern taxpayers' leagues wanted the opposite: government that was worse, small, and ineffectual. The Redeemers were highly successful in their quest for low taxes, low spending, and weak state governments after 1877. In Mississippi, for example, between 1875 and 1885, Democrats cut the state budget by more than half and slashed taxes.[34] The connections between organized tax resistance in the South and the commitment to good citizenship, public virtue, and the rule of law that most Northern taxpayers' organizations evidenced was attenuated at best and often absent altogether.

Taxpayers formed new taxpayers' groups to resist taxation between 1900 and 1929. Before the Great Depression, however, taxpayers' associations were neither numerous nor a significant presence in American public life. In 1930, taxpayers' organizations probably numbered no more than fifty.[35] Their creation and activities were episodic and almost always reactions to specific local problems. When the stock market collapsed in 1929, the taxpayers' league was an inchoate institution with only modest influence on a national scale.

The history of taxpayers' associations in the United States spans more than 150 years. One of the most remarkable attributes of such organizations prior to the Great Depression, however, was their caducity. Like the lilies of the field, they sprouted up, flourished for a season, then faded away. The Great Depression was transformative in this way, as in so many other ways. In the five years following the 1929 stock market crash, the taxpayers' association rapidly evolved into a permanent and enduring institution in American society, a part of the fabric of civic and political life in the United States. By the mid-1930s, it had become, to paraphrase historian Fernand Braudel, one of the "structures of everyday life" in this country.[36]

2

The Tax Revolt, 1930–1941

The "Taxpayers Are Rising" and "Want to Pay Less for Government"

Mary Belle Parrish created quite a stir when she attended the annual artists' costume ball in Marblehead, Massachusetts, on July 31, 1935. The eighteen-year-old daughter of a chauffeur and a maid appeared at the function wearing only a barrel with the moniker "Tax Payer" emblazoned on it. Mary won first prize for her costume, by which she declared that increasingly onerous tax burdens had stripped the American taxpayer of everything, even the clothes on her back.[1] This sentiment was widespread, and images of the hapless taxpayer clothed in nothing but a barrel appear with some degree of frequency in publications in the 1930s.

Depression-era tax protests were not, however, confined to theatrical demonstrations by individual taxpayers. On the contrary, in these years taxpayers organized to contest their taxes to an extent and with a fervor hitherto unseen in the United States. On the eve of the Great Depression, the taxpayers' association had been on the scene in the United States for two generations, but it was still a relatively nascent and anemic institution that operated on the periphery of American civic life. In 1932, the National Association of Real Estate Boards' records indicated that "on January 1, 1930, there were just 33 organized groups of taxpayers in the entire country."[2] An online search of newspaper archives from the 1920s reveals that most of the collective tax resistance that was reported in the print media occurred in the western United States, including Nevada, New Mexico, Texas, and, especially, California and Utah.[3] The Fresno Taxpayers' Association in California was a particular beehive of activity.[4] Organized taxpayer efforts, though, were the exception, not the rule, and can hardly be said to have constituted a movement, much less a sustained or nationwide one.

Prior to 1930, the formation and undertakings of taxpayers' associations were occasional, and usually responses to immediate local or regional issues and stresses. The creation of the Taxpayers' League in Lawton, Oklahoma, in October 1905, for instance, was "the outgrowth of the storm sewer contract, which the taxpayers viewed as an unnecessary burden, and one of the prime objects of the organization [was] to bring an action . . . to enjoin the city from proceeding" with the contract.[5] In the same year, the citizens of Reading, Pennsylvania, came together to form the Reading Taxpayers' League because of the "general distrust of city councilmen which exists among the people" as a consequence of allegations in open court that a local corporation had won a municipal contract by bribing the councillors.[6] A fiscal crisis in Adams County, Mississippi, in 1921 prompted the Adams County Taxpayers' League to investigate the administration of county affairs, and the league's published report "stir[red] up [the local] citizens."[7] Four years later, taxpayers in Milwaukee, Wisconsin, established the Northwest Taxpayers' Association for the "purpose . . . [of] oust[ing] Mayor W. Hoan and several other city officials, who they charge 'played politics' in the naming of the new fire chief."[8] Perhaps the most notable example of regional dynamics prompting taxpayers to organize was the formation of taxpayers' associations in the states of the former Confederacy during Reconstruction. The conditions that encouraged joint action by taxpayers generally were short-lived and localized; consequently, such activity in those decades shared those same temporal and geographic characteristics.

The onset of the Great Depression completely transformed this economic, political, and civic landscape. The American economy, the incomes of most Americans, and the revenues of many American businesses shrank far more precipitously than did local and state government expenditures in the early 1930s, producing crippling taxes for many. American workers who paid the rents and purchased the goods that enabled landlords and businesses to pay their taxes experienced massive job losses and a severe contraction in their purchasing power. Homeowners suffered comparable job losses, which further reduced consumer spending. The national unemployment rate, 3.2 percent in 1929, surged in the next four years, peaked at 24.9 percent in 1933, and remained above 20 percent for the next two years. Between 1929 and 1933, the average weekly earnings of workers in manufacturing decreased by one-third, and those of workers in the durable goods sector decreased by almost 40 percent.⁹ Farmers also experienced a precipitous decline in their incomes: nationwide, annual net farm income dropped by more than two-thirds from 1929 to 1932.¹⁰ The scope and size of the tax problem were apparent to citizens from all walks of life and were an incessant theme of public discourse.

In a 1933 article entitled "Taxation Nears a Crisis," William B. Munro painted a bleak picture of systemic dysfunction in American taxation. Munro, a professor of history and government at the California Institute of Technology, a former president of the American Political Science Association, and the author of several books on public administration, argued that the "tax situation in the United States has reached a stage of seriousness which the average citizen does not appreciate. The burden of national, state, and local taxes has become one of the most formidable obstacles in the path of economic recovery." Munro endeavored to quantify the growth of what he termed the "incubus" of taxation:

> In 1929 the national income of the United States . . . was estimated to be about $85,000,000,000. Our total tax bill for that year was estimated at about $10,000,000,000. In other words, the entire tax levy of 1929, lumping together all federal, state and local assessments, amounted to about 12 percent of the national income. For the year 1932 . . . this national income has dropped to about $40,000,000,000, or less than half what it was three years ago, while the total amount levied in taxes receded only about 10 percent. It ran to almost $9,000,000,000 for the year, which means that it devoured over 20 percent of the national income.

He argued that governments "do not begin by determining that public expenditures must be trimmed into line with the existing revenues" but that, instead, "for the greatest part they proceeded to bridge the gap by piling on more taxes. Consequently, the taxes go up at the very time that people as a whole can least afford to have them go in that direction."¹¹

Munro accurately identified the crux of the taxation dilemma but probably missed the mark in surmising that average Americans did not comprehend its seriousness. The very real difficulty that many Americans experienced in paying their taxes and otherwise making ends meet made them keenly aware of the crisis in taxation and illustrated the aphorism that experience is often the best teacher. Contemporary sources bear this out. In January 1933, a journalist in Nebraska wrote that "tax-consciousness is a new addition to the vocabulary of many Americans. It is the term they use to account for the rising tide of tax rebellion."¹² In an address to the Kentucky General Assembly on March 4, 1932, Melvin A. Traylor, president of the First National Bank of Chicago, observed that the cost of government had become "an unbearable burden on the backs of American citizens" and that the magnitude of the tax problem "has brought disaster to thousands of taxpayers in every part of the country."[13] Various speakers in a series of radio addresses and roundtable discussions in the "You and Your Government" series sponsored by the National Advisory Council on Radio in Education in 1932 and 1933 emphasized the taxpayer's plight. In one, Murray Seasongood, the president of the National Municipal League, noted that the "American taxpayer is bearing an intolerable burden."[14] In another, Thomas Reed, a professor of political science at the University of Michigan and the Chairman of the Committee on Civic Education by Radio of the National Advisory Council on Radio in Education, declared that the "taxpayer is groaning under his burden. He would like to lighten it."[15] In a third, Dr. Lent D. Upson, a public administration scholar at Wayne State University and the director of the Detroit Bureau of Municipal Research from 1916 to 1944, rued the fact that the "embattled taxpayer . . . is harassed by private worry."[16] When he addressed the National Conference on Government in November 1933, Seasongood reiterated that the "taxpayer is resentful; he revolts at the heavy needless burden he is made to bear."[17]

Business leaders and taxpayers echoed this sentiment. In 1933, Chicago attorney Claude Tharp examined the methods of controlling the cost of local government through taxpayers' associations precisely because public awareness of the tax exigency had become so pervasive and prominent. He began his study by noting that "the problem of mounting tax burden of local government and methods of control have been the occasion of much discussion for the past two years." He maintained that

> as the demands for government services increased, the waste involved in the vast number of local governmental units, often duplicating each other, became more noticeable and burdensome . . . resulting in unreasonable demands upon the resources of the Taxpayer. . . . Taxpayers are now awakening to the deficits of the present financial systems, and it seems a most opportune time to analyze and evaluate existing methods of controlling finance that are in use in the various states.[18]

In a January 1933 radio address sponsored in part by the American Taxpayers League, F. Robertson Jones, general manager of the Association of Casualty and Surety Executives, likewise declared that "the American people have suddenly become aware of the crushing tax burden which has been saddled upon them during a decade of spendthrift government."[19] In October 1931,

Edgar C. Rust, chairman of the Massachusetts division of the New England Council, "called upon leading business executives of the state to join in a campaign to prevent further handicap to business, through augmented tax burdens, by the widespread creation of local taxpayers' associations." In his letter to the council members, Rust argued that "the present burden of taxation in Massachusetts is rapidly approaching, if it has not already passed, the economic limit. . . . If taxes go beyond this economic limit, that is, the ability of the community to pay, the result is the depreciation of property values, crippling of industry, unemployment and the flight of capital in industry."[20] The following summer John C. Percival, while speaking to the local Kiwanis Club in Lowell, Massachusetts, about the objectives of the recently formed Lowell Taxpayers' Association to which he belonged, claimed that "tax burdens have reached a confiscatory stage to an alarming degree" and urged taxpayers to organize "in a determined effort to relieve the taxpayer of some of his burdens that he may retain ownership of his property."[21] Twenty-two local taxpayers' associations in Massachusetts came together to form the Middlesex County Taxpayers' Association in early 1933, during what they described as "these times of stress" in which "the taxpayer . . . is already bearing more than he is able in the matter of taxes."[22] Fear and pessimism dominated the March 1933 organizational meeting of the Taxpayers' League of Letcher County in eastern Kentucky, at which its members declared that "taxes on real estate . . . are so outrageously high and out of reason that it amounts to confiscation of our properties" and worried that "unless the taxpayers get some relief from the unjust burden it will only be a short time until the bulk of our properties will be forfeited to the state and county because we are unable to pay our taxes."[23] A speaker at a county taxpayers' association meeting in Minnesota was hyperbolic on the subject of property taxes, telling the audience that "when I was auditor of Stearns County, the tax delinquent list was infinitesimal" but that the "last printing of the delinquent tax list almost forced The Times to deliver it with trucks."[24] The tax crisis was omnipresent in the United States in the early 1930s and palpable to almost every adult.

Although the economic pain of the Great Depression was inflicted on nearly all Americans, the middle class suffered the most from property taxation. The propertyless poor had no compelling reason to participate in tax protests, and there is no evidence that they did so to any meaningful degree. For the most part, property taxes did not consume a substantial portion of the disposable income of the wealthy, so the "tax burden" was not that oppressive for them. Some members of the business community who hoped that shrinking government revenue streams would reduce the size of government supported the efforts of tax resisters.[25] Prominent among these antistatists was Merle

Thorpe, editor of the *Nation's Business*, the United States Chamber of Commerce's official publication. Large business property owners were also involved in some taxpayers' associations, including the Kentucky Tax Reduction Association.[26] The vast majority of organized taxpayers, however, were from the middle class. Typical members of taxpayers' associations included small business owners, landlords who owned one or perhaps a few commercial or residential properties, farmers, homeowners, people engaged in trades and in clerical occupations, and real estate agents. The thirty thousand–member Association of Real Estate Taxpayers (ARET) in Chicago, for example, was comprised mainly of people of modest means, such as the owners of small businesses (restaurants, drug stores, plumbing outfits, laundries, grocery stores, photography studios, and so forth); persons engaged in clerical and sales employment; and unskilled, semiskilled, and skilled workers. ARET's largest single group of members was skilled blue-collar workers (carpenters, painters, plumbers, electricians, tailors, machinists, and mechanics).[27] Hal Steed's Taxpayers' League of Atlanta and Fulton County was similarly representative of middle-class tax resistance. Merchants, an automobile dealer, the owner of several office buildings, other "real estaters and property owners," small and struggling landlords like Steed, and a loan agent were among its members, although they did enlist a wealthy retired "dry-goods jobber" to serve as chairman.[28] The taxpayers' association movement of the 1930s was fundamentally a middle-class undertaking, impelled by the anxieties, concerns, and interests of middle-class Americans.

One consequence of this tax crunch was a rapid and substantial increase in organized tax resistance between 1930 and 1933. The number of taxpayers' associations and the extent of their programs grew astronomically in these years. Edward M. Barrows wrote in the *National Municipal Review* in May 1933 that taxpayers' organizations "are hurrying into action everywhere."[29] At almost the same time the Governmental Research Association, "an organization of individuals professionally engaged in governmental research" and based in Chicago, found that "taxpayers [are] organizing now in all parts of the country."[30] Thomas Reed warned that "the taxpayers are rising."[31] The National Municipal League's Committee on Citizens' Councils for Constructive Economy declared that "every local government in the country today is being subjected to terrific pressure . . . from organized taxpayer groups hit hard by the depression."[32] The foreword to a legal periodical symposium on the tax collection process and real estate tax delinquencies affirmed that "accentuation of the tax burden by the depression has led to the organization of important pressure groups working for a variety of measures which may be subsumed under the slogan, 'relief for real estate.'"[33]

Public officials and public administration experts employed a number of colorful metaphors and descriptions to highlight the rapidity with which taxpayers' associations were proliferating. They complained that taxpayers' leagues "sprang up like weeds" throughout the United States and observed that organized taxpayer activity was "sweeping across the country like a prairie fire." They recognized that "this throng of citizens' tax reduction organizations unquestionably represents a new force of unknown potential strength" in "countless American communities" and pondered how to harness that energy to the cause of good government reform.[34]

The widespread establishment of taxpayers' associations was proceeding full force by 1932. Early in his radio address sponsored by the National Advisory Council on Radio in Education, Murray Seasongood observed that "there can be no doubt of the strength and sincerity of taxpayer sentiment for economy. Taxpayers' organizations have sprung up all over the country to enforce demands for economy."[35] Lent Upson noted that "all over the country big and little industrialists and bankers, shop-keepers and home-owners, are being marshaled into regiments of economy leagues, tax reduction associations, and other agencies for united action."[36] In October 1931, the New England Council was advocating for the creation of numerous local taxpayers' leagues because by that time they already had "been found the most effective means of dealing with the [tax] situation."[37]

Many public administration academics and professionals acknowledged the potential efficacy of taxpayers' organizations in dealing with the tax crisis if they were guided by relevant expertise. In 1932, Thomas Sewall Adams, a government finance scholar who served as the first editor of the *Bulletin of the National Tax Association*, declared that "to achieve the desired end" of controlling government costs, "it is probable that the taxpayers of every state will find it necessary to organize permanent associations, guided by leaders of broad views and assisted by experts who give their entire time to the work of reducing costs and increasing efficiency."[38] Edward M. Barrows believed that the taxpayers' association movement "has possibilities" and "contains within itself the germs of a thoroughgoing government house cleaning such as this country has never before witnessed," if assisted by "the trained advocates of better government."[39] Lent Upson predicted that the "success of the contest between [organized taxpayers] and intrenched politics will depend upon determination, intelligent leadership,—and facts," which critical information Upson and other experts in government finance and administration were prepared to provide to taxpayers' groups.[40]

By mid-1933, taxpayers' leagues likely numbered in the thousands. Edward Barrows estimated that there were between three thousand and four thousand, and local and regional figures bear out this estimate.[41] Claude Tharp identified thirty-nine state taxpayers' associations operating in thirty-three states and the District of Columbia as of 1933.[42] This number did not include organizations at the municipal and county level, where the real growth was occurring, because, as Tharp observed, "local governments [were] the largest spenders of public funds."[43] In his July 1932 speech, Lowell Taxpayers' Association officer John C. Percival noted that "in Massachusetts there are now taxpayers' associations in over 14 cities and towns . . . with many additional associations now in the process of formation."[44] Indeed, eight months later there were twenty-two taxpayers' groups in Middlesex County, Massachusetts, alone, which collaborated to form the Middlesex County Taxpayers' Association.[45] According to the Governmental Research Association, whose findings were well researched and generally reliable, there were 140 active taxpayers' associations in Massachusetts in October 1933, an increase of 60 from September 1932, and the largest, the Worcester Taxpayers' Association, had more than ten thousand members.[46] At the annual meeting of the Minnesota Taxpayers' Association on February 27, 1934, "fifty-seven counties sent delegates to the convention" and the association's secretary "reported 70,000 enrolled members in eighty of eighty-seven counties in the state."[47] In late 1935, New Haven Taxpayers Inc. in Connecticut, which had been organized as a municipal research agency in July 1933, had 1,760 dues-paying members, representing far more than one-third of the city's property owners.[48] In 1932, there had been only seventy-four local taxpayers' groups in New Jersey.[49] By December 1936, the New Jersey Taxpayers' Association had evolved from a "small group of citizens" to a "large and powerful organization composed of county and local taxpayers' associations affiliated with the parent organization from 250 communities" and having several hundred thousand members.[50] As of 1933, the Tennessee Taxpayers' Association had established county taxpayers' leagues in sixty-three of the state's ninety-five counties, and New Mexico had local taxpayers' organizations in almost every county.[51] That same year Claude Tharp declared that "taxpayers' associations have developed beyond the experimental stage and now play an important role in the fiscal affairs of the majority of states."[52] During the 1930s, the taxpayers' association movement became one that was nationwide and of enormous magnitude. Americans' participation in taxpayers' organizations in this period was unprecedented and remains unsurpassed.

One rough indicator of the scope and intensity of organized taxpayer activity is the extent to which it was covered in the print media. Such news coverage in the *Lowell Sun* in Lowell, Massachusetts, is illustrative. Between 1909 and 1911, that newspaper mentioned taxpayers' associations 114 times in articles covering the activities of taxpayers' organizations in the United States. From 1912 to 1926, there is not one reference to taxpayers' associations. Between 1930 and 1936, they are mentioned over 1,200 times.[53]

The overarching purpose for which taxpayers organized was to reduce their tax bills. A letter from an Iowa farmer, whom Wheeler McMillan quoted in the January 1933 issue of the *National Municipal Review*, expressed the taxpayer's mindset at its most basic level:

> My taxes are more than twice what they were a few years ago. My products sell for about a third of what they used to bring.... We buy fewer clothes, make fewer improvements (or none), buy fewer groceries, use our car less and longer—and so on with every item under my personal control. I would also like to buy less government.... At least I would like to pay less for whatever government I have to have.[54]

McMillan, an author and lecturer on American agriculture, declared that "farmers are not very particular as to what devices are adopted for reducing taxes, just so taxes are reduced."[55] The same was true of taxpayers from all walks of life. One means to this end was the enactment of constitutional and statutory tax limits. Another, the Massachusetts division of the New England Council observed, was for taxpayers "to exert a measure of control over public expenditures."[56] Claude Tharp described this strategy as comprising efforts "to reduce expenditures and reorganize governmental structure with a view to introducing features of control and economy." Most experts in the field of public administration agreed with Tharp's contention that "centering activities about expenditures and the control of government costs is the most direct and effective approach" to cutting taxes.[57]

Accordingly, taxpayers' associations sought to make municipal, county, and state government both cheaper and better, or, as the Fitchburg, Massachusetts, Taxpayers' Association put it, they had "the double object of reducing the cost and increasing the efficiency of . . . government."[58] Taxpayers' organizations consistently espoused these dual objectives. The Lowell Taxpayers' Association, for instance, was formed "for the purpose of fostering, encouraging and promoting a non-partisan interest and a study of the activities of federal, state, county and municipal agencies, as such activities may affect the taxpayers of Lowell," and "cooperating with such agencies [in order] to assist in effecting economy and efficiency."[59] The twenty-two taxpayers' groups in Middlesex County, Massachusetts, declared that it is "the purpose of these associations to cooperate with the Local Taxpayers' Associations of Massachusetts to reduce state and county governmental costs without impairing necessary and efficient public service."[60] The Arizona Taxpayers' Association organized to "cooperate with and assist private citizens and public officials in eliminating waste and extravagance from the conduct of public affairs, and to bring about the practice of genuine economy consistent with efficiency throughout every department of government."[61] The theme of "genuine economy consistent with efficiency" appeared repeatedly in the statements of goals and principles of taxpayers' organizations.

Taxpayers' leagues sought to attain these general aims through a number of specific objectives. Claude Tharp argued that "one of the first objectives of a taxpayers' association should be the directing of its efforts toward securing a sound budgetary and accounting system for the state and localities."[62] When the New Jersey Taxpayers' Association was urged to endorse a tax strike in 1933, its members refused to do so and instead "reiterate[d] our determination to work unceasingly . . . for the relief of the overburdened taxpayer, by searching for new ways to reduce public expenditures. . . . To accomplish the objectives of the Association," it called for the passage of legislation to provide "absolute control" of government expenditures, to require budgeting for all state expenses, to improve management of the state highway department, to reform public debt processes, and to limit public debt. It also urged the state legislature to adopt a "pay-as-you-go" policy in government, consolidate municipalities where possible, reduce public education costs, and regulate local government finances, among other things.[63] The Teaneck, New Jersey, Taxpayers' League, whose "only declared object . . . was to secure and maintain a non-partisan, efficient municipal government," adopted thirteen principles to achieve that end, including the "reduction of taxes by efficient, progressive and economical government"; institution of a city manager form of government; the "employment of qualified, disinterested and efficient public servants"; a civil service system for subordinate employees; the semiannual publication of detailed municipal financial statements; the "comprehensive planning and execution of public improvements . . . without extravagance"; and no construction of highway, sewer, and water projects "without financial protection to the general taxpayer."[64] The CTA's aims encompassed the following: improving the budgeting, reporting, and auditing procedures in local and state government; avoiding any increase in existing tax rates; enacting legislation regulating the issuance of bonds; making public education "more efficient and economical" by consolidating school districts; eliminating duplication of government functions; implementing centralized purchasing systems; depoliticizing and professionalizing the unemployment relief system; making the rural police system more efficient and effective by adopting a state police system; and working to "arouse citizen interest in government."[65] Some or all of these same goals appeared in the platforms and statements of principles of most taxpayers' groups.

The nature of Depression-era taxpayers' organizations highlights a number of salient features of American society and of political protest and civic engagement in the United States. The taxpayers' league was, first, an economic phenomenon. The taxpayers' association was a complex, multifaceted organism—part political action group, part legal advocacy entity, part public education instrument, part social club—but at its core it was an economic creature because its raison d'être was economic: to reduce taxes. Its diverse political, legal, educational, and legislative activities had a common focus, which was to contain and, where possible, to lighten the burden on taxpaying members. The astounding proliferation of taxpayers' organizations and the enormous expansion of their activities in response to the economic catastrophe of the Great Depression is further evidence of their essentially economic character.

Second, taxpayers' associations were primarily a middle-class phenomenon. Although some wealthy taxpayers, including individuals and large business enterprises, belonged to or otherwise supported taxpayers' leagues, it was mainly those Americans in the economic middle ground between the wealthy and the propertyless poor who organized, led, and sustained taxpayers' organizations because they felt most acutely the pinch of paying taxes during the Great Depression. The middle class sometimes considered itself overlooked by the Roosevelt administration, which focused on revitalizing industry and creating jobs for the unemployed, yet it was this demographic from which the most was asked to pay for the cost of government and its recovery efforts. Taxpayers' groups multiplied and attained considerable success in these years because they were supported by such a large swath of middle-class Americans.

Third, collective tax resistance was for the most part a white male enterprise because in the 1930s it was white men who owned most of the businesses and real estate that were subject to property taxation. The leaders and members of taxpayers' organizations, with few known exceptions, were white men. The names of women appear infrequently in contemporary sources concerning taxpayers' associations. The speakers, officers, and participants at their meetings and demonstrations who are identified in newspapers and other print media are men. Photographs of their rallies and other gatherings usually depict a sea of white men with seldom a woman or nonwhite person to be seen. Women, however, were not completely absent from the tax revolt. In the early 1930s, according to historian Anthony Badger, "farmwomen storm[ed] county courthouses in Colorado . . . to ease the weight of property taxes."[66] Sometimes women appeared in an ancillary role, such as displaying posters for a membership drive.[67] There were a few gender-specific (i.e., women's) taxpayers' associations scattered across the United States, including local groups in Medford, Massachusetts; Chadron, Nebraska; and Washoe County (Reno), Nevada.[68] Two women's organizations, the State Federation of Pennsylvania Women and the Pennsylvania League of Women Voters, belonged to the Pennsylvania Tax Forum, a statewide association.[69] The most active women's taxpayers' league was the New Jersey Women's Taxpayers' Association, formed in February 1934, because there had "developed a spontaneous demand throughout the state to support the program of the New Jersey Taxpayers' Association for expenditure reduction and control." Like Depression-era taxpayers' organizations generally, this group took a balanced approach toward reducing taxes and cutting government expenses, arguing that "schools must be kept open. Public health must be protected. Functions of government must be adequately relieved of the unbearable burden of taxation."[70] Organized tax resistance by women in the 1930s, however, was the exception, not the rule. The available evidence indicates that neither minorities nor women were a significant presence in the taxpayers' association movement.

Women, white and black, were actively involved in the poll tax repeal movement in the 1930s. This manifestation of tax resistance, however, differed in kind from the taxpayers' association movement. Opposition to poll taxes was fundamentally a civil rights struggle, since the poll tax was a direct impediment to exercising the right to vote. Women in the poll tax repeal movement grounded their efforts not only in voting rights but also in civil rights and women's rights.[71] Taxpayers' organizations simply sought to lower taxes so as to obtain financial relief, not to vindicate constitutional rights.

A final important feature of the taxpayers' association movement was its spontaneous, indigenous, and local character, which was apparent to contemporary observers. The populist impulse behind tax resistance during the 1930s was powerful and national in scope. Early in the decade, House majority leader Henry Rainey, an Illinois Democrat, declared that the tax "rebellion is general. . . . The sentiment against heavy local taxes and heavy cost of government is the most conspicuous present manifestation of politics in the United States."[72] Although collective tax protests emerged in many states, they did not represent a coordinated, national movement but, rather, a local, grassroots one, in which citizens engaged in what historian Meg Jacobs has termed "state-building from the bottom up."[73] National Municipal League staffer Howard P. Jones found the speed with which taxpayers' associations were being established and their nationwide distribution especially remarkable in light of their spontaneity, and he noted that "there were few paid organizers, traveling the highways and byways, to weld such groups together."[74] Commentators on local government finances, such as Edward M. Barrows and Murray Seasongood, noted that "taxpayers' organizations . . . have sprung up like mushrooms over the country."[75] Barrows characterized taxpayers' leagues as "amateur" and concluded that "they are no part of any 'national movement,' though they represent public opinion in an even truer sense, for they personify the popular thought of thousands of communities crystallizing into national sentiment." He further observed that taxpayers' groups were "organizations of voters within a given political area that are formed to deal primarily with problems of taxation and all its implications within the boundaries of that area" and that "the campaign to reduce taxes consists of many minute, independent local efforts."[76] The spontaneity of the Depression-era tax revolt was equally obvious to taxpayers. The Indianapolis Chamber of Commerce tax committee, for example, emphasized toward the end of the decade that "'the spontaneous outburst of taxpayer interest' has strengthened its position in promoting [its] work" to check the "four-year rising tide of taxes."[77]

This is not to say that there was no attempt to coordinate the efforts of tax resisters, but such attempts were few and did not alter the fundamentally local character of the movement. The only instance of formal interstate taxpayers' league collaboration that Claude Tharp found in his 1933 study was the Western Taxpayers' Association, comprising associations in twelve western states that met annually "to discuss tax problems of common interest."[78] In November 1931, American Taxpayers' Inc., an organization based in New York City, launched the *American Taxpayers' Quarterly*, a journal that purported to speak on behalf of the American taxpayer because he "is himself largely inarticulate."[79] This journal did not speak for long, however, since this first issue was apparently also the last. The taxpayers' association movement remained a decentralized, bottom-up one. As late as 1938, the Tax Policy League observed that "many of these [taxpayers'] organizations are small local groups, many of which spring up overnight and speedily pass out of existence" and that "no register of such groups had ever been compiled."[80] Such indigenous political and civic movements are typical in the American political system, in which local government and principles of federalism occupy key places.

Collective tax resistance in Connecticut encapsulates the material characteristics of the taxpayers' association movement. Taxpayers began organizing in 1931, prior to which there was only one noteworthy taxpayers' league in the state. During the next two years, citizens founded taxpayers' organizations in "most of the large cities and in many of the important towns," including Hartford, New Haven, Manchester, Bridgeport, Bristol, Waterbury, New

Britain, Enfield, Plainville, Terryville, and Winsted. The Hartford City Property Owners Protective League, established in February 1932, was, according to the *Hartford Courant*, "most active in spreading the gospel of taxpayers collective action to surrounding towns." The *Courant* reported that by January 1933, the work of organized taxpayers had "assumed the aspects and proportions of a 'movement.'" These taxpayers' associations "all represent[ed] essentially the same class in their communities, the payers of property taxes on small real estate properties." They attracted some "malcontents" and "some of the radical fringe of the old political parties" but mainly "solid citizens of all parties." The founders, leaders, and members of these taxpayers' groups included a number of men identified by name and "other business men," but the *Courant* makes no reference to any female participants. The organizations concentrated on the cost of local government and tax relief. Nearly all of the taxpayers' groups were "organized to meet some sharply defined, local situation which threatened the purses of the property owners," and each was "formed independently of the others." In Manchester, the "local condition that brought action" was a proposed $90,000 expenditure to improve a street; in Hartford, it was the city's decision to reduce the "rents paid by the city to poor families" that in turn slashed the income of rental property owners. Taxpayers' associations in Connecticut, as elsewhere, were local, spontaneous, economic, male, middle-class creatures.[81]

The relationship between the taxpayers' association movement and the politics of the Depression at the national level was complex and significant. The flow of influence between the tax revolt and the Hoover administration was a one-way street. Hoover was as unresponsive to the widespread taxpayer protests as he was to the other symptoms of the collapse of the American economy. The federal government's actions and inactions during his tenure, though, worsened many of the economic conditions underlying the Depression and, in doing so, accelerated and intensified the antitax movement. The flow of influence between organized tax resistance and the New Deal, on the other hand, was bidirectional. The scope and strength of the tax revolt informed and shaped key New Deal policies, and those policies, by providing critical assistance to desperate taxpayers, in turn abated taxpayer hostility to some extent.

During Hoover's last two years in office, collective tax resistance had no discernible impact on the federal government's response to the economic crisis, and a number of its decisions and policies caused the domestic economy to contract further. The Federal Reserve's decision in 1931 to reduce the money supply choked credit availability. Declining federal tax revenues heightened Hoover's concerns about a balanced budget, which he insisted was "the most essential factor to economic recovery" and "the first necessity of the Nation." An antistatist, Hoover opposed federal spending for unemployment relief or to control agricultural output and support crop prices. Even as the economy continued to deteriorate, Hoover remained firm in his antistatist worldview, vetoing a relief bill in 1932. That same year Congress compelled the president to allow the Reconstruction Finance Corporation to lend funds to states for relief, but his administration erected so many hurdles to obtaining those loans that most of the relief and public works funds that Congress had authorized remained undisbursed when Roosevelt took office. Tone-deaf to the urgent cries of American taxpayers, Hoover pressed Congress to raise taxes and, when it obliged, signed into law the Revenue Act of 1932, which, according to historian Elliott Brownlee, "imposed the largest peacetime tax increases in the nation's history."[82]

At a time when what the United States economy needed was economic expansion and greater consumer spending, the federal government's actions diminished consumer purchasing power, shrank the economy, and made matters worse for nearly all Americans, including taxpayers. By aggravating the economic crisis and the tax crisis, the federal government elevated taxpayer anxiety across the country and galvanized the tax revolt.

In contrast, the taxpayers' association movement had meaningful impacts on the Roosevelt administration's response to the Depression and the crisis in taxation. Taxation, agriculture, and housing policy were the areas in which the tax revolt had the greatest influence. For obvious reasons, tax policy had a high likelihood of generating taxpayer hostility. As historian Molly Michelmore has observed, New Dealers understood the need "to insulate the administration from the kind of taxpayer hostility that had produced a vibrant and powerful grassroots antitax movement" in the preceding three years, and, consequently, they crafted tax policy to address "popular hostility to new and direct federal taxes." One strategy New Dealers employed to this end was to eschew income taxation of the middle classes and instead tax the wealthy and attack concentrations of wealth.[83] The Revenue Act of 1935, which increased effective income tax rates on the rich by almost one-half and hiked the maximum estate tax rate to 70 percent, embodied this approach. A second was to rely on taxes that were largely obscured from the taxpayer's view, such as processing and excise taxes, and therefore evoked little opposition from taxpayers. A third was to market tax proposals in such a way that taxpayers did not regard the exactions as taxes. Roosevelt utilized this approach in rolling out the Social Security Act of 1935, which enjoyed broad public support despite the fact that Social Security payroll taxes were both regressive and highly visible. The administration characterized the payroll contributions as insurance premiums with which workers were purchasing an annuity to which they had a vested right, and most Americans accepted this characterization. New Dealers' emphasis on hidden taxes was effective in deflecting taxpayer hostility and served them well politically: in a 1939 survey, almost 25 percent of respondents indicated that they "didn't happen to pay any taxes." The New Deal tax regimes reveal how widespread and powerful tax resistance at the local and state levels shaped and constrained federal tax policy under Roosevelt.[84]

The Roosevelt administration was also alert to the political danger posed by the discontent and anger that pervaded the farm community. Between 1929 and 1932, crop prices and farm incomes plummeted while farm debt remained at an all-time high. Many farmers, unable to keep their real estate taxes and mortgage payments current, lost their properties. This state of affairs drove the farm community to act. In 1932, farmers organized farm strikes, in which farmers refused to ship their products to market until they received their "cost of production." In Iowa, the protests went further: taxpayers belonging to the Farm Holiday Association obstructed shipments of crops, blocked roads, damaged vehicles, and on one occasion stopped a freight train and removed its cargo of cattle. Farmers also interfered with foreclosure and tax sales of farms, threatening auctioneers and prospective bidders and forcing the sale of the property back to the owner for one cent.[85]

The New Dealers responded to the crisis in agriculture with the Agricultural Adjustment Act and the Farm Credit Act, both enacted in the spring of 1933. The measures that provided the most direct and immediate benefits to struggling farmers were the Agricultural Adjustment Act's acreage reduction contracts, in which the federal government paid farmers to cut back their acreage in production, and the Farm Credit Act's loan program, through which farmers were able to refinance their properties on favorable terms. Twenty percent of all mortgages were refinanced within eighteen months, and, according to historian William Leuchtenburg, "on an average day, the Farm Credit Administration saved three hundred farms from foreclosure." The New Deal's agricultural initiatives increased net farm income from $2 billion to $4.6 billion between 1932 and 1939, though it still remained below the 1929 level of $6.1 billion.[86]

Housing policy was also front and center in the minds of New Deal policymakers. When Roosevelt took his oath of office in March 1933, vast numbers of taxpayers had already lost their homes to tax and foreclosure sales (250,000 homes in 1932 alone), and in the first six months of 1933, home foreclosures were exceeding one thousand a day. The Roosevelt administration went to work on proposed legislation immediately, and in June 1933, Congress created the Home Owners' Loan Corporation (HOLC), which provided low-interest, longer-term, lower-payment mortgage loans to homeowners. Over the next two years, 10 percent of all homeowners refinanced their homes through the HOLC, and over time the HOLC refinanced one-fifth of homes in American cities. The HOLC required borrowers to use a portion of the loan proceeds to pay their delinquent real estate taxes. As such, HOLC loans not only enabled taxpayers to save their homes but also improved the fiscal positions of local and state governments. Daniel Hoan observed that the HOLC "must be credited with invaluable help in reducing tax delinquency" in Milwaukee from more than $26 million in April 1933 to just under $12 million in December 1935. In its first three years of operation, more than $200 million in HOLC loan proceeds were applied to past-due real estate taxes.[87]

Other New Deal measures also affected Americans, including taxpayers, broadly. The direct relief, work relief, and public works programs injected huge amounts of money into the economy, provided assistance and employment to many, and generally improved the lot of taxpayers, although the impacts of these initiatives on taxpayers were more macroeconomic and diffuse than those of the agricultural and housing policies that targeted specific taxpaying constituencies. New Deal spending also injected billions of federal tax dollars into the treasuries of state and local governments, bolstering their revenue systems, which had been devastated in the first years of the decade by a combination of a sharp drop-off in tax revenues and rising demands for unemployment relief. The magnitude of this transfer of federal funds was significant, representing more than 10 percent of local and state revenues at its high point.[88] By fortifying the finances of local and state governments, New Deal spending allowed the public officials running them to be more accommodating to the demands of taxpayers' organizations to hold down taxes. In sum, while a number of New Deal programs had indirect, incidental, or generalized impacts on American taxpayers, it was the housing, agricultural, and taxation policies that powerfully acted on large classes of taxpayers and that, in turn, were shaped by the taxpayers' association movement.

The attitudes of tax resisters toward the New Deal were a complicated and sometimes incongruous mix. Although some die-hard antistatists participated in taxpayers' organizations, most of their members' views of the federal government's response to the Depression ranged from outright support to ambivalence. Two factors account for the overall lack of opposition to the New Deal from citizens who were protesting vigorously their local and state taxes. First and foremost, New Deal programs were conferring direct, concrete benefits on many of these taxpayers. "Roosevelt won loyalty," William Leuchtenburg notes, "not simply to the New Deal as an abstraction but to particular agencies which acted directly on people as government rarely had before."[89] HOLC and Farm Credit Administration loans had saved many tax resisters' homes and farms from tax sale and foreclosure, and the Public Works Administration (PWA), the Civil Works Administration, the Works Progress Administration, and other federal agencies had furnished employment and a financial lifeline to millions of Americans. Consequently, many members of taxpayers' groups understandably welcomed, and some expected, the federal government's intervention in the domestic economy. Even taxpayers with an individualistic, antistatist mindset tended to have mixed feelings about the New Deal, harboring suspicions of big government but recognizing their need for assistance from the Roosevelt administration and grudgingly accepting it. Conservative taxpayer ambivalence was the norm in places where hostility to top-down federal authority was powerful and common. The "long-lasting legacies" of the New Deal in Oklahoma, observed one New Deal scholar, "included a reverence for President Roosevelt and fear and distrust of 'federal bureaucrats.'" In a similar vein, another found that "in their political attitudes, most Montanans accepted the new federal role, but they did not necessarily applaud it. Many local farmers and stockmen enjoyed the benefits of New Deal subsidies while continuing to maintain their conservative political philosophy, distrusting and criticizing the federal government."[90]

The New Deal tax regime also helps to explain why tax resisters campaigned for economy and efficiency in local and state government while simultaneously supporting, or being agnostic about, New Deal spending. The Roosevelt administration refused to consider taxing the income of the middle classes and instead relied mainly on taxes on the wealthy and corporations, on indirect or hidden consumer taxes, and on taxes (like Social Security payroll taxes) that taxpayers did not think of as taxes. New Deal tax policy aroused strong opposition from the business community and the rich but did not produce significant tax awareness among or tax resistance from the middle classes.[91] By and large, taxpayers who participated in collective tax resistance at the local and state levels did not perceive New Deal spending to be adding to their tax burdens.

Regardless of the extent to which New Deal programs may have altered tax resisters' views of federal spending, the federal government, or its role in economic recovery, the New Deal did not meaningfully or broadly change organized taxpayers' stance on local and state government spending and taxes or slow their efforts to reduce those taxes. Admittedly, two New Deal initiatives did have some impact on the degree to which taxpayers' associations invoked two of their tax-reduction tools. The HOLC loan outreach contributed to a reduction in the number of tax strikes in two ways. HOLC loans enabled the borrowers to pay their past-due property taxes, and the loan conditions that required them to do so and to keep their taxes current precluded them from participating in tax strikes and effectively aligned the taxpayer's interests in the timely collection of real estate taxes with those of the local governments to which the taxes were due. The popularity of PWA projects, which injected federal funds into local communities and created local jobs, reduced the utility of tax limitation measures because PWA policies made it harder for counties and municipalities that were subject to inflexible tax caps to qualify for those projects.[92] Although taxpayers' organizations relied less on tax strikes and tax limits as the HOLC's and PWA's operations expanded, taxpayers continued to form new groups and to engage in extensive constructive economy, political, and litigation activities during the height of New Deal activism between 1933 and 1937, and beyond.

Organized taxpayer activity in the 1930s reflects the complex interaction between obligations and rights in Americans' conceptions of citizenship. Because "a citizen is one who rules and is ruled in turn" in the United States, there exists a "reciprocal relationship between state and citizen" in which Americans both "exercise the rights and bear the obligations of citizenship."[93] Depression-era Americans recognized that a principal obligation of citizenship was paying taxes. That obligation, however, was accompanied by a concomitant right to hold government accountable for how it spent taxes and to insist on good government. Sometimes this right was characterized as a duty. For example, *Nation's Business* editor Merle Thorpe, who in 1932 gave sixteen radio addresses under the general title "In Behalf of the Delinquent Taxpayer— Present and Prospective," stated that "it is on the books that we must pay taxes. But it is just as much the obligation of citizenship that we should find out where our money goes and why." Thorpe went on to commend citizens who participated in taxpayers' associations and other organizations committed to fiscally responsible government and who, by doing so, "recognize their duties of citizenship in its highest sense; if need be, to give some of their time and some of their energy to the enormously important business of governing themselves well."[94] More often, though, the people's prerogative to ensure that tax dollars were prudently spent was framed as a right of citizenship. The Teaneck, New Jersey, Taxpayers' League, for instance, claimed that it was created in 1929 when local government finances had "reached a crisis" and, as a result, "the people of Teaneck awoke to the principles set forth in the Declaration of Independence that whenever any form of government becomes destructive, it is the right of the people to alter it and to institute a new government, laying its foundations on such principles, and organizing its powers in such form, as to them seem most likely to effect their safety and happiness."[95]

This dual characterization of the interest that Americans had in the operation of their government as a privilege or right, on one hand, and as a duty or obligation, on the other, may well reflect the fact that in the 1930s the culture of citizenship in the United States was beginning to evolve from one in which obligations were emphasized to one in which rights were ascribed greater importance. Christopher Capozzola has argued that as late as the early 1920s a culture of obligation remained ascendant because the United States was still "bereft of institutions at the local or national level to create and nourish a meaningful culture of rights" and that it was only in the last half of the twentieth century that a view of citizenship grounded in rights came to predominate.[96] The economic crisis of the Great Depression compelled Americans to think hard about how government was run and financed, a development that good government expert Edward M. Barrows termed "the present recrudescence of public interest in matters of government," and to emphasize their rights as citizens regarding these matters.[97] Taxpayers' leagues were an important instrument through which they asserted those rights. The sheer magnitude of the taxpayers' association movement and the extent to which Americans invoked and enforced those rights through such organizations in turn contributed to and encouraged the transition to a more rights-based conception of citizenship. In this sense, the taxpayers' association movement was both derivative, a product of its times, and constitutive, helping to transform Americans' notions of citizenship.

Americans at the time understood the integral connection between citizenship and taxpayers' organizations and that the latter were products of and pragmatic exercises in citizenship. For Hal Steed, the Taxpayers' League of Atlanta and Fulton County and its successes were what one expected to occur "when good citizens get together."[98] A 1932 editorial in the *National Municipal Review* observed that "citizens' organizations are springing up in many cities and demanding material cuts in city budgets," and it praised those "wise political officials [who] are cooperating with irate citizens."[99] The National Municipal League appealed to the taxpayers' sense of civic duty in calling for the creation of local citizens' councils for constructive economy, which would, "in cooperation with constituent groups, . . . speak for the public at large, with adequate consideration of the city's needs and obligations, and . . . secure such action as is clearly in the public interest."[100] Citizenship in its broadest sense encompasses legal status, membership rights and obligations, and civic involvement, and all of these attributes were represented in the taxpayers' associations of the 1930s.

The crisis in taxation in the early 1930s and the ensuing "conflicts over taxation brought to light differing conceptions of the state's proper role in society."[101] This ideological struggle was fundamentally a contest between statism and antistatism, tax resistance being, as Julian Zelizer has noted, "the most concrete manifestation of antistatism."[102] On one hand were those who favored the expansion of government; on the other were those who believed that the "price of government should undergo the same measure of deflation" as the economy and, therefore, advocated for smaller, or at least cheaper, government.[103] The clash of expanded-government sentiment and small-government sentiment was a central dynamic of the tax resistance movement.

Those on the far-right end of this spectrum clung to a Gilded Age, Big Business view of the state. Merle Thorpe typified this wing of antitaxers. To Thorpe the problem was that "'Let Government Do It' has become the national slogan of thoughtless, indifferent Americans," that "government has an inborn itch to supervise," and that "we, as a nation, are galloping toward socialism by the way of taxation" and "swinging our government in [Moscow's] direction." Because the "greatest obstacle to business recovery is taxation," the solution was plain to Thorpe: "only by reducing the number of government activities will we get at the cause of taxes. . . . The sooner we deflate government, the sooner normal living and working conditions for all of us will return."[104] Sterling E. Edmonds, a St. Louis attorney, was equally alarmed at the growth of government bureaucracy, the sinister nature of which he conveyed in the alarmist title of his 1933 law-centered treatise, "The Federal Octopus in 1933: A Survey of the Destruction of Constitutional Government and of Civil and Economic Liberty in the United States and the Rise of an All-Embracing Federal Bureaucratic Despotism."[105]

Most of this hardline antistatism came together in opposition to the New Deal under the umbrella of "free enterprise," a nuanced and protean view of government that its proponents continued to develop and refine in the 1930s and the ensuing decades.[106] Dire warnings of the dangers that the New Deal and "statist tyranny" posed to "capitalistic individualism," the autonomy of business firms, and the liberty and freedom of individuals permeated free enterprise rhetoric.[107] By the late summer of 1933, historian Lawrence Glickman noted, "the language of the state as an umpire, not an actor, a servant, not a master, a subordinate, not a ruler of business, had become commonplace" among free enterprisers. They assailed excessive federal spending, especially for welfare, and taxation, which they contended was producing a "militant, tax aroused electorate."[108] Free enterprisers sought to appeal to the taxpayers who were driving the tax revolt against local and state governments, regularly depicting the middle-class taxpaying citizen as "the new forgotten man." Merle Thorpe was a creative force behind this antistatist ideology that prominent figures in the business and political communities espoused.[109] In 1934, Daniel Hastings, the chairman of the Republican Senate Campaign Committee, promised to "undo" many New Deal programs, "abolish at least 90 percent of the bureaucracy now existing in Washington," and thereby "restore American liberty to American people." Two years later, Herbert Hoover argued that the New Deal philosophy of government was "founded on the coercion and compulsory organization of men . . . which would weaken the vitality of American freedom." He also boasted that as president he had "vetoed the idea of recovery through stupendous spending to prime the pump" and had thrown "out attempts to . . . centralize power in Washington" because "these things . . . in the end . . . would shackle free men."[110] Antistatism and its free enterprise strain were potent forces among portions of the American electorate in the 1930s, including business elites, in the South, where distrust of strong central government dated back to the colonial period, and in the less populous, less industrialized, more rural states in the Great Plains and the Rocky Mountains, where self-reliance, individualism, and other nineteenth-century frontier values still had wide appeal.[111]

The other end of this continuum was populated by individuals who believed in the virtue and efficacy of state activism. These included the architects of the New Deal, which was the political embodiment of faith in state intervention in domestic economic affairs. Good government experts and other public administration professionals, whose thinking about the state had been shaped by Progressivism's confidence in the ability of government to remediate social and economic ills and to promote a better society, generally supported vigorous government action and opposed tax resistance. Not surprisingly, public officials, who spent tax dollars and whose salaries were paid with tax dollars, endeavored to protect and expand their bailiwicks and their revenue streams, though the contraction of the national economy made many mindful of the need for efficiency in government. Milwaukee mayor Daniel Hoan, himself a socialist, would have welcomed a national gallop toward socialism.

Some tax resisters were determined small-government types, but most taxpayers inhabited the moderate middle of the big government–small government debate. Some taxpayers' groups even embraced big-government policies. In Berlin, New Hampshire, the members of the Berlin Taxpayers' Association created the Berlin Farmer-Labor Party, whose platform called for the public ownership of utilities.[112] Taxpayers' associations often opposed policies that would cripple state and local governments or unduly cut back the delivery of government services. Nearly all taxpayers wanted the *price* of government to undergo the same measure of deflation as the economy, but they also wanted to maintain the government services that they needed and used. Most taxpayers, like the Iowa farmer, did not necessarily want less government. Their main quarrel was with its cost, not its size or reach. What they really desired was less expensive government. Taxpayers in Kentucky were typical of this worldview: they "advocate[d] retrenchment in all governments" not because they were small-government devotees but because they wanted to achieve "a reduction in the cost of all government."[113] It was here, in the quest to control and reduce the cost of government, that the worldviews of the majority of taxpayers and of good government experts intersected and bolstered one another.

Taxpayers embarked on this quest by organizing across the country. As a consequence, taxpayers' associations were a principal vehicle by which middle-class Americans came together to engage in political and legal activism in the 1930s. Pressure from taxpayers took a variety of forms and achieved significant results. Nearly all taxpayers' organizations experimented with the types of activities in which Hal Steed's taxpayers' league engaged. They conducted investigations of government operations and audits of government finances, made recommendations to public officials, educated the public, sponsored legislation that promoted good government, and opposed legislation that threatened the public treasury. These constructive economy efforts represented the traditional, coactive strain of organized tax resistance and stemmed from the Progressive Era's good government movement. In the early 1930s, taxpayers' leagues also experimented with three avenues of assault on tax spenders that were more aggressive and adversarial: politics, tax strikes, and litigation. Taxpayers, manifesting the populist impulse in American politics, turned to politics with three goals: electing taxpayer-friendly officials, forcing state and local governments to reduce expenses and taxes, and enacting tax limitation measures. Adapting the workplace stoppages employed by the American labor movement, taxpayers' organizations from time to time threatened, and occasionally called for, collective action by taxpayers to suspend payment of their real estate taxes until public officials made concessions that taxpayers demanded. Taxpayers filed scores of taxpayers' lawsuits to enjoin unlawful spending and other illegal acts of local government. In doing so, they exhibited an instrumental view of the law that had been on the rise for decades. These diverse activities, their roots, and their legacies are central to the taxpayers' association movement.

Taxpayers' groups' use of sharper tactics after 1930 is not to suggest that they abandoned their previous constructive economy measures. On the contrary, taxpayers' leagues continued to rely primarily on research, legislation, public education, and collaborative engagement with public officials. Still, after 1930, the taxpayers' association movement expanded into new activities and was characterized by a greater degree of heterogeneity, complexity, and nuance.

3

Taxpayers' Associations' Legislative and Education Programs

The Pursuit of "Constructive Economy"

In November 1932, as the nation sunk deeper into economic depression, the CTA announced that it would "present an economy program to the 1933 session of the legislature which will make . . . possible" a $35 million savings "in the cost of state government for the next biennium." Dr. Milbank Johnson, chairman of the CTA's board of directors, explained that the CTA's "suggestions for economy are based on two year's [sic] intensive study of all departments and functions of state government" and that the findings and legislative recommendations had been reviewed by the CTA's State Affairs Committee, "made up of prominent Californians representing all taxpaying groups of the state." Johnson argued that the "condition of public finances in the state . . . makes necessary the enactment of basic and fundamental economy legislation, which, while rigidly economizing and retrenching, will not permanently injure government institutions." Johnson then articulated the CTA's twenty-seven-point legislative program aimed at promoting economy and efficiency in California government.[1]

The CTA's activities reflect the collaborative strain of organized taxpayer activity in the 1930s. In these endeavors taxpayers constructively engaged public officials with the overarching goal of reducing taxes. The means to this end were research, education, and legislation. Taxpayers' associations conducted hundreds of investigations concerning state and local government administration and finance. They used their findings to persuade public officials of the necessity and wisdom of implementing reform measures, to assist them in doing so, and to generate the requisite public support. They further shaped public policy by securing the passage of legislation that codified good government reforms and taxpayer-friendly budgets.

For the most part, taxpayers' groups eschewed radical proposals and extreme measures in their efforts to refashion the structures of state and local governments and to constrain their budgets. The legislative agendas of taxpayers' organizations reflected a cautious, mainstream approach in which taxpayers sought to work with, not against, public officials. Like the Taxpayers' League of Letcher County, Kentucky, taxpayers' groups overwhelmingly "offer[ed] suggestions and constructive criticism on and about" local and state governments and vowed "to cooperate fully with every department of . . . government."[2] Taxpayers' leagues made, as Milbank Johnson stated, "suggestions for economy," not strident demands, and provided legislators and public administrators with the information and data they needed to evaluate those suggestions and make informed decisions.

Contemporary public administration academics and experts assigned the label "constructive economy" to these moderate programs of taxpayers' associations that sought to achieve economy without causing permanent damage to the institutions of government. Political scientist Thomas Reed summarized the objects of constructive economy as follows:

> Constructive economy will save the good while destroying the bad. It will lead to permanent reform in the processes of government which will be doing good long after the present depression is merely a bad dream. Constructive economy selects for pruning those things that need pruning.

Good government professionals acknowledged the need to reduce the cost of local and state government "during periods of depression" but insisted that such cost cutting must be thoughtful, measured, and targeted at the structures of government, warning that the "mere indiscriminate reduction of expenses is never constructive economy and may turn out not to be economy at all." A. R. Hatton, a Northwestern University professor who specialized in municipal government and political reform, maintained that the "elements of a program of constructive economy" must be directed at changing "certain governmental and political conditions in the United States," including government units that were excessive in number; tax systems that were overlapping, badly organized, inefficient, and obsolete; inadequate processes for budgeting, accounting, and purchasing; little or no long-range planning; and "partisan interference in administration." Constructive economy measures focused on how state and local governments were organized and operated and how they provided services, whereas destructive economy efforts sought only to reduce the amount of government expenditures.[3]

Depression-era taxpayers' associations were not breaking new ground with their legislative, investigative, and educational programs. On the contrary, their collaborative activities hark back to the good government agenda of Progressive reformers in the late nineteenth and early twentieth centuries. Scholars were mindful of the Progressive Era roots of the constructive economy strategies of taxpayers' leagues. In making the case for the importance of reorganizing county governments if their costs were to be reduced, public administration academic Lent Upson urged taxpayers' groups to build on the foundation laid by earlier good government advocates:

> In the field of city government, usable facts about the necessity of public services and their costs have been gradually accumulating for a quarter of a century. It was in city government that a few interested and public-spirited citizens of a generation ago, the so-called professional reformers, and the teachers of government in the universities, made their first attack on incompetent and wasteful government.[4]

Ordinary taxpayers may not consciously have associated their aims and actions with those of Progressives. Nevertheless, Progressivism's good government elements infused and shaped the legislative programs and other cooperative efforts of taxpayers' organizations during the Great Depression.

Progressivism and Good Government Reform

Progressives pursued two main lines of attack in seeking to secure honest and efficient state and local government. One was to engage in traditional political activity with a view to ensuring election integrity and electing reform-minded individuals. Progressives formally organized in a number of major cities to advance these goals. In New York City, for example, younger Progressives created the City Club of New York, the purposes of which included "securing permanent good government for the City of New York through the election and the appointment of honest and able municipal officers." In furtherance of this objective, the City Club sought to organize Good Government Clubs in every assembly district. These clubs were dedicated to "securing honesty and efficiency in the administration of city affairs" and "procuring the election of fit persons to city offices." The City Club maintained that the efforts of Good Government Clubs "made possible the election of a reform mayor, William L. Strong, in 1894." New York City Progressives were also able to cobble together the political coalitions necessary to elect Fusion Party candidate Seth Low as mayor in 1901 and reform Fusion candidate John Purroy Mitchel as mayor in 1913.[5]

The reformers' other line of attack was to reform the structures and operation of government. Organized taxpayers in the 1930s who employed the collaborative tactics that Claude Tharp examined were the heirs to this strand of Progressive good government reform. Progressive structuralist reformers emphasized the need to rationalize and refashion public finance and administration along business and scientific principles in order to promote government that was open, honest, efficient, and capable of meeting the challenges confronting cities in the late nineteenth century. The Progressive model of city government included the following elements: a functionally departmentalized organizational structure, a strong city government having a centralized administration in which executives had the powers they needed to get things done, a merit-based civil service system, scientific and transparent systems of accounting and budgeting, the general professionalization of government, and the involvement of policy-generating experts to transform the structures of municipal government and the employment of experts to assist in operating it. The first two features targeted the organization of municipal government, the next three concerned its administration, and the last was directed at both.[6]

The Progressive urban reformers' approach to good government included both organizational and administrative innovations. Perhaps the most fundamental organizational reform was the institution of a municipal administrative structure of function-based departments, in which each department carried out a core function of city government. This administrative structure provided clear spheres of responsibility and clear lines of authority. In doing so, it promoted efficiency, competency, and accountability, and it reduced redundancy and waste. The functional division structure enabled cities to expand the scope and quality of public services; improve public education, health, sanitation, safety, and transportation; and generally enhance the quality of urban life.[7]

In addition to organizational reforms, the Progressive good government model contemplated a number of innovations in administration. The earliest to become widespread was a merit-based civil service system that was insulated from politics.[8] A second important administrative reform was the introduction of scientific and open systems of accounting and budgeting. The evil at which this measure was directed was the sorry state of municipal fiscal systems and records in the late nineteenth century. In most cities fiscal "systems" were decidedly unsystematic, and municipal finance records were disorganized at best and chaotic at worst. San Francisco, for example, did not even attempt to categorize or otherwise organize municipal expenditures by department, project, or function, but merely kept a running, chronological list of disbursements. As a consequence, municipal governments generally had no idea how much it cost to provide a particular service or unit of service or to run a particular department, which made budgeting and prudent management of city finances nearly impossible. It also meant that taxpayers, like their public officials, had no meaningful understanding of how and on what tax dollars were being spent. In addition, muddled financial records and opaque systems of public finance provided the perfect breeding ground for graft and corruption. In a 1908 speech to the American Statistical Association, Simeon N. D. North, the director of the United States Census Bureau, declared that the "most prolific source of municipal graft, its securest hiding place, its most effective agency in seeking immunity, is the chaos existing in municipal bookkeeping and in the classification of municipal accounts."[9]

The solution, good government Progressives argued, was to apply scientific and business principles and methods to public finance. William H. Allen, a political scientist who in 1905 organized the New York Bureau of City Betterment to further the reform of New York City government, maintained that "the adoption of scientific methods of accounting and of reporting the details of municipal business with a view toward facilitating the work of public officials" was crucial to achieving the bureau's goals. The product of this "scientific" approach to good government reform that had the most far-reaching and significant impacts was the National Municipal League's creation of a uniform municipal accounting system. Another important innovation was the adaptation to municipal finance of "unit cost accounting," in which financial inputs were compared with physical output in order to determine the cost of units of municipal functional service. This was made possible by the Federal Census Bureau's development of statistical reports concerning physical units of each such service (e.g., cleaning one square mile of city streets) that could be correlated with statistics on expenditures for those services. Good government experts also devised and put in place central purchasing systems and modern audit and budgeting procedures. The benefits derived from the implementation of these measures included far more accurate budgeting, better and more cost-effective municipal services, and more efficient and better-managed city government. Bringing order and openness to municipal fiscal affairs also meant that meaningful financial information was readily accessible to both public administrators and the public, made the detection of financial impropriety easier, and reduced the incidence of public officials' misappropriation and other misuse of public funds.[10]

Two elements of the Progressive good government agenda, the professionalization of government and the use of experts in that process and in devising and implementing structural reforms, were closely related. The drive to professionalize government flowed inexorably from the growing recognition of "public administration" as a discrete academic discipline and as a profession. Good government advocates considered the adoption of a city manager form of government as essential to this professionalization process. Under the city manager plan, a nonpartisan public administration professional oversaw a centralized administrative structure of function-oriented departments, each headed by a nonpartisan professional in the field relevant to that department's municipal function, including accounting, engineering, public transportation, public sanitation, public finance, public recreation, public education, and so forth. The push for professionalization was impelled by the fact that the administration and operation of a late nineteenth-century city having a population of more than thirty thousand required a level of specialized knowledge, training, and expertise that traditional municipal hiring practices, shaped by networks of patronage and nepotism, could not provide. There was a significant correlation between the success of municipal government reform and the extent to which cities utilized experts to manage and administer them.[11]

Policy-generating experts brought their expertise to bear in the transformation of municipal government from the outside and the inside. In the early twentieth century, organizations were established to conduct research in areas relevant to municipal administration and to offer recommendations to improve the machinery of government so as to make it more effective and efficient. These research bureaus also conducted audits of city departments and assisted in implementing their policy proposals. Some of these entities took the form of independent, nonprofit bureaus of municipal research. Local governments also created in-house departments of experts for this purpose. Des Moines, Detroit, Los Angeles, New York City, Madison, Norfolk, Rochester (New York), Cleveland, Kansas City (Missouri), Philadelphia, Sacramento, and San Francisco, among others, had public-sector or independent bureaus of efficiency. Two large cities, Chicago and Milwaukee, had both independent and in-house bureaus. State governments, including Washington, Kentucky, Maryland, and New York, also established departments to promote economy and efficiency in government, as did several county governments (e.g., Los Angeles County and Cook County, Illinois) and public school districts. The Government Research Association was established in 1914 to serve as a nationwide clearinghouse for these various good government research efforts.[12]

The Progressive vision of good government was a coherent framework whose constituent parts were interrelated to a considerable degree. The general professionalization of government depended on both a merit-based civil service system, in which appointment and promotion were based on qualifications and not connections, and the separation of politics from administration. Similarly, the efficacy of a functionally departmentalized organizational structure hinged on a centralized administrative structure through which department actions and programs could be coordinated and managed effectively and on being staffed by capable professionals. Scientific systems of public finance also required some professionals to operate them. Political scientists and other good government experts designed these reform measures and articulated their rationales.

Progressive Era reformers achieved modest success in refashioning and improving the structures and processes of city government. By 1908, a majority of large cities in the United States had adopted the National Municipal League's uniform system of accounting. In the second decade of the twentieth century, the functional theory of city government was generally understood and accepted, if not yet put in place, by public officials across the nation. Merit-based civil service systems had been established in many states and large cities before 1930. Efficiency bureaus made important contributions to municipal government reform in those cities that had them. Buffalo, Cleveland, and Detroit were especially successful in implementing significant structural reforms. New York City made reasonable progress in making city government more efficient and honest, at least until the Tammany machine returned to City Hall in 1918. In assessing municipal reform efforts in this period, historian Kenneth Fox concluded that "city residents of the late 1920s were 'better off' as a result of the expenditures and activities of their city governments than the city residents of 1904" and that "functional innovation appears to have aided in producing at least a modicum of municipal progress."[13]

Progressives produced only modest progress in the reform of municipal government in large part because Progressivism's good government impulse was neither grassroots nor widely diffused across the nation. Urban good government reform was primarily the province of urban elites, who had the time, resources, and motivation to pursue it. Most proponents hailed from cities' upper class and upper-middle class, and many were businessmen, lawyers, and other professionals. For example, of the 165 persons who founded the Citizens Union, a political reform organization in New York City, in 1897, "40 were lawyers, 28 businessmen, 24 merchants, 24 professional men, 14 bankers, 11 labor union leaders, 6 manufacturers, 2 were classified as workingmen, and 20 were not classified by occupation." Contemporaries sometimes derisively characterized these elite urban reformers. For many good government proponents, their motivation was a sense of civic obligation, spurred by notions of noblesse oblige. A less noble reason for some was the fact that municipal reforms enhanced the relative influence of urban elites because they weakened the patronage system that political party machines used to finance themselves and diminished the machines' political power.[14]

Whatever the motivation, urban good government reform in the Progressive Era remained a top-down affair in which a relatively small number of Americans participated and that, with a few exceptions, was confined to a modest number of large cities. Progressive reformers focused their efforts on the larger cities because that is where they mostly lived and worked and because it was those cities, by virtue of their size and complexity, that faced the most serious challenges in administering municipal government and delivering municipal services efficiently and effectively. Broad swaths of the American public did not agitate for good government reform prior to the Great Depression because their tax burdens were not that onerous and, consequently, they were not overly conscious of them.

The economic collapse after 1929 changed all that. Within a year or two, average taxpayers like Hal Steed faced ever-increasing tax bills and had become mindful of the cost of state and local government. Taxpayers determined to do something about it, establishing thousands of taxpayers' associations nationwide. In contrast to Progressive municipal reform, the good government impulse in the 1930s was a spontaneous, broad-based, grassroots phenomenon having wide support from the middle classes. Drawing on the foundation of good government measures and ideas that Progressives had developed in the previous generation, taxpayers' groups set out to implement a vision of economic and efficient government at the state and local levels. Taxpayers' leagues in the Great Depression consistently adapted and applied the salient features of the Progressive good government model in devising and executing their investigative, education, and legislative policies and programs.

The Constructive Economy Activities of Depression-Era Taxpayers' Associations

The moderate programs and activities of taxpayers' organizations were diverse, extensive, and directed at "constructive economy" in government.[15] Claude Tharp surveyed organized taxpayer activity at the state level as of 1932. He found that the main functions of taxpayers' associations were (1) research and investigation, (2) use of the information thus obtained to educate the public and government officials and to shape public policy regarding government administration and spending, (3) active engagement in the budget processes of state and local governments, and (4) a vigorous legislative program.[16] In these ways, taxpayers' leagues sought to cooperate and collaborate with local government officials and engage them constructively to promote good and affordable government and thereby reduce their taxes.

The research activities of taxpayers' associations were foundational in that they formed the basis for many of their other efforts. The larger organizations maintained paid staffs of accountants, lawyers, and other professionals to investigate subjects relevant to controlling government finance. The Arizona Taxpayers' Association had auditing and legal departments that analyzed state, county, and municipal budgets in order to cut costs. Moreover, "proposed bond issues are investigated and the influence of the Association is used to defeat those which appear unnecessary or excessive." The CTA conducted numerous assessments of government finance and administration in 1932. That same year, many tax levies in Montana were reduced as a result of the Montana Taxpayers' Association's examination of levies across the state and its subsequent recommendations. The Tennessee Taxpayers' Association completed three surveys on local government finance, and its work product was apparently sufficiently impressive that the governor selected the association's staff to act as a fact-finding body for the state legislature. Tharp noted that since 1915, the Taxpayers' Association of New Mexico had been "the only agency for assembling the material for the budget submitted to the legislature by the Governor" and that it was also involved in the formation of local government budgets. Many of the state taxpayers' organizations shared their professional staffs with local associations, especially at budget time, including those in California, Indiana, New Jersey, Louisiana, and Utah.[17]

Local taxpayers' groups likewise participated in the preparation of county and municipal budgets. A "carefully planned program of economy" prepared by the Washington County Taxpayers' Association in Tennessee led to a substantial budget reduction.[18] A. C. Rees, secretary of the Utah Taxpayers Association, boasted that the association had "succeeded in having all local budgets analyzed by the local taxpayers and, in the case of all larger units, to have definite demands made upon public officials for reduced expenditures. Despite the unprecedented shrinkage in assessed valuations, the old levies have been maintained, or reduced."[19] Harry Miesse, the Indiana Taxpayers' Association secretary, declared that in Indiana it had been "possible through the operation of county associations of taxpayers for members to watch the preparation of budgets, attend local hearings which are required by law—and advise with their own local officials as to what expenditures are proper and what are not."[20] Taxpayers' associations quickly learned that cooperation and interaction with public officials during the budget process were essential to controlling government spending.

The legislative program was a core activity of taxpayers' leagues for two reasons. First, many of the specific aims of taxpayers' associations, such as instituting sound accounting and budgeting systems for state and local governments or improving processes related to incurring public debt and issuing bonds, could be achieved only by enacting new laws or changing old ones. Second, often the unnecessary or excessive expenditure of public funds, such as imprudent public works programs or public contracts awarded without competitive bidding, could be prevented only by promulgating or stopping the passage of new legislation.

The necessity of an effective legislative program was self-evident to the leaders of taxpayers' groups even before the crisis in taxation after 1930. In a 1928 address to the National Tax Association, A. C. Rees had emphasized that

> good legislation promotes economy and efficiency in government. In this field, the taxpayers' association can wield a tremendous influence . . . by contacting with the legislators during the entire course of the session, assisting them to analyze proposed legislation, preparing digests, supplying data and in general serving as an official advisory council to the legislature.[21]

Speaking to the same body three years later, Harry Miesse placed greater stress on the importance of organized taxpayers sponsoring and opposing legislation. A taxpayers' association, he insisted, should not "sit meekly and watch the introduction of bills in the legislature to make it easier for the public to be plundered." It must "watch every bill introduced, study its possibilities, and then oppose it with all the vigor possible if it threatens a raid on the public treasury. Watching pending legislation, supporting good bills and fighting bad ones has been part of the program of the Indiana Taxpayers' Association."[22] Claude Tharp also highlighted the significant legislation-shaping and budget-shaping activities of other state taxpayers' associations, including those in Arizona, California, Kansas, Massachusetts, Minnesota, New Jersey, Tennessee, and New Mexico. For example, as a result of an extensive educational outreach to local officials and the public, the Minnesota Taxpayers' Association "had a prominent part in securing a 20% reduction in property taxes since 1930."[23]

Taxpayers' organizations performed a vital educational function by disseminating relevant information to the public and to public officials. Their officers spoke to civic clubs and chambers of commerce, gave radio addresses, and issued press releases. Many taxpayers' associations had their own publications. The CTA published a monthly magazine entitled *Tax Digest*. The New

Jersey Taxpayers' Association issued a monthly "Taxegram" as well as weekly bulletins. The Wisconsin Taxpayers' Alliance prepared a semimonthly magazine named *The Wisconsin Taxpayer*. These publications were generally regarded as reliable sources of information regarding public finance. In 1934, for example, the Governmental Research Association described *The Wisconsin Taxpayer* as a "wealth of information and valuable data with reference to Wisconsin's state and local government . . . as well as many interesting governmental facts and developments in other states."[24] The Taxpayers' League of Letcher County's goal of "educat[ing] the tax paying public on questions of taxation" was among the express purposes of nearly all taxpayers' groups.[25]

Taxpayers' associations after 1932 expanded the scope and intensity of the activities that Tharp had identified. In the mid-1930s, there were many more taxpayers' organizations, and those established before 1930 did much more of the same things because the exigencies of the Great Depression required it. Research and investigation continued to be a central, and perhaps the most common, activity of organized taxpayers. In 1933, the Lake County Taxpayers' Association in Gary, Indiana, conducted a study of county employee salaries to serve as the basis for proposing a general reduction in those salaries if necessary. The Taxpayers' Association of New Mexico, convinced that the absence of a scientific system of property valuation had produced significant disparities in property assessments, undertook a survey of property assessments in Santa Fe County "as a demonstration of a method which might be applied by taxing authorities in establishing a scientific basis for assessing property." The Kentucky Tax Reduction Association, established in December 1932, examined local government in six counties to establish an empirical basis for proposing a new county budget law. Partly as a result of the association's efforts, in early 1934 the Kentucky legislature passed a county budget statute that required uniform budgets for all counties and established budget commissions in every county. In Tennessee, the Hamilton County Taxpayers' Association audited certain city departments and prepared reports of its findings, which "contained many specific suggestions for achieving greater efficiency and economy." The Tennessee Taxpayers' Association's survey of Campbell County produced detailed recommendations for improving budgetary, purchasing, and accounting systems. Other research and investigation projects of taxpayers' leagues in 1933 reported by the Governmental Research Association in the *National Municipal Review* included those of the Taxpayers' Research League of Delaware, the Taxpayers' League of St. Louis County in Minnesota, the Utah Taxpayers Association, the New Bedford (Massachusetts) Taxpayers' Association, the Wisconsin Taxpayers' Alliance, and the Pierce County Taxation Bureau in Tacoma, Washington.[26]

The research activities of taxpayers' associations accelerated in subsequent years. The Taxpayers' Research League of Delaware embarked on an ambitious program to assess the public highway system, administrative procedures in county offices, methods of financing bonds for construction projects, state government costs, municipal financial data, and the state tax system.[27] In Connecticut the New Haven Taxpayers' Association formulated and began "a comprehensive program of research" concerning all city departments and functions with a view toward making recommendations designed to promote efficiency and economy in government.[28] The Tennessee Taxpayers' Association and the Hamilton County Taxpayers' Association engaged in a joint survey of the county's finances and administration and produced a 151-page report whose recommendations for "improving the administrative machinery" and for "effecting economies and retrenchment," if implemented, would reduce county expenses by 10 percent.[29] The Tennessee Taxpayers' Association increased its research activities significantly in 1934, and a summary of its projects for that year was published in the January 1935 edition of the *National Municipal Review*.[30] There was also a spike in the investigative efforts of the Lake County (Indiana) Taxpayers' Association, which examined the finances and budgets of the county and four cities and planned "much more thorough investigations of the proposed budgets for local units" in 1935.[31] In New Bedford, Massachusetts, the local taxpayers' group made a thorough study of tax abatements with the goal of making abatement procedures more equitable, and it also published a report on the city's financial condition that "pointed out how impossible it was to restore any pay cuts this year and was effective in forestalling such action."[32] The Stark County Tax League in Canton, Ohio, made recommendations to the governor on county reorganization based on its research of county governments, and it analyzed the impact of a tax limitation amendment that reduced the maximum property tax rate by one-third.[33] The state taxpayers' association in New Jersey "expanded its work in the field of local activities and its program of analytical research on public administration problems" and published reports, many of which were distributed to more than three hundred civic organizations, on a plethora of subjects, including the city manager form of government, highway policy, tax exemptions, the operation of the civil service, public welfare, public employee pensions, property tax delinquencies, consolidation of municipalities, tax limits, and proposed new taxes.[34] Taxpayers' organizations in Louisiana; Woonsocket, Rhode Island; Wisconsin; and New Mexico also completed numerous research projects in 1934.[35]

In 1935, the CTA commenced a study, after just completing one that advocated the establishment of a statewide police force, to "determine what constitutional and statutory changes are necessary in order to establish an appropriate state police system."[36] The Taxpayers' League of St. Louis County published a report highlighting excessive per-pupil costs in Duluth, Minnesota, schools and the fact that the school board's operating budget had exceeded the 20-mill statutory tax limit. It also assessed the "problem of public debt and the decreasing proportion of local revenues that are available for operating expenses after debt payments have been made." It used the information generated by the first study to litigate a declaratory judgment action that established the tax limit as binding on the school district, and it marshaled the evidence produced by the second one in a lawsuit in which it was "successful in preventing the city from adding additional bonds to the outstanding debt by attempting to issue bonds under emergency powers when in fact no 'emergency' existed."[37] The Tennessee Taxpayers' Association continued to expand its research programs. After the state legislature asked the governor to have all state government departments audited, the governor requested the association to supervise this task. It selected a public administration consulting firm to head the study, and it furnished its research services at no charge. The final report "revealed many opportunities for securing greater economy and efficiency in the conduct of the state's business." In 1935, the association also developed a comprehensive fiscal plan for the governor to present to the legislature, completed its fourth annual survey of state government finances, and undertook an investigation of public finances in each of Tennessee's 95 counties and in 145 municipalities.[38] Research projects were also carried out in 1935 by state taxpayers' associations in Kentucky, New Jersey, and Wisconsin and by local organizations in Worcester, Massachusetts; Fort Wayne, Indiana; Utica, New York; Santa Clara, California; and Woonsocket, Rhode Island.[39]

    The research, investigation, and public education activities of taxpayers' organizations proceeded full throttle in the ensuing years, all with the same overall objective. The director of the New Bedford Taxpayers' Association reported in May 1936 that the "association has continued its work of fact-finding and fact presentation, to the end that efficiency in government may be obtained."[40] Between legislative sessions the Wisconsin Taxpayers' Alliance "devoted most of its efforts to supplying taxpayers and citizens with information about ways and means by which their governments may be improved."[41] In June 1937, the Fitchburg, Massachusetts, Taxpayers' Association declared that in its "five years of service to taxpayers and public officials alike, the association has endeavored to promote efficiency in governmental administration by presenting scientific solutions to public problems."[42]

    Good government research remained high on the agendas of taxpayers' leagues because, in their view, experience had proven its worth. In 1936,

M. W. Madden, the research director of the Lake County Taxpayers' Association in Gary, Indiana, opined that "the need for unbiased governmental research organizations has been satisfactorily demonstrated in many parts of the country. Sporadic individual appeals and protests are seldom heeded, and only by organized efforts can taxpayers hope to hold governmental costs at sane levels." The Tennessee Taxpayers' Association contended that the improvements in state government administration resulting from its research activities had enabled Tennessee to close the fiscal year ending June 30, 1936, "with a continuation of about the same $5,000,000 annual reduction in expenditures that has occurred for three successive years." The same year the Taxpayers' Research Association of Fort Wayne, Indiana, reminded taxpayers that local taxes had been reduced 40 percent from 1931 to 1936 and asserted that "a major factor in this reduction of local governmental expenditures has been the work of the Taxpayers' Research Association, which was organized . . . to fight waste and extravagance with an array of facts and analyses by which adequate budgets for good local government at the lowest possible cost could be scientifically determined."[43] In 1937, the Fitchburg, Massachusetts, Taxpayers' Association maintained that its research efforts during its five-year existence had "been a major factor in the improvement of governmental administration" in the city.[44]

The other prominent constructive economy activity of Depression-era taxpayers' associations was their legislative programs. Through these programs organized taxpayers exercised both hard, or direct, legislative power and soft, or indirect, legislative power. "Hard" legislative efforts refer to those activities aimed at improving the laws affecting state and local government finance and administration by changing them and opposing laws on those subjects that taxpayers' leagues deemed imprudent, ill-advised, or otherwise contrary to the interests of taxpayers. Those measures were embodied in state constitutions, state statutes, local laws and ordinances, and municipal charters. Taxpayers' groups often worked closely with legislative bodies (state legislatures, county commissions, city councils, boards of selectmen, and so forth) in crafting new statutes and ordinances and revising existing ones, and they also were instrumental in obtaining public and legislative support for the approval or enactment of such laws. On other occasions they worked to defeat proposed legislation. Such hard legislative efforts focused on the law itself, as it related to the management and finance of government.

"Soft," or indirect, legislative efforts were aimed not at the law itself but at influencing, independently of the law, those policies, processes, procedures, and operations of government units, and actions of public officials, that could be influenced apart from the law. Taxpayers' associations endeavored to do so through a combination of cooperation, collaboration, negotiation, advocacy, and confrontation with public officials. The ends to which these means were directed were the perennial twin goals of economy and efficiency in government. Perhaps the area in which taxpayers' leagues exercised "soft" legislative power with the greatest effect was in the budget processes of municipalities, counties, and states. They also achieved considerable success in implementing improvements in government administration and operations.

The larger taxpayers' organizations, by virtue of their greater resources, generally had the most extensive and effective legislative programs. The Kentucky Tax Reduction Association drafted and sponsored nine bills dealing with county and local government in the 1934 state legislative session, five of which were "enacted into law and afforded the means of saving the taxpayers of Kentucky an estimated $5,000,000 a year." One of these measures was the new county budget law that established a uniform budget process for all counties. After this bill was passed, the association's staff worked with state officials in preparing the budget to be used by the counties pursuant to the legislation. Another statute abolished the office of county jailer and transferred the jailer's functions to the county sheriff, resulting in an estimated savings of more than $600,000 annually. In the 1936 legislative session, the Kentucky Tax Reduction Association defeated an attempt of the jailers' association to have this provision repealed.[45] A third measure, requiring annual audits of county finance records, had resulted in "substantial sums . . . being returned to local treasuries" by 1935. During the 1934 legislative session, the association also helped prevent the approval of a number of bills that, "if passed, would have done serious damage to the cause of good county government," according to John W. Manning of the University of Kentucky, who failed to identify these supposedly injurious bills.[46] The Kentucky Tax Reduction Association exerted hard legislative power to get important reforms enacted into law and to prevent the passage of other bills as well as soft legislative power to assist in implementing the county budget law.

The state taxpayers' association in neighboring Tennessee worked closely with the state legislature, especially in connection with budgetary matters and appropriations bills. The Tennessee Taxpayers' Association assisted the legislature in drafting the appropriations bills enacted in 1933, which reduced state government expenditures by 35 percent from the prior year, and the 1935 biennial appropriations act "assure[d] a continuation of most of the large reductions in the cost of government originally provided through the 1933 appropriations act." The association was also involved in the installation of the state's new central accounting system in the fall of 1935. In the 1937 legislative session, the taxpayers' group extended its legislative efforts to the subject of county government administration.⁴⁷

Taxpayers' organizations played an important part in securing the adoption of the manager form of government in many localities. In Nebraska, for instance, the Association of Omaha Taxpayers, formed in February 1932, was "instrumental in securing the adoption of several important reform measures" in 1934, including a manager form of government for Douglas County. City and county manager plans for government were a critical component of the business model of government, one premise of which was that government units would be better and more professionally run or managed by individuals with professional training and expertise in public administration than by nonprofessional elected officials. Reformers who had advocated for a business model of government in the Progressive Era argued that government administration had become an increasingly complex and demanding business requiring the application of "practical business methods" and "techniques of business management in government" by skilled professionals.⁴⁸ Consequently, manager plans for local government were a centerpiece of the agenda of good government organizations. In January 1935, the *National Municipal Review* touted Douglas County's adoption of a county manager plan of government as a model for other local government units.⁴⁹ The National Municipal League believed the manager form of local government to be essential to "the solution" of "the problem of curtailing budgets without abandoning services" and a great improvement over what it called "inefficient, archaic forms of government" typical of most municipalities and counties.⁵⁰ Good government professionals and taxpayers also supported the manager plan of government because it was nonpartisan and "keeps politics out" of local government administration.⁵¹

In 1936, the CTA "played an important role in the enactment of the 5% expenditure limitation law." It was also actively involved in efforts to streamline local government in Los Angeles County and was represented on the Committee on Governmental Simplification.⁵² That same year the Taxpayers' League of St. Louis County in Duluth, Minnesota, sponsored and secured voter approval of an amendment to the city charter establishing a tax rate limit, and it also persuaded county officials to implement many of its recommendations for improving purchasing and accounting procedures.⁵³ The Minnesota Taxpayers' Association, the Montana Taxpayers' Association, and the Massachusetts Federation of Taxpayers also had active legislative programs.⁵⁴

The New Jersey Taxpayers' Association maintained a vigorous and comprehensive hard legislative program, scrutinizing all bills introduced in the state legislature and preparing proposed legislation. It was particularly effective in bringing public pressure to bear on legislators. In 1934, it "led the opposition to a sales tax, and on this occasion organized the largest meeting of citizens ever assembled at Trenton to attend a public hearing conducted by a committee of the legislature. The legislation was defeated." Two years later it advocated revisions to the state's proposed local budget act and "was able to convince the legislators of the wisdom of its arguments and was successful in having the bill held in committee until the objectionable features," which would have substantially increased local tax rates, were stricken. It also succeeded in continuing a freeze on the salaries of municipal and county employees through its ability "to convince the legislators, at the public hearing on the question, of the insurmountable financial burden which would result . . . if such suspensions were not continued."[55]

The legislative program of the Taxpayers' Association of New Mexico included significant hard and soft efforts. The association's director worked with state legislative commissions to recommend needed legislation. The association also participated in drafting a variety of new legislative measures and facilitated their passage. Among these was a statute allowing taxpayers to pay delinquent taxes in installments, and the association "conducted an intensive campaign to acquaint taxpayers with this provision and it is believed that this effort was responsible for the collection of a large amount of delinquent levies." The Taxpayers' Association of New Mexico promoted good government legislation and then worked hard to make it effective. In 1935, the state legislature passed an act consolidating state revenue collection agencies, a measure for which the association had pressed for several years. Another principal activity of the association was assisting in the preparation of local government budgets and representing taxpayers at public hearings on budgets.[56]

The indirect legislative efforts of the Worcester Taxpayers' Association in Massachusetts are representative of such activities by large local taxpayers' associations. Formed in 1931, by 1935 it had nearly twelve thousand members. It organized and directed "a strong popular demand for continued economy toward city hall," successfully opposing the recission of public employee salary reductions, persuading local officials to install modern inventory and cost accounting systems, and obtaining larger shares of federal funds for the city. It also "made the most militant campaign in the history of the city to compel the city council to reduce the budget" in 1935. According to its executive director, the association prevented "fourteen unnecessary police department appointments made by the outgoing mayor," saving the taxpayers $30,000 annually, and put a halt to a number of proposed PWA projects because, it maintained, they would have required the city to incur substantial debt and the "maintenance of these new buildings and other projects would impose a large permanent cost on the local taxpayers." The Worcester Taxpayers' Association also endeavored to shape state legislation, but the exercise of such hard legislative power took a back seat to its soft legislative activities.[57]

Numerous other local taxpayers' leagues had vital legislative programs during the mid-1930s. Local organizations drafted and facilitated the passage of state legislation affecting state and local government and of municipal ordinances in their own communities. Through the legislative process, collaborative efforts, and public pressure, they exerted a powerful influence on the content and amount of state and local government budgets and of contracts entered into by local and county government units. In a host of ways, organized taxpayers at the local level in Fitchburg, Springfield, and New Bedford, Massachusetts; Chattanooga, Tennessee; San Jose, California; Utica, New York; New Haven, Connecticut; Gary, Indiana, and elsewhere promoted efficiency and economy in government, lowered their taxes, and shaped the structures of local government in their communities.[58]

Near the end of the decade John Elting, a contributor to *Forbes* magazine, surveyed organized taxpayer activity at the municipal level and found that the constructive economy approach continued to dominate taxpayers' efforts to control taxes. Elting noted the significant extent to which taxpayers' groups worked closely, cooperatively, and effectively with public officials. They engaged mainly in fact-finding, public education, and collaboration in developing budgets and streamlining operations. In Wheeling, West Virginia, a nonpartisan citizens' organization assisted the city council in preparing annual budgets, informed the public by distributing pamphlets and publishing weekly news bulletins in the local newspaper, and secured the adoption of a city manager system of government. The Taxpayers' Research Association in Fort Wayne, Indiana, "comb[ed] the budget, item for item, to shear off waste and duplication," yielding a tax rate for 1939 that was the lowest in ten years and the lowest per capita debt for any city of its size in the nation. The Indianapolis Chamber of Commerce's tax committee made line-item recommendations for reducing taxes that lowered tax requests by almost $2.2 million and cut 1939 tax levies below their 1938 levels. Taxpayers in five Massachusetts towns succeeded in scaling back municipal expenditures or tax rates in 1939. The constructive economy programs of organized taxpayers in South Bend, Indiana, prevented the city from issuing $6 million in bonds "for unnecessary public improvements," persuaded the city to adopt a "scientific system" for real estate assessment, and produced tax rates for each year from 1931 to 1939 that averaged 16 percent less than the rates initially proposed. The municipal research bureau in Baltimore "work[ed] quietly" with city officials to put in place a number of good government measures, among which were monthly financial analyses and coordinated accounting and purchasing systems, that produced "tremendous savings," cutting public debt by $16 million and pre-Depression departmental expenses by $3.4 million. The St. Paul, Minnesota, Bureau of Municipal Research, established in 1921, "worked unceasingly to present the facts to the voters," scrutinized budget proposals, succeeded in having a proposed bond issue for building a school lowered by $3 million, assisted in modernizing government operations, and curtailed government expenses by approximately 16 percent from 1930 to 1938. Other cities that Elting examined in which taxpayers "rel[ied] on cooperation with local government officials to cut taxes" included Warren, Ohio; Wichita, Kansas; El Paso, Texas; Shreveport, Louisiana; Roanoke, Virginia; Chicago; and Cincinnati. He found that economy programs and "intelligent tax-fighting" had decreased local government spending in Wheeling from $1,750,000 in 1930 to 1,150,000 in 1938, slashed South Bend's annual tax bill from $5.5 million to $2 million between 1932 and 1938, lowered Wichita's 1938 taxes to 79 percent of the 1930 levy, and reduced Cincinnati's municipal debt by more than 20 percent.[59]

Elting found that county and state taxpayers' associations pursued constructive economy with equal vigor. The Massachusetts Federation of Taxpayers, representing 150 local groups, achieved substantial spending reductions in the 1938 state budget by issuing press releases and bulletins, publishing a monthly newsletter, broadcasting radio programs across the state, compiling and sending to "more than 300,000 homes" the "voting records of state legislators on important spending matters," and closely scrutinizing legislation in order to "focus . . . the attention of legislators on specific measures." The Pennsylvania Economy League was a "non-political, non-partisan, fact-finding research organization" that "operate[d] on a platform of quiet cooperation with officials." It worked with the Taxpayers' Forum of Pennsylvania, which concentrated on legislation and, "using the facts supplied by the Economy League, sponsor[ed] legislation aimed to reduce government expenditures and increase efficiency." In Minnesota the state taxpayers' association employed "radio broadcasts, newspaper stories and magazine articles" to "tell . . . the story of government costs and high taxes to the public." Elting concluded that its "methods apparently have been successful: During ten years, more than $100,000,000 in local taxes has been saved." He also found that the Inter-Organization Conference in Ohio "had a large share in preventing the imposition of any new taxes since 1935" and maintained that the organization's research and publicity programs illustrated how "education in tax matters brings results" by "getting the facts" to the taxpayers and state legislators. The Washington State Taxpayers' Association's monthly publication had a circulation of approximately one hundred thousand, and it influenced spending and tax legislation and decisions in that state.[60] Sylvia F. Porter, an economist who at the time was the financial editor of the *New York Post* and later authored a number of widely read books on investment, surveyed taxpayers' organizations across the nation in 1940 and corroborated Elting's findings regarding the nature, extent, and efficacy of the constructive economy activities of taxpayers' associations.[61]

The constructive economy programs of taxpayers' organizations were diverse and local, targeting the particular deficiencies endemic to state and local government in the municipality, county, or state in which each taxpayers' league operated. Yet they all had at least three things in common. In their legislative activities, taxpayers' leagues aimed to effect structural changes in state and local government administration and finance, and many implemented lasting reforms. Crucial to these successes was the significant degree to which large taxpayers' groups and small, local ones worked together, the large organizations providing the resources and expertise that the smaller ones lacked and the smaller ones contributing the grassroots energy and the local support and connections that powered the taxpayers' association movement. Equally important were the law and legal institutions, to which organized taxpayers resorted regularly.

The efforts of taxpayers' organizations in California reflected all three of these features of the constructive economy facet of organized taxpayer activity in the 1930s. Leaders in business, industry, and agriculture established the CTA in 1926. It was an outgrowth of a series of earlier taxpayers' associations, the first of which, the Taxpayers' Association of California, had been formed in 1916. The CTA's board of directors was comprised mainly of executives from utility companies, railroads, insurance companies, banks, mining enterprises, agricultural producers, and other business interests.[62] The board included at least one academic, William B. Munro, a professor of history and government who wrote extensively on taxation and public administration.[63] Business interests were the moving forces behind the CTA because it was businesses that paid most state taxes in California at the time.[64] Local governments were financed almost entirely by property taxes that counties and municipalities assessed.[65]

The CTA's overarching purpose was to "work for economy and efficiency of government and reduction of taxes." To this end, the CTA vowed to promote "economies . . . in the collection and expenditure of public monies," "advise and cooperate with public officials" to achieve these goals, "conduct non-partisan and non-political research studies" of public administration and finance in state and local government, and educate the public and public officials regarding government administration.[66] By 1936, with a decade of experience under its belt, the CTA had articulated more specific objectives to advance its general goals, including (1) improving the auditing, budgeting, and reporting procedures of government units; (2) reducing the number of independent taxing bodies; (3) eliminating redundant or overlapping government functions; and (4) centralizing the purchasing processes of state and local government units.[67]

Contemporary observers differed sharply in their assessments of whose interests the CTA was promoting. According to Elmer Staffelbach, director of research for the California Teachers Association, the CTA was "largely financed and directed by representatives of the public utility and other corporations actuated by a desire to escape equitable taxation."[68] Franklin Hichborn, a left-leaning progressive investigative journalist, likewise viewed the CTA primarily as a front for corporate interests who sought to shift the tax burden to the "plain citizen taxpayer," and he described Milbank Johnson as "a reactionary of the most pronounced type." Although Hichborn recognized that some "excellent citizens" were members of the CTA, he contended that the CTA mainly represented the interests of the class of taxpayers "who can help themselves shift part of their just proportion of the tax burden to the shoulders of the class that cannot help themselves."[69] On the other hand, Claude Tharp argued that the taxpayers' associations that he studied, including the CTA, were fairly "representative of the diverse interests of the state" and of all taxpayers, were nonpartisan, and were "promoted and headed by men of character who have held consistently to a constructive and progressive program."[70] In 1939, John Elting gave the CTA positive ratings across the board. He commended the CTA for its belief "in research, working with officials and publicity of tax facts," and he argued that its "work is made effective by strong support from public opinion" shaped by "the tremendous newspaper coverage of tax stories released by the association": 3,219 in one year.[71]

The truth about the CTA probably lies somewhere in the middle of these two contrasting perspectives. The lion's share of the CTA's financing and leadership came from the business world, and reducing taxes on public utilities, railroads, and other corporations was certainly high on its agenda. Nevertheless, the CTA also supported limitations on state and local government expenditures as well as reforms to promote economy and efficiency in government, which benefited not only corporations but also small property owners and individual taxpayers. Business interests likely dominated the CTA, but many of the proposals it advanced lightened the tax burden on the average citizen taxpayer too. Moreover, the CTA collaborated with and assisted the many local taxpayers' organizations that were established in the early 1930s and that represented "the plain citizen taxpayer" for whom Hichborn advocated.

In the 1930s, the CTA was at the center of taxpayers' efforts to bring about constructive economy in government by revising the state constitutional provisions and statutes and the local ordinances that dictated how state and local governments financed and conducted their operations. Organized taxpayers in California invoked the law in two principal arenas to meet the fiscal challenge that the Great Depression presented to state and local government. First, they played an important role in bringing about the constitutional overhaul of California's fiscal system. In addition, the CTA and local taxpayers' organizations collaborated on a number of projects that helped refashion public administration and finance. Taxpaying citizens relied on the law and legal institutions in a variety of ways in their government reform and tax resistance efforts.

Organized taxpayers' most enduring and far-reaching legislative accomplishment was in the area of taxation reform. The CTA and other California taxpayers' organizations worked with the state legislature to secure the passage of amendments to the taxation provisions of the state constitution in 1933. When the stock market crashed in 1929, state and local government units in California were raising revenues by means of a dual taxation system that Californians had implemented by constitutional amendment in 1910. It was a dual tax system in that the state, on one hand, and municipal and county governments, on the other, derived their revenues from completely separate and distinct sources. The state's revenues came from a gross receipts tax on public utility companies, a gross premiums tax on insurance companies, a corporate franchise tax, a bank capital stock tax, and a gift and inheritance tax. In the 1929–1930 fiscal year, the public utilities gross receipts tax alone accounted for 52.5 percent of state revenues. In contrast, local governments were financed almost entirely with taxes assessed on real and personal property.[72] As a practical matter, local governments did not "collect any tax for state purposes, and properties taxed for state purposes no longer [paid] directly any county or city tax."[73] This taxation system was unable to finance government or to adapt when the business revenue sources and property tax values on which it depended began contracting in the early 1930s.

The crisis in taxation provoked intense responses by California taxpayers. Corporations had long found unsatisfactory a fiscal system in which they paid nearly the entire cost of state government. Property owners and small businesses, faced with declining incomes, insisted on property tax relief. Local taxpayers' associations and the CTA lobbied legislators and garnered public support to enact constitutional changes to the state's fiscal system.

In 1933, voters approved the Riley–Stewart amendment to the state Constitution. It was named after Ray Riley, the state controller, and Fred Stewart, of the California Board of Equalization, who had presented the initial proposal to the state legislature. The amendment completely transformed California's public finance system. The gross receipts tax on public utilities was to be eliminated and utility company property returned to local property tax rolls, which expanded the local property tax base. The amendment required the state to furnish additional aid to local schools and to raise further revenues to cover that cost. It also limited spending increases by state and local governments, on which taxpayers' leagues had been especially insistent.[74] The additional revenues mandate prompted the state legislature to enact a retail sales tax in 1933 and a personal income tax in 1935. Because personal incomes increased far more rapidly than property valuations in the ensuing years, the base for the income and sales taxes likewise grew much faster than the property tax base. One unintended consequence of the Riley–Stewart amendment was that the changes in the mix of taxation may have reduced property taxes but created a flexible system of taxation that allowed government to expand rapidly in the ensuing decades.[75]

The measure received broad support from organized taxpayers. Public utilities were pleased to be rid of the gross receipts tax, and corporations generally benefited from creating a more elastic fiscal system that expanded the tax base to include personal incomes and reduced the government's reliance on business taxes. Small businesses and property owners emphasized the amendment's limitations on state and local spending and the property tax relief they would bring. Consequently, local taxpayers' leagues as well as the CTA promoted the Riley–Stewart amendment.[76] Still, some Californians, such as Hichborn, argued that the sales and income taxes imposed following its adoption further shifted the tax burden from corporations to "the general taxpayer."[77]

Organized taxpayer activity in California also was representative of the extent to which state taxpayers' associations throughout the nation worked with municipal and county taxpayers' organizations to promote good government reform at the local level. The CTA primarily assisted local taxpayers' organizations through its research and legislation programs. It maintained a paid staff of, or hired when needed, lawyers, accountants, public administration experts, and other professionals to examine subjects relevant to advancing good government and reducing its costs and to advocate for taxpayer-friendly legislative changes. Even before local taxpayers' groups began multiplying after 1930, the CTA worked and shared its expertise with municipalities and counties to facilitate "economies and efficiencies" in government, including Los Angeles, San Diego, Fresno County, and Sonoma County.[78] Once local taxpayers began organizing, the CTA frequently cooperated with them to advance their shared goals of containing the cost of local government and reducing local taxes. Most local taxpayers' associations could afford little in the way of relevant expertise. The CTA not only shared its professional staff with local organizations, especially at budget time, but also conducted numerous research projects regarding local government. As early as 1932, the CTA had more than thirty studies in progress concerning, among other things, budgeting, bonding and accounting processes, and the organization and operation of local government units and departments.[79] The next year the CTA completed a survey of all departments in Alameda County government, a budget review "at the request of the Santa Anna city council to effect a 20% reduction in the city's 1933–34 budget," audits of the administration of the juvenile home and welfare department in Santa Barbara County, population estimates to aid in projecting government expenditures and revenues, and an extensive examination of administration and finances in Los Angeles County.[80]

The CTA also worked with local taxpayers' leagues to shape legislation pertaining to local government and local taxes. CTA experts frequently appeared before public officials during the budget process and succeeded in influencing municipal and county budgets. The CTA had input into legislation affecting public finance and administration through its representation on various public bodies. In 1932, the CTA was appointed to the State Advisory Council of the Tax Research Bureau "to enable taxpayers to participate actively in an official study being made for the guidance of the legislature."[81] It also had a seat on the Committee for Governmental Simplification and convinced the legislature to adopt a 5 percent expenditure limitation law.[82]

The collaboration between local taxpayers' associations and the CTA was vital to their success because the symbiotic relationship provided a means by which each could draw on resources unique to the other, with their combined impact being greater than the sum of the individual parts. Working in tandem allowed organized taxpayers to harness the spontaneous energies of local taxpayers' leagues, to which most organized taxpayers belonged, and to avail themselves of the financial resources and professional expertise that the CTA brought to the table. In doing so, taxpayers' organizations optimized taxpayer zeal and taxpayer assets.

The constructive economy activities of taxpayers' associations proved, in most instances, to be constructive and effective when it came to refashioning the structures of state and local government and to promoting good government reform. Organized taxpayers were pivotal in securing the implementation of the good government reforms that Progressives had articulated a generation earlier.[83] Functionally departmentalized organizational structures increasingly became the norm, as states, counties, and municipalities streamlined their administrations, eliminated redundant functions and departments, and consolidated agencies. They also centralized their administrative structures and administrative authority in executives. The adoption of the manager form of government by many cities and counties not only promoted the Progressive model of strong local governments but also contributed to the overall professionalization of government by ensuring that it was overseen by public administration professionals. Equally crucial to making government more professional, more efficient, and less expensive was the frequent use by state and local governments of experts in fields relevant to public administration, many of whom were employed or recommended by taxpayers' organizations, to assist in devising and implementing good government reforms, and the employment of such experts to operate government agencies and departments.

The Progressives' notion as to the necessity of applying "scientific" principles to the problems of public administration also gained wide acceptance as a result of the constructive economy activities of taxpayers' leagues. Taxpayers' associations undertook to establish "a scientific basis for assessing property"; to develop scientific and transparent budgeting, purchasing, inventory, and accounting systems; to project government revenues and expenses on the basis of population studies; to "scientifically determine" adequate budgets; to promote uniformity in budgeting; and to make government effective and efficient "by presenting scientific solutions to government problems."[84] In these efforts taxpayers' organizations exhibited a data-driven, evidence-based, empirical approach to meeting the challenges of public administration and good government reform in the Depression era.

Sometimes, however, taxpayers' leagues went too far in their enthusiasm to slash public expenditures, and their "constructive economy" efforts produced destructive results. In these cases, government revenues were reduced to such an extent as to undermine the ability of state and local governments to fulfill all of their core functions until public officials, usually quite soon, developed streams of replacement revenue. Such instances were uncommon and short-lived, since most taxpayers had an interest in having government provide an adequate level of the necessary public services on which they depended.

Public officials and administrators, teachers' unions, municipal creditors and bondholders, and others whose interests were threatened by unsystematic, across-the-board budget cuts tried to steer organized taxpayer energy into constructive economy channels. In 1932, the National Municipal League created the Committee on Constructive Economy in State and Local Government, predicated on its organizers' belief that the "great body of taxpayers undoubtedly desire wise economy if they only knew how to get it." This committee in turn undertook to establish citizens' councils for constructive economy in states and cities that would "consider the problems of maintaining essential community services in the face of the need for reduction of public expenditures . . . to the end that the present widespread demands for reductions may produce actual and permanent improvements in government, the tax system, and the services rendered by public and semi-public agencies." These citizens' councils assisted taxpayers' groups with their research, education, and legislative programs and often provided them with relevant expertise. The National Municipal League's Citizens' Councils for Constructive Economy initiative was active until 1936, when the league discontinued it because by then organized taxpayers had largely abandoned tax strikes, indiscriminate budget cuts, and other "destructive" actions that threatened the revenue streams of counties and municipalities or "the preservation of those [government] services which are necessary in a civilized society."[85]

The proponents of constructive economy in academia, public education, banking, and public administration were not, however, the driving forces behind the constructive economy activities of Depression-era taxpayers' associations. State taxpayers' organizations had developed mature public education, research, and legislative programs in the two decades prior to the stock market crash in 1929. In response to the post-1930 taxation crisis, taxpayers' groups significantly expanded these activities and developed new ones at the state and local levels. Good government experts and the National Municipal League's constructive economy program did reinforce the constructive economy strain of organized taxpayer activity, but they did not initiate or control it. Taxpayers' leagues vigorously pursued constructive economy in government even after the National Municipal League pulled the plug on its constructive economy outreach in 1936.

The taxpayers' associations' constructive economy programs were also constructive in their approach to reforming government and lowering taxes. Before 1930, organized taxpayers confined themselves almost exclusively to education, research, and legislative activities. The taxpayers' organizations that Claude Tharp examined in 1932 had adopted a nonpartisan, cooperative posture in which they sought to engage constructively with public officials. As Hal Steed put it, "My idea was to conciliate them, not fight them."[86] Even in the late 1930s, John Elting found that many taxpayers' organizations "operate[ed] on the theory that the most effective way to improve local government and reduce taxes is to work cooperatively with public officials" and that organized taxpayers generally preferred "working with, not against, city officials in lopping off expenditures."[87] Although contention between taxpayers and tax spenders was to some extent inevitable, pre-1930 taxpayers' leagues emphasized collaboration, not confrontation, and clashed with state and local government officers infrequently and only as a last resort.

The swift and severe contraction after 1930 of the property and income tax bases from which government raised revenue, however, impelled organized taxpayers to consider and employ additional, more adversarial means in the tasks of refashioning and controlling the cost of government. Taxpayers' associations continued to maintain vigorous research and legislative programs, but the economic exigencies of the era convinced taxpayers of the need to pursue three aggressive strategies: traditional and sometimes partisan political activity that included campaigns for property tax caps, litigation, and calls for collective action by taxpayers to withhold their real estate tax payments until tax spenders agreed to reduce property assessments, public spending, and taxes. Organized taxpayers had engaged in electoral politics and had filed taxpayers' lawsuits before 1930, but in the next decade they committed more time and resources to these efforts. Tax limits and tax strikes were new additions to the taxpayers' arsenal, products of the desperation engendered by the Great Depression. Taxpayers' groups experimented with these activities as they endeavored to navigate the taxation crisis.

4

The Populist Politics of Taxpayers' Groups

"Vox Populi, Vox Dei"

In 1933, citizens of Berlin, New Hampshire, organized the Berlin Taxpayers' Association after they learned that the city tax collector had misappropriated taxes, and the mayor and city council not only were unwilling to do anything about it but reappointed the tax collector to another term.[*] Later that year, 150 unemployed workers, agitated by municipal corruption, business bankruptcy and belt-tightening, and continued joblessness, united under the National Recovery Administration guidelines and formed the Coos County Workers Club. By January 1934, it had four thousand members (in a city whose population peaked at 20,018 in 1930), many of whom also belonged to the Taxpayers' Association, and the Workers Club "proposed to launch an independent political party in the coming city elections." To facilitate this objective, in February 1934, the Workers Club began publishing a newspaper, the *Coos Guardian*, which pledged to "be the official mouthpiece of the Coos County Workers Club, the veterans, the farmers, the taxpayers, and all other individuals or groups who have a just cause." The publication's perspective and purpose were exemplified in its populist motto, "*Vox Populi, Vox Dei*" (the voice of the people is the voice of God), which warned political leaders that the people's wishes are irresistible.

---

[*] Portions of this chapter originally appeared as "Citizens with a 'Just Cause': The New Hampshire Farmer-Labor Party in Depression-Era Berlin." *Historical New Hampshire* 62, no. 2, 117–137. © 2008 New Hampshire Historical Society. Used with permission.

The Taxpayers' Association, the Workers Club, and other civic organizations and individuals came together to create the Berlin Labor Party (later renamed the Berlin Farmer-Labor Party). The new party's stated raison d'être was to address "the real issues affecting our bread and butter" and to "more justly distribute" the "burden of the depression." Its candidates for mayor and three city council seats were elected in March 1934, and in the 1935 election the Farmer-Labor Party gained control of city government.[1]

These efforts by New Hampshire taxpayers are among the many instances in which Depression-era taxpayers' groups engaged in traditional politics to promote economy and efficiency in state and local government and to reduce their taxes. Taxpayers had three specific political objectives. The first was to elect candidates for public office who were sympathetic to their plight and promised tax relief. The second was to persuade public officials to reduce government spending by bringing political pressure to bear on them. The third was to amend state constitutions and statutes in order to limit the amount of taxes that states, counties, and municipalities could levy on property. Taxpayers in the 1930s achieved modest success in electing candidates of their choice and much success in achieving the other two goals.

Taxpayers' political activities were part of a populist political wave that swept the nation in these years. The wave, in turn, found its source in a populist impulse in American politics that extended back to the eighteenth century. Organized taxpayer politics during the Great Depression are best viewed through the prism of the inveterate tradition of populist politics in the United States.

Populism in America: From the Early Republic to the Great Depression

Populism is an elusive and contested concept that has proven extraordinarily resistant to definition or synthesis.[2] Michael Kazin has described populism as "more an impulse than an ideology" and as a "flexible mode of persuasion" that numerous and diverse segments of "the people" have employed throughout the history of the United States. He defined it as "a language whose speakers conceive of ordinary people as a noble assemblage not bounded narrowly by class, view their elite opponents as self-serving and undemocratic, and seek to mobilize the former against the latter." Cas Mudde views populism as an antielitist "thin-centered ideology" that divides society into two opposing groups, the "pure people" and the "corrupt elite," and to which "thick-centered" or "full" ideologies (for example, socialism or nationalism) are attached. Lawrence Goodwyn approached the subject from a popular agency perspective, in which the populist impulse mobilizes "the people" to promote their common interests through mass democratic movements.[3] Populism is reformist, not revolutionary: populists generally do not seek to destroy the existing political order but to enhance their status and power within it. Populism is often the product of discontent (economic, social, political, or a combination thereof) and associated with the attendant emotions of discontent, resentment, and frustration. In the United States, populism is usually characterized as a bottom-up, spontaneous phenomenon.[4]

The populist politics in which taxpayers engaged in the 1930s exhibited many of these characteristics. It was a "people's" or mass democratic movement in which broad swaths of the American public invoked the language and spirit of populism to influence both elections for public office and the spending habits of public officials and to promote ballot initiatives concerning taxation. Taxpayers used populism as a vehicle (or, in Mudde's words, "a thin-centered ideology") to which they harnessed their antitax and efficient government agendas. Taxpayers' political activities were not revolutionary but reformist. They did not seek to upend political institutions but to reform government, lower taxes, and increase their influence within the existing political order. Like the taxpayers' associations themselves, their political efforts were grassroots and indigenous.

American populism also has temporal attributes. It is both long-standing and episodic, omnipresent but latent more often than not. Populism may be understood as a thread inextricably woven into the fabric of American political history that harks back to the days of Thomas Jefferson and Andrew Jackson. The populist impulse is an undercurrent in American politics, available to be tapped by political actors and movements, erupting from time to time with considerable power and impact and then subsiding. Populist movements have abated for a number of reasons. Sometimes the political establishment co-opts the populists' agendas and actors or finds other ways to counter them. In other instances, times simply change: the circumstances that precipitated the populist episode have been ameliorated or disappeared. In still others, the populist wave has simply run out of energy. As Richard Hofstadter observed with respect to the People's Party of the 1890s, each populist episode may be considered "to be merely a heightened expression, at a particular moment in time, of a kind of popular impulse that is endemic in American political culture."[5]

There were four major populist episodes in the United States from the nation's founding through the Great Depression. The first peaked in the 1790s, included a strain of plebian Anti-Federalism, provoked the young nation's first tax rebellion, and generated the guiding principles of American populism's worldview. The second lasted from the 1820s to the 1840s and was associated with Jacksonian Democracy. The movement most commonly identified with the term "populism" in the United States is the populist revolt in the late nineteenth century, which began with the agrarian discontent of the 1870s and 1880s, consolidated with the formation of the People's, or Populist, Party in 1892, and reached its high-water mark in the 1896 election. The crisis of the Great Depression precipitated the fourth populist episode, in which tax leaguers were among the many voices of populist protest seeking to advance the interests and enhance the status of ordinary Americans.[6]

The 1794 Whiskey Rebellion was the first significant populist outburst after the ratification of the Constitution.[7] An armed tax insurgency was not, however, the only significant feature of this populist episode in the republic's early years. Of more lasting significance were the contributions of various Democratic-Republican thinkers that were to influence and inform populism and populist rhetoric in the United States. Thomas Jefferson had founded the Democratic-Republican Party in 1792 to formalize political opposition to Hamilton and the Federalist Party. In the 1790s, these Anti-Federalists refined and articulated several key, and closely related, themes in Democratic-Republican thought that formed a kind of populist heritage on which populist movements would draw from that time forward. These included the agrarian myth, suspicion of the "money interests," and a theory of labor value grounded in a producer ethic.

The agrarian myth was a prominent feature of Jeffersonianism. Jeffersonians imagined a republic peopled by a large class of small freeholders whose industry, virtue, and self-sufficiency would form a bulwark against the corrupting influences of commerce and finance. "Those who labor in the earth," declared Jefferson, "are the chosen people of God, if ever he had a chosen people, whose breasts he has made his peculiar deposit for substantial and genuine virtue." In Jefferson's view, agrarian labor and virtue were inextricably connected: "I repeat it again, cultivators of the earth are the most virtuous and independent citizens." Only such virtuous and, therefore, patriotic citizens could be depended on to sustain the republic and preserve liberty against the malign influences of pro-British, Federalist elites. For this reason, Jefferson concluded that the "small land holders are the most precious part of the state."[8]

The other side of this Jeffersonian coin was an antipathy toward commerce, industry, and banks, whose leaders tended to be pro-Federalist and pro-British. Jefferson regarded these segments of the national economy, and the eastern seaports and large cities in which they were based, as conduits of corrupting British influences that he feared would undermine the republic. In the early 1790s, Hamilton's national bank was a principal target of such Jeffersonian hostility. John Taylor, a Virginian who was one of the more radical Jeffersonians, argued that the Bank of the United States replicated an English system of finance that would by its very nature corrupt American politics. He characterized those who owned bank stock as "false citizens" and posited,

> If a number of the members of Congress are stockholders, or bank directors, then an illegitimate interest is operating on the national legislature—then the bank has seduced away from their natural and constitutional allegiance, the representatives of these states—and then, even foreigners—our late most malignant and inveterate enemy—have obtained an influence on our national councils, so far as they have obtained bank stock. The English who could not conquer us, may buy us.

William Manning, a tavernkeeper from Billerica, Massachusetts who reflected the plebian end of the Jeffersonianism spectrum, shared Taylor's suspicion of the Bank of the United States. Manning considered the bank an instrument of the wealthy to promote their interests at the expense of the interests of the debtor classes, whose labor was ultimately responsible for the creation of wealth.[9]

This idealization of the yeoman farmer and demonization of bankers and merchants combined to contribute to Jeffersonians' development of a theory of labor value rooted in producerism that proved foundational to the language of populism in America. Its proponents divided society into two groups: a laboring producer class whose members generated wealth, and a parasitic, nonlaboring, nonproducing class whose members reaped the fruits of the producers' labor. The former consisted of artisans, shopkeepers, laborers, farmers, and small manufacturers. The latter included bankers, merchants, large landowners and manufacturers, physicians, ministers, and lawyers. Among the most forceful expositions of the producer theory of labor value was *The Key of Liberty*, a 1798 treatise authored by William Manning, the Massachusetts tavernkeeper. Manning argued that "Labour is the sole parrant of all property" and a fount of republican virtue, that, in contrast, "those that live without Labour are ever opposed to the prinsaples & operation of a free Government," and that there was a fundamental "Difference of Interests Between those that Labour for a Living," who he described as "the Many," and "those that git a Living without Bodily Labour," who he described as "the few." "A free Government," Manning maintained, "is a government of laws made" and "executed according to the will & interest of a majority of the hole peopel and not by the craft, cunning & arts of the few." Jefferson likewise subscribed to producerism and saw politics as a struggle between the industrious, virtuous, and productive many—the people—and the self-interested, nonlaboring, unproductive few—an antirepublican elite. Thenceforth, the producer ethic would infuse populist notions of "the people" and "the elite."[10]

The primacy of "the people" and the producing classes and suspicion of the money interests and commercial elites became key elements of American populism and recurring themes in subsequent populist episodes. The Age of Jackson witnessed a surge in populist energy and discourse. The populists of this era drew heavily on the concept of American society that Jeffersonians had crafted. "The people" figured prominently in Jacksonian rhetoric, and Andrew Jackson promised to vindicate "the will of the people." Laborers and other ordinary Americans considered Jackson their champion and representative. His political supporters described him as "one of the people," and he was widely regarded as a "friend of the people" and as being "on the side of the people."[11] Class conflict between the workingman and the businessman, and the producer ethic on which it was based, were also central elements of Jacksonian political thought.[12] Jackson's 1832 message to Congress, in which he vetoed the bill to recharter the Second Bank of the United States, typified populist discourse in this period. In true Jeffersonian fashion, he aligned himself with the producing many, the people, against the privileged few, the money power. The "rhetoric of the Bank veto," historian Harry Watson has observed, "would become the language of protest," and "its populist uses would expand in the future."[13]

The populist revolt that culminated in the formation of the Populist Party in the 1890s invoked and built on the tenets of the Jeffersonian conception of American society. The populists of this era adapted the rhetoric of Jackson's Bank veto to rally their followers, persuade others, and protest the existing political system. They regularly extolled the producers and maligned the ubiquitous money power that, populists maintained, was engaged in a vast international conspiracy to impoverish the producing class and enrich the "monied aristocracy." The Populist Party's platform decried the fact that "from the same prolific womb of governmental injustice we breed the two great classes—tramps and millionaires," and reminded Americans that "wealth belongs to him who creates it." Despite such inflammatory language and the presence of radical elements in the People's Party, late nineteenth-century populism was on the whole a reform, not a revolutionary, movement that sought change within the existing political framework. The Omaha platform characterized the People's Party as a "party of reform," and Populist leader Ignatius Donnelly's declaration that "we do not believe that the path of reform is through the torch and the rifle" but "through the ballot box" is representative of mainstream populism in this period. The platform also demanded that state revenues "be limited to the necessary expenses of the government economically and honestly administered," a cause that Depression-era taxpayers' associations were to embrace and strive to implement.[14]

The taxpayers' association movement in the 1930s was one manifestation of the next significant populist episode in the United States. This populist moment is most commonly associated with three individuals: United States senator Huey Long of Louisiana, Father Charles Coughlin, and Dr. Francis E. Townsend. In the mid-1930s, they and their respective movements garnered considerable political support among ordinary Americans who felt that the First New Deal programs had not adequately addressed the economic crisis.

Long was a populist demagogue who had been elected governor of Louisiana in 1928 and to the Senate in 1931. He attributed the Depression to a single fundamental cause: extreme wealth inequality and the consequent strangulation of mass consumer spending. Long's solution, which he announced in 1934, was his "Share Our Wealth" program, in which a confiscatory tax scheme would limit the amount of wealth any person could possess, the amount that could be passed on to heirs, and one's annual income. The wealth thus appropriated from the "plutocrats" would be redistributed to the "common man," with the government providing every family with a $5,000 household allowance and guaranteed annual income of between $2,000 and $2,500. Long correctly identified wealth concentration as a serious structural flaw in the American economy, but his plan had its own fatal flaws in that there simply was not enough concentrated wealth to fund it and much of that wealth was not liquid and, therefore, not easily redistributed. Nevertheless, in 1935, prior to Long's assassination in September of that year, there were approximately twenty-seven thousand Share Our Wealth Clubs with seven million to eight million members, and polls indicated that Long could attract as much as 12 percent of the vote as a third-party presidential candidate.[15]

Father Coughlin was a Catholic priest in Michigan who began broadcasting his sermons on radio in 1926 but, in 1930, shifted his focus to the nation's dire economic situation and political solutions to them. He blamed the Great Depression on a perennial populist bugaboo: the money power, the bankers whom he demonized as the "money changers in the temple" and whose "private control and creation of money" he challenged. Coughlin denounced the gold standard and the "cursed famine of currency money which blights our progress and multiplies starvation." In November 1934, he set forth "Sixteen Principles of Social Justice" designed to shift control of the money supply from private bankers and the Federal Reserve Bank to a "government-owned Central Bank" that would increase the money supply, facilitate affordable credit, and thereby provide a job-creating stimulus to the economy. To promote these goals, Coughlin established the National Union for Social Justice, whose nationwide membership peaked at nearly one million.[16]

Townsend was the third of these populist critics of the New Deal. He claimed that his crusade for old age economic security was the product of an epiphany he had in late 1933, when he observed three old women scavenging for food from garbage cans in an alley. He began promoting his Townsend Old Age Revolving Pension Plan, under which the federal government would pay a $200 monthly pension to persons over sixty, on the condition that they spend it within a month, which would be financed with a 2 percent transaction tax. Local Townsend Clubs were established throughout California in 1934 and had proliferated across much of the nation by early 1935, with nearly five hundred thousand paid members. Although the enactment of the Social Security Act in 1935 took some of the wind out of the Townsend forces' sails, his Townsend Clubs, historian Alan Brinkley observed, "survived and prospered, developing into a large and vibrant national movement, infiltrating the fabric of insurgent politics in nearly every region of the country."[17]

By 1935, the three movements were interacting and overlapping. Many Americans belonged to both Share Our Wealth Clubs and Townsend Clubs and also followed Coughlin's broadcasts. Polls indicated that Long could receive modest support as a third-party candidate in the 1936 presidential election, but his assassination in September 1935 left the Long, Townsend, and Coughlin forces without a viable national candidate. Nevertheless, in 1936, Coughlin formed the Union Party, which nominated North Dakota congressman William Lemke for president. That same year Gerald L. K. Smith, who had succeeded Long as the face of the Share Our Wealth Club, allied with Townsend, and in June they declared their support for Lemke. Coughlin proved impossible to work with, however, and the Union Party was plagued by divisions. In November, Roosevelt was reelected in a landslide.[18]

Although their foray into presidential politics failed spectacularly, the Long, Townsend, and Coughlin movements did impact national politics and public policy. Roosevelt's move to the left in 1935 with the Second New Deal was, to some extent, an acknowledgment of the First New Deal's shortcomings. It was also, though, a response to the popular support for these three populist dissidents and sought to co-opt that political support. The Second New Dealers brought a more pro-labor, antibusiness bent to promoting economic recovery and a new emphasis on tackling the problem of wealth inequality.[19]

Despite the strong and distinctive personalities of their respective leaders, the Long, Coughlin, and Townsend movements shared important characteristics. The policies and programs that each advocated aimed to remedy real and perceived deficiencies of the New Deal, under which the economic recovery had been slow and fitful. Their constituents, like those of contemporaneous taxpayers' organizations, were not mainly the poorest Americans but the middle classes, the "more substantial citizens who had been laid low by the Depression." The ideologies of all three drew heavily on the populist tradition in American politics, including populism's affirmation of community and the principles of local control and accountability that also guided taxpayers' associations in this period.[20]

Taxpayers' Leagues and the Politics of Depression

Organized taxpayers' political aims in the 1930s were threefold: to change the people who governed cities, school districts, counties, and states; to slash government spending by convincing elected officials that it behooved them politically to do so; and to obtain property tax relief by limiting the amount of property taxes that state and local governments could assess. Taxpayers' associations engaged in traditional electoral politics with a view to electing candidates who represented, or were at least mindful of, the taxpayer's situation. If taxpayers' organizations could seize control of government, especially at the local level, they would be in a better position to implement fiscal and administrative policies directed at reducing taxes. Failing that, taxpayers' leagues applied political pressure to public officials to streamline government and cut expenses. Finally, organized taxpayers effectuated fundamental structural change to state fiscal systems by amending state constitutions and statutes in order to cap the amount of property taxes that states, counties, and municipalities could levy to finance their operations. To this end, organized taxpayers proposed and campaigned for constitutional tax limitation ballot initiatives in dozens of states. They also advocated a variety of statutory property tax limitation measures in many states.

In the first three decades of the twentieth century, taxpayers' associations largely eschewed traditional political activity, especially of a partisan nature. Leaders of taxpayers' organizations and those who examined them maintained that taxpayers' leagues should encourage good people to run for office and work collaboratively with elected officials to promote economy and efficiency in government but that they should not participate in electoral politics. In Claude Tharp's estimation, it was imperative that "a taxpayers' association . . . declare its intention to remain non-political" and that "no one group representing a certain . . . political party dominates."[21] A. C. Reese, while secretary of the Western Taxpayers' Association, declared in 1928 that the duty of promoting good legislation regarding state and local government "must now be assumed by some representative, non-political organization, such as a taxpayers' association."²² Three years later Harry Miesse, the Indiana Taxpayers' Association's secretary, insisted that a taxpayers' association

> must be non-partisan in theory and in fact. Its greatest strength will come through enlisting the membership and active participation of representatives of all political parties to the end that they may sit down together as citizens and as taxpayers rather than as partisans, and consider what is wisest and best as a whole. Because of its non-partisan character, a taxpayers' association must remain aloof from political campaigns.²³

These sentiments represented the dominant worldview among organized taxpayers through 1931. Taxpayers' organizations participated in political campaigns only infrequently, and when they did so they tended to emphasize the nonpartisan nature of their efforts. After the five candidates favored by the Teaneck Taxpayers' League were elected to the city council in the 1930 election, for instance, the league later stressed that all five were "non-partisan candidates" and that the "league did not have among its members a single person then active in partisan politics."²⁴

Many taxpayers' groups continued to shun partisan politics in the 1930s. The members of a county taxpayers' league in Kentucky exemplified this approach to tax reduction, declaring that "this organization shall be non-partisan and non-political" and "shall have no political leanings whatsoever, but shall be ever alert to the interest of the tax paying public."²⁵ Speakers at a 1934 Minnesota county taxpayers' association gathering stressed that "we are not a political organization," are "not affiliated with any party," and "do not want to see taxes mixed up with politics." The questionnaire that the New Jersey Taxpayers' Association mailed to all candidates for public office concluded with the admonition that "we owe it to our families as well as to ourselves, to be first of all a taxpayer, second, a Democrat or Republican or any other party we choose." In New Jersey, some members of a local taxpayers' league severed their ties with it and formed a competing "nonpartisan" organization because the first group had "injected politics into their association."²⁶

In the early 1930s, however, there was a moderate, though not seismic, shift in the attitudes of organized taxpayers toward traditional political activity. Some actions took the form of indirect educational efforts with respect to elections. The Minnesota Taxpayers' Association and the New Jersey Taxpayers' Association, for example, prepared and distributed to candidates for state and local office a questionnaire on taxation and then published the candidates' responses in newspapers and furnished them to local taxpayers' leagues.

The Minnesota organization also prepared and published tax platforms for state legislature candidates.[27] Officials and candidates for elective office solicited support from taxpayers' groups at election time. The Worcester Taxpayers' Association proclaimed that in the 1935 city election "the candidates of both parties strove to outdo each other in stressing their interest in the taxpayer . . . , and it was impressed upon the political aspirants that the path to success at the polls was along the idea of pledging economy during the campaign."[28] Likewise, the three gubernatorial candidates in New Jersey felt compelled to address the New Jersey Taxpayers' Association at its annual meeting during the 1934 campaign.[29] In 1932, the Stearns County, Minnesota, Taxpayers' Association backed and helped to elect candidates to the state legislature, but two years later it declined to endorse any candidates because its members were satisfied with the incumbents' tax reduction efforts.[30] Prior to the 1936 state elections in Massachusetts, local taxpayers' associations distributed pamphlets disclosing waste, inefficiencies, and massive budget shortfalls in numerous communities. "The publicity worked," reported *New York Post* finance editor Sylvia Porter. "When the . . . election returns were counted, 17 out of 19 legislators whose records showed they stood for extravagance had been defeated."[31]

The political strategies of organized taxpayers generally came under the umbrella, well understood by public officials, of political pressure. Journalist Gordon Gaskill examined this aspect of taxpayers' associations' programs to learn "how thousands of aroused citizens are cracking the whip against public extravagance in their communities." Gaskill captured the essence of taxpayer political pressure in his conversation with a "veteran of the tax wars," who explained that the "secret" of effective tax resistance

"Can be solved by working the old seesaw."
"The seesaw?" I echoed, puzzled.
"Sure. You know—when one end goes up, the other goes down?"
"Of course, but what goes up and what goes down?"
"Well, you raise hell and lower taxes."

Taxpayers understood full well the capacity of this strategy to bend the conduct of officeholders to the voters' will. Some taxpayers' groups even codified it in their charters and organizational documents. When taxpayers in Letcher County, Kentucky, established their taxpayers' league they adopted bylaws providing that the "purpose of this organization shall be to bring concerted effort and pressure for the needed tax reforms."[32]

Organized taxpayers regularly undertook such concerted efforts. The power of political pressure is seen in the Washington State Taxpayers' Association's observation that "since our monthly publication now has a circulation of some 100,000 copies, we find [the] inclination of [public officials] to assist [us] is more apparent." This statement prompted John Elting to argue that "votes speak a language that officeholders understand. As soon as they know voters are on their trail, they will begin to do something about cutting expenses and taxes." In her survey of taxpayers' leagues, Sylvia Porter likewise found that in "every section of the United States taxpayer groups are proving their ability to force the politicians to trim their sails," as when "more than 6,000 New Yorkers descended upon the state capital to impress upon their legislators the meaning of a cent to a man who earns $15 a week." Porter commended taxpayers' organizations for their belief "that the democratic way [to cut taxes] is to eliminate needless expenses by exerting the influence of the ballot, publicity, and eternal vigilance." In 1931, the Philadelphia Taxpayers' Association's members marched on city hall and "forced the City Council to cancel a proposed increase" in real estate assessments. The relationship between increasing political heat on public officials and reducing taxes was borne out by the experience of organized taxpayers in Massachusetts, where, according to Elting, in 1938 the Massachusetts Federation of Taxpayers "put heavy pressure on state legislators" and thereby defeated "spendthrift legislation" that would have cost taxpayers more than $48 million.[33]

Small but vivid abuses, as well as large ones, by public officials who were tone-deaf to the cries of the beleaguered taxpayer had the potential to fire up taxpayers and coalesce their political energies. The following anecdote exemplifies this phenomenon:

> Suddenly the police radio rasped to life, and all over Worcester, Mass., officers in patrol cars bent forward to listen. "Calling Car 6," . . . the radio droned grimly. "Bring two sardine sandwiches to the police station. That is all." Thanks to that frantic appeal, Worcester taxpayers today are saving thousands of dollars every year. The call was picked up by a listening post of the Worcester Taxpayers' Association, which was on the warpath against waste in the police department. The association knew that police cars were being used as glorified personal taxicabs for high officials, but it needed a striking incident to rouse the citizens. Sardine sandwiches did it. . . . In the end the department was overhauled. The little luxuries and extravagant trimmings were sloughed off.

Other examples of inefficiency, fiscal carelessness, and "extravagances" that drove taxpayers to distraction and then to action include a "luxuriously equipped" dogcatcher's vehicle in a Michigan town; a second, unnecessary telephone on each desk in an Arkansas city hall that increased the city's annual telephone bill by more than $1,000; a sheriff's use of expensive engraved stationery; a county government spending $5,000 replacing a boiler rather than $150 to refurbish it; the assignment to each garbage truck in a Midwestern city of six workers (a driver, four laborers, and one inspector, though nobody could "explain what the inspector was supposed to inspect"); excessive travel reimbursements; a $130 monthly salary paid to a municipal swimming instructor three years after the city had closed its swimming pool; a New Jersey town that maintained the same number of teachers to staff its schools even after student enrollment had decreased by three thousand and thereby reduced the number of teachers required by nearly one hundred; $10 wastebaskets in a Massachusetts municipality; and an $8,000 pigpen at a county farm in Indiana. Taxpayers' organizations were able to eliminate much unnecessary spending by publicizing it, attending public hearings and confronting tax spenders with the evidence thereof, reminding officeholders that it was in their political interest to be frugal with tax dollars, and voting out of office those who did not heed the taxpayers' message.[34]

These many instances of waste and inefficiency would not have struck most taxpayers in 1939 or 1940 as mere "extravagant trimmings." The substantial annual cost of one hundred teachers' salaries and benefits is self-evident. The $130 monthly salary for the municipal swimming instructor is equivalent to $2,442 in 2021 dollars, and the $10 wastebaskets would cost $187 today. At the time public officials were incurring these expenses, the national unemployment rate was 14.6 percent and the average weekly earnings of manufacturing workers was $25.20, or the cost of two and a half wastebaskets.[35]

Taxpayers' leagues also actively promoted their own candidates and tickets for state and local office. New Jersey was a hotbed of such political activity. The Newark Taxpayers' Association contributed to the ouster of four of the five incumbent city commissioners in the 1933 election. Two of the victorious candidates, Reginald Parnell and Austin Waldron, had accused four of the incumbent commissioners of "graft and corruption in the government, and pledg[ed] a $2.50 tax rate" to reduce taxes, and they had "received their unusual independent vote from supporters in the Newark Taxpayers' Association, of which they were among the principal organizers." In the same election cycle, the Audubon Taxpayers' Association conducted but lost "a spirited fight" against the Republican organization in the Audubon borough election.[36] In the fall of 1933, the Citizens and Taxpayers' Association of Asbury Park, New Jersey, put forth a slate of candidates for five vacancies on the city council, and all five won.[37] The Jersey City Taxpayers' Association spearheaded the creation of a fusion political movement that sought unsuccessfully to oust the incumbent Democratic administration, which had rejected the association's demands for cuts to the municipal budget, in the May 1933 municipal elections.[38]

The rough-and-tumble politics of the New York City metropolitan area were even rougher than usual for the Taxpayers and Rentpayers Association of West New York, New Jersey, during the 1935 city election campaign. The association had initiated a fusion movement against the local Democratic machine to unseat the five Democratic city commissioners in the May 14 municipal election. On the night of April 17, there was an attempt to murder Irwin Rubinstein, the leader of the fusion movement and legal counsel to the association. As Rubinstein drove home on dimly lit Broadway Street, a sedan with four men in it forced his vehicle to the curb. One man got out of the car, put a pistol through the driver's window of Rubinstein's vehicle, and fired two shots, but as he did so Rubinstein struck the assailant's arm and the shots went wild. Rubinstein drove away and narrowly escaped. He carried on the political battle, and the anti-Democratic fusion movement "carried all its five candidates to victory."[39]

Hal Steed's Taxpayers' League of Atlanta and Fulton County expressed some ambivalence about the extent to which it should engage in political activity. Steed favored a cooperative approach, preferring "to conciliate [officeholders], not fight them." Others "insisted that we go into politics," declaring that "the elections will be coming on soon. . . . We must pick our candidates." For a time, the tax leaguers adopted something of a compromise stance, seeking to have input in the election of state legislators who had the power to enact "our proposed reforms, notably consolidation of local governments," but not taking sides in local elections. When an effort to recall the public works superintendent whom the league supported was made, however, the league went into high gear politically, elicited the largest voter registration ever at the time, and "we taxpayers won." Steed and other moderates headed off a tax strike by convincing taxpayers that the "remedy is not in striking, but in orderly cure at the polls." Although the league's experiments with vote control were inconsistent, it engaged in traditional political activity when its leaders deemed it appropriate.[40]

John Elting identified several communities in which taxpayers took "a wholehearted plunge into local politics, organizing along political lines and trying to put into power men who will get results of the kind wanted." In Indianapolis, petitions opposing tax increases garnered more than thirty thousand signatures and more than three thousand citizens attended a public hearing on the matter, "all of which," Elting observed, "is dynamite to any political officeholder." South Bend, Indiana, taxpayers "organized, like a political party, into regions, districts, and sections," enlisted 1,500 members who "demand[ed] action," and compelled local officials to control expenditures and modernize the machinery of government. Organized taxpayers in St. Paul, Minnesota, "support[ed] economy-minded city officials who themselves cut proposed budgets." In 1938, Roanoke, Virginia, citizens were "so wary of spending borrowed money . . . that in the September election nine out of ten proposed PWA building projects were beaten." Elting concluded that "it pays to back economy-minded officeholders to the limit, for they can get results which non-officeholders cannot."[41]

Local taxpayers' associations in Connecticut made inroads both at the ballot box and on the political pressure front. The taxpayers' organization in Manchester was able to elect two of its leaders to the board of selectmen in 1931 and to reelect them in 1932 through the "concerted efforts of members and sympathizers." In Windham organized taxpayers were influential in reducing public employee salaries and other public expenses. The taxpayers' group in Manchester pressed for and realized significant cuts in the 1931 and 1932 budgets. The Hartford Taxpayers' League convinced the Board of Finance to slash the salaries of city employees by 10 percent. In early 1933, a journalist who reported on taxpayers' associations in the state was sufficiently impressed with the results they had obtained to predict that "a new voice will be heard at the State Capitol, the voice of organized taxpayers whose pocketbooks are directly affected by whatever the Legislature finally will decide to do" on "matters of taxation."[42]

The Farmer-Labor Party in Berlin, an industrial city in northern New Hampshire, is a good example of the connection between organized taxpayer political activity and political party formation in this period. When taxpayers realized that the city officials were indifferent to the tax collector's thievery, they formed a taxpayers' association. In October 1933, the Berlin Taxpayers' Association filed a taxpayers' lawsuit against the mayor and city council, and it prevailed in the trial court four months later. This litigation occurred contemporaneously with the establishment of the Coos County Workers Club and was a catalyst for the creation of the Berlin Farmer-Labor Party by the Taxpayers' Association, the Workers Club, and other organizations.[43]

The Workers Club publication, the *Coos Guardian*, which vowed to speak for the workers, taxpayers, farmers, and others who had been battered and left behind by the Great Depression and which also spoke for the Farmer-Labor Party, reflected many of the populist themes that were resonating throughout the nation. Its focus was on the producing classes, whose "wages are lagging behind the cost of living" and "have gone as low as can be and yet permit a working man's family to live." While acknowledging that "there is much dispute as to whom and what caused this depression," the *Guardian* was clear about who was not to blame:

> The depression has brought forth among the laboring class unnecessary and undue suffering that is not yet relieved. . . . Yet the class of people who had the least to do with bringing about the depression nevertheless has to suffer the most, simply because they are not in government.

The fundamental problem, the *Guardian* maintained, was the excessive concentration of wealth in the hands of a few and the consequent diminution in the purchasing power of ordinary Americans. It observed that the "original theory behind the [National Recovery Administration] codes was to arrive at a restoration of prosperity or normalcy by increasing public purchasing power. . . . Hence the problem was to get more money into the hands of the unemployed." But the National Recovery Administration had failed to do so, having "discarded" the "'wage before profit' policy" that had been intended "to effectuate an increase in the general purchasing power." The *Guardian* concluded that "increasing purchasing power is simply another way of saying shifting or redistributing wealth. A partial redistribution of wealth is the only solution."[44]

The Berlin Farmer-Labor Party applied these principles when it came to the consumption and cost of local government services and to protecting the interests of taxpayers. Its March 1934 platform declared that "the city must practice economy in this depression is no news any more than the fact that real estate under our taxation system is overburdened. Taxes must be lowered, and the sooner the better." Accordingly, it pledged that "strict economy . . . be practiced in all city expenditures in view of reducing taxes to within the real estate values and revenues" and, with a view toward partial wealth redistribution, that "all necessary payroll economies . . . be practiced on the higher paid employees and not inflicted on the rank-and-file of the departments." The latter policy was a response to the fact that, under the Democratic city administration that the Farmer-Labor Party was seeking to oust,

> when employment is to be curtailed and wages reduced, they begin at the foot of the ladder. The man who is getting only enough to buy the necessities of life is slashed; those at the top overlooked or cut slightly. . . . We believe that economy at the top is in order as being more just and also more of a saving.

In this respect, the Berlin Farmer-Labor Party reflected both its populist "*Vox Populi, Vox Dei*" motto and the bottom-up political reform efforts typical of taxpayers' organizations. In the fall of 1934, the Farmer-Labor Party struck a similar populist tone, proposing a platform that "realized that fundamental changes are necessary in our society, that the burden of making a living may be equalized and made more uniform in order that everyone may be provided with the necessities of life now denied to a great many of our fellow citizens."[45]

In the March 1934 city elections, Farmer-Labor Party candidates won three (out of nine) city council seats and the mayoralty. The success of the Berlin Farmer-Labor Party attracted the attention of the *Boston Sunday Globe*, which observed that if the party should "begin missionary work in other industrial centers of the State, the old party leaders would have something to think about." The following March Berlin citizens voted overwhelmingly in favor of the entire Farmer-Labor slate of candidates, including attorney Arthur Bergeron, who had represented the Berlin Taxpayers' Association in its lawsuit against the city and was the editor of the *Coos Guardian*, for mayor. During Bergeron's first administration, all of the 1934 platform pledges were fulfilled, and Berlin taxpayers realized significant property tax relief.[46]

The Farmer-Labor municipal government worked closely and effectively with Brown Company, one of the largest pulp and paper manufacturers in the United States and the city's largest employer, which initiated bankruptcy reorganization proceedings in the fall of 1935. To assist the ailing firm, the city allowed Brown Company to pay its 1935 property taxes at a reduced rate. In 1936, the city entered into and renewed a cooperative unemployment wood cutting contract with the state, Brown Company, and the Reconstruction Finance Corporation to finance the harvesting of timber necessary for the company's operations by using the city's unemployed men. Under the plan, the Reconstruction Finance Corporation loaned money to the city, which used the funds to finance the company's logging operations. In turn, Brown Company repaid the "loan" by purchasing wood from the city in increments based on the company's market demands for wood and its ability to pay for it. Constructive engagement with Brown Company was a consistent theme in Farmer-Labor Party policy. In the run-up to the 1937 city elections, the party reminded citizens "of the pleasant and mutually profitable relations that existed between Brown Company and the City" and called on them to vote "straight Farmer-Labor" and reelect the Farmer-Labor mayor and city councillors so as to "assure full cooperation with the Brown Company in a fair and equitable manner to all concerned and protection to both wage earners and taxpayers."[47]

In anticipation of the 1936 general elections, Farmer-Labor activists across the state formed a New Hampshire Farmer-Labor Party and chose a slate of candidates for statewide offices, but the fledgling party received just 1 percent of the vote. In the March 1936 municipal elections in Berlin, however, the Farmer-Labor administration had been reelected, and the Farmer-Labor Party remained in power until 1938. Brown Company, having benefited from the cooperation of the Farmer-Labor city government, experienced the beginnings of a financial recovery that would continue through the next decade. Philip Glasson, the secretary of the Berlin Farmer-Labor Party, later recalled that "by 1937 Brown Company got profitable again" and rehired the employees it had laid off.[48]

As the local economic recovery gained momentum, the Berlin Farmer-Labor Party's political position was increasingly undermined. In the 1938 city elections, the Farmer-Labor candidate for mayor, Edward Legassie, one of the more left-leaning socialist members of the party, lost to the Democratic nominee. The following year Berlin voters elected a more moderate Farmer-Labor Party mayoral nominee, Amie Tondreau, who served as mayor until 1943. Nevertheless, after 1938, the Farmer-Labor Party ceased to be a dynamic force for political change as its raison d'être became increasingly irrelevant in a burgeoning local economy.[49]

The Berlin Farmer-Labor Party was representative of the populist protest movements springing up in response to the Great Depression, and it manifested key elements of the populist impulse in the United States. It embraced producerism, focusing on the plight of workers and farmers and on implementing economic measures intended to improve their lot. An editorial in the *Guardian* suggested that "perhaps the reason why Labor should enter and stay in politics is best explained in a little poem," which included the following stanza:

> *The ones that do the useful work*
> *Are poor as poor can be,*
> *And those who do no useful work*
> *Live in luxury.*

The poem's author is unknown, but Jeffersonians, Jacksonian Democrats, and late nineteenth-century populists had all penned similar sentiments. The Berlin party championed "the People" and the "common man" in their quest for economic justice. Its leaders and members were suspicious of national elites, whose First New Deal policies had failed to increase the purchasing power of the general public and whose June 29, 1934, National Recovery Administration code hearing concerning proposed revisions to the pulp and paper code Bergeron derided as "a plain farce and a bluff." They were likewise distrustful of the local elites who had mismanaged city government to the detriment of workers and taxpayers and had turned a blind eye to the tax collector's malfeasance.[50]

The Farmer-Laborites of Berlin also evinced that curious mixture of radicalism and pragmatism that characterized American populism. They were radical in their advocacy for a partial redistribution of wealth as necessary to rectify the prevailing economic inequities and in their firm opposition to existing political power structures. In this respect they reflected the long-standing American tradition of hostility toward large accumulations of wealth that may be traced at least as far back as plebian Anti-Federalism and that manifested itself politically from time to time. Fundamentally, though, the Farmer-Laborites were practical individuals, not die-hard ideologues, who were motivated primarily by a desire to mitigate the harsh economic circumstances facing their community. They sought to reform capitalism, not uproot it, and to moderate its operation and effect. Indeed, although the Berlin Farmer-Labor Party railed against concentrations of wealth and promoted workers' rights, it never sought to undermine Brown Company but, rather, worked collaboratively with it and endeavored to put the company on a firmer foundation.[51]

Populist politics, the law, and evolving notions of citizenship combined in the crucible of organized taxpayer activity in Berlin to produce a viable third-party political movement. The taxpayers' association's lawsuit and the ensuing political reform activities of the taxpayers were galvanized by the economic dimension of citizenship and by the rights-based conception of citizenship that was becoming ascendant in the 1930s. Taxpayers locked horns with tax spenders over how the latter were spending—and in the case of the tax collector, stealing—public funds. The taxpayers' suit played a crucial part in generating the political critical mass necessary for the creation of the Farmer-Labor Party in Berlin. In turn, the party engaged in bread-and-butter politics in order to increase citizens' purchasing power and lighten their tax burden. These same dynamics of American law, populism, and citizenship animated much of organized taxpayers' political activities in the 1930s, including their quest for property tax relief through the adoption of tax limitation measures.

Intense and widespread advocacy of tax limits was the other facet of organized taxpayer political activity. Some states had experimented with tax limitation measures in the previous three decades, but they were not common before 1930. Two developments provided the impetus for the adoption of property tax caps: a precipitous decline in the assessed value of taxable property and a marked increase in tax rates and tax delinquencies as the U.S. economy contracted in the early 1930s. In Ohio, the total assessed value of taxable property plummeted from almost $13.5 million in 1932 to just over $8 million in 1933, and in the same period accumulated tax delinquencies spiked from approximately $63 million to more than $164 million, or 91 percent of the taxes levied in 1933. In Michigan, the general property tax base shrunk by more than 30 percent between 1930 and 1933, the average tax rate reached a record high in 1932, and in the 1932–1933 fiscal year the tax delinquency rate reached 35 percent in Detroit, an average of 40.5 percent in the rest of the state, and 92.5 percent in the Detroit suburbs. Increasingly unable to pay their property taxes and desperate for relief, taxpayers actively promoted constitutional and statutory tax limits in numerous states.[52]

Taxpayers developed two approaches to capping their property taxes, both of which prohibited the amount of taxes from exceeding a certain percentage of assessed valuation. Many states enacted a single percentage maximum that applied to all types of taxable property. Voters in Michigan approved one of the earliest such measures in 1932, amending the state constitution to cap the total amount of property taxes at 1.5 percent of the assessed valuation. During 1932 and 1933, organized taxpayers also secured the passage of constitutional amendments establishing property tax ceilings in New Mexico (2 percent), Ohio (1 percent), and Oklahoma (1.5 percent). Other states adopted a more calibrated methodology that provided different percentage limits for different classes of property. In November 1932, West Virginians amended their constitution to divide taxable property into four classes and impose a tax limit on each class: 0.5 percent on Class I property (tangible and intangible personal property), 1 percent on Class II (residential property and farms), 1.5 percent on Class III (real and personal property located outside of municipalities, other than property in Class I and Class II), and 2 percent on Class IV (real and personal property within municipalities other than Class I and Class II). That same year voters in the state of Washington, in response to organized taxpayer protests, approved by a two-to-one margin a ballot initiative that imposed a maximum property tax of 4 percent on urban property and 2 percent on rural property. Most of these tax limitation measures were incorporated into state constitutions, but in some states taxpayers secured them through legislation. Washington's tax limit was initially statutory, and legislatures in Indiana, Delaware, Minnesota, and Nebraska also enacted various statutes circumscribing property taxes.[53]

Taxpayers' associations were not, however, in the vanguard of this tax limitation movement. Rather, its principal impetus came from organized real estate interests, in particular the National Association of Real Estate Boards and its affiliated divisions at the state and local level, whose members had a direct and significant interest in capping taxes on their real estate. The rationale for tax limits was simple: real estate was being taxed disproportionately in comparison with other forms of taxable property or with taxable income. The real estate organizations that were among the main backers of the tax ceiling in Washington argued that it was necessary because taxable real estate constituted "only about 35 percent of the wealth, but bear[s] 85 percent of the taxes" and that "the cost of government must be forced down." Tax limitation measures proved to be somewhat effective in reducing the property tax bills of real estate owners and shifting some of the overall tax load to others, but they did little to reduce the cost of government.[54]

Agitation for tax limits was not an explicit element of the programs and activities of most taxpayers' associations. Indeed, at least one, the Stark County Tax League in Ohio, complained that the adoption in November 1934 by Ohio voters of a further reduction in the tax ceiling would shrink revenues faster than a commensurate reduction in the cost of government could be achieved.[55] Such opposition to tax caps shows that taxpayers' organizations were not simply antitax entities. Rather, they sought to balance the level of necessary government services against the taxpayers' ability to pay for those services. Still, many of the members of the real estate organizations that backed tax limits also belonged to state and local taxpayers' associations, so there was considerable support for tax limitation measures in taxpayers' associations even if there is little evidence that most openly promoted them. In any event, the taxpayers themselves, whom the taxpayers' associations represented, clearly and overwhelmingly supported constitutional and statutory tax ceilings, as is demonstrated by the fact that voters approved such revisions in at least twenty states during the 1930s, including Washington, Michigan, Ohio, Nevada, West Virginia, Indiana, New Mexico, Oklahoma, Arkansas, Minnesota, and Nebraska.[56]

The effects of these measures were immediate and significant. On the one hand, they did fulfill the taxpayers' expectation that their property tax bills would be reduced. After West Virginia adopted its tax limit, property tax levies were cut by between one-half and two-thirds. The other side of this coin, though, was the corresponding reduction in property tax revenues that were the main source of funding for most local governments. After Washington adopted its 4 percent/2 percent tax cap in 1932, the following year state revenues from the general property tax fell approximately 60 percent, and city and county tax levies also experienced large reductions. Ohio's 1 percent maximum diminished revenues by roughly $40 million the next year. Government cost cutting could not keep pace with revenue losses and, consequently, states enacted business, sales, and other new taxes to make up the revenue shortfall. Most of the benefit of tax ceilings flowed to large property owners, and small taxpayers saw little shrinkage in their taxes in the aggregate.[57]

The tax limitation laws adopted between 1932 and 1934 produced a host of unforeseen and undesirable consequences. "Local officials were faced with the dilemma of how to obtain sufficient revenues for operating purposes."[58] In the short term, they often were unable to do so, resulting in a dramatic curtailment of local government services, as occurred in West Virginia and Ohio, among other states. In the long term, public officials found replacement revenues from other sources, such as taxes on business revenues and alcoholic beverages, the effect of which was not to reduce the public's overall tax load but merely to shift it from one class of taxpayers, owners of real estate, to others.[59] By arbitrarily restricting the revenue-raising capacity of government units, tax limits also undermined municipal credit. As Frederick L. Bird, the director of municipal research for Dun & Bradstreet, observed, a municipality's "ability to borrow, and the rate at which loans can be secured, are contingent upon the risk involved to the lender, and such risk is manifestly increased when arbitrary limits are placed upon a municipality's ability to tap its resources for repayment."[60]

As one might expect, tax spenders were vehemently opposed to tax limitation measures. Many political scientists, public administration experts, and tax officials harshly criticized these laws as being unduly rigid, throttling the delivery of services by state and local government, and ineffective in reducing the overall tax burden, as taxes were merely shifted from owners of real estate to other taxpayers.[61] One of the earliest such critiques was put forth by Joseph P. Harris of the University of Washington, who examined the likely impacts of the property tax caps that Washington voters had approved in November 1932. He concluded that "every indication points to a period of drastic retrenchment in governmental activities all along the line, except for welfare and public works financed by bond issues, which will pile up financial troubles for the future."[62] The National Municipal League, a nationwide citizens organization committed to good government, devoted almost the entire November 1935 issue of the *National Municipal Review* to the negative consequences of real estate tax limitation. In an editorial introducing this symposium on tax ceilings, the National Municipal League argued that "tax limitation represents probably the most serious immediate menace with which local self-government and sound public finance is faced at the present time."[63] Simon E. Leland of the Illinois Tax Commission likewise maintained that the adoption of tax limitation proposals would "have disastrous effects upon governmental activity in Illinois amounting to chaos and the complete breakdown of many services in various sections of the state. . . . These schemes have so frequently curtailed government service and produced fiscal chaos that the plan has been permanently discredited."[64]

The push for tax limitation measures continued after 1934 but slowed appreciably. In 1935, many more proposals were rejected than adopted. Delaware, Indiana, Minnesota, Nebraska, and Utah tinkered with tax limits, but these provisions were, one commentator observed, "of minor or emergency character." Ohio adopted two proposals that added some flexibility to its 1 percent tax cap. Initiatives that failed to pass included a 1.5 percent property tax maximum in Utah; a reduction in Ohio's 1 percent limit to a 0.5 percent limit; 1 percent constitutional limits in Arizona, Florida, Nebraska, Texas, and Illinois; a 1.5 percent constitutional ceiling in Iowa; constitutional limitations in Minnesota, New York, Massachusetts, and Maryland; and statutory tax cap proposals in New Jersey, Illinois, and Minnesota. In late 1935, Jens P. Jensen, a professor at the University of Kansas who wrote about these developments, wondered with cautious optimism whether it was "a warranted conclusion that the tax limitation epidemic has lost its virulence."[65]

One explanation for this trend is that taxpayers and legislators came to realize that the criticisms of tax ceilings as unreasonably rigid and not particularly efficacious were, to some degree, justified. The most probable one, though, is that tax limitation had its limits; that is, taxes could be restricted only so much without causing the engines of state and local governments to seize up completely. Between 1932 and 1934, organized taxpayers succeeded in enacting scores of tax limitation measures, but by 1935 further circumscription was not all that feasible.

Evaluating the efficacy of organized taxpayers' political strategies yields mixed results. Tax limitation measures were blunt, inflexible, inefficient instruments of tax relief. They restricted only government revenue derived from certain sources, mainly property taxes, but not government spending. In the short term, tax ceilings undermined municipal credit and forced public officials to curtail, sometimes significantly, government services. In a November 1935 editorial, the National Municipal League asserted that "a series of experience reports on the operation of tax limitation laws" had shown that "wherever tried, such laws have resulted in a practical breakdown of local government and chaos in municipal finance." In the longer term, state and local governments identified replacement revenue sources and transferred the tax burden to other taxpayers. "The citizen soon discovered that lower property tax levies did not necessarily mean tax savings." As a press opinion in a Kentucky newspaper wryly observed,

> Tax shifting is by way of becoming the most popular legislative sport. Levies are taken off real estate—and put on investment. Personal property taxes are reduced—and an additional tax is placed against incomes. The assessor sends a new and different blank—but the check that goes back is as large or larger than before.

In 1935, John Sly of Princeton University argued that "all taxes . . . ultimately come back to the wealth of the state," that "unless expenditures are reduced the gross load upon that wealth is substantially unchanged," and that the "control of local expenditures . . . is the surest road to tax relief." Tax limits were no substitute for good government reform that actually reduced the cost of government and the overall tax load.[66]

The traditional political activities of taxpayers' associations were far more effective in achieving tax relief. Taxpayers' organizations educated elected officials and voters about the necessity for and means to good government reform and insisted that public officials implement such reforms. In many communities organized taxpayers helped to elect candidates who were responsive to their demands for economy and efficiency in local government. As a consequence of political pressure by taxpayers, municipal and county administrators in many jurisdictions made progress in implementing the elements of the Progressive good government model. Local officials, mindful of local conditions and of the particulars of the county and city governments they were running, were able to approach the refashioning of the machinery of government in a way that was precise, measured, and practically adapted to the local realities of how that government functioned. Tax caps were dull tools of tax policy directed at revenues, whereas good government reform was aimed at the control of local government spending, the source of the "tax problem," and could be targeted and flexible. The experiences of organized taxpayers with their political programs validates Princeton University political scientist John Sly's conclusion that tax limits "cannot be expected to produce permanently the relief which the taxpayer desires. This must come through the improvement of his government, rather than through his solemn vows to tax himself no further."[67]

Both prongs of organized taxpayer political activity were rooted in the nation's populist heritage. Through the medium of political activism, taxpaying citizens sought to constrain tax spenders and to bend the elites running local governments to the will of the people when it came to taxing and spending. Like their mainstream populist forebears, Depression-era taxpayers mainly worked to reform and improve government, not disrupt or overthrow it. The "money powers" with whom taxpayers vied for elected office and battled about public spending were the tax spenders—those officials and candidates for public office for whom realizing economy and efficiency in the public sector was not a priority. Tax limitation laws served to tie the fiscal hands of those same money powers. Populism was the thin-centered ideology to which taxpayers hitched their substantive antitax agenda, as had the whiskey rebels 150 years earlier, in pursuit of tax relief. Historian Alan Brinkley observed that the political protest movements that Huey Long and Father Coughlin launched in the 1930s "gave evidence . . . that the long tradition of opposition to large, inaccessible power centers, a tradition that stretched from the American Revolution to the populist revolt and beyond, continued to survive."[68] The political programs of organized taxpayers in this period likewise demonstrated the continuing vitality of the populist impulse in the United States.

During the Great Depression, taxpayers' organizations also invoked another feature of the populist tradition, producerism, to justify and advance their most militant strategy, the tax strike. In the taxpayer's view, just as workers produced the goods and services on which the economy depended, so too taxpayers provided the revenues on which government relied. For more than two generations organized labor had employed work stoppages in its the struggle with industrial elites to obtain better pay and working conditions. The collapse of property values and the property tax base by 1931 drove American taxpayers to consider, threaten, and, on occasion, resort to tax strikes in an effort to rein in the tax-spending elites running local government.

5

The Specter of Tax Strikes

"Shutting Off the Money"

The nation's largest and longest tax strike in the 1930s, centered in Chicago, was hardly inevitable. In May 1930, a handful of affluent real estate owners organized the ARET of Illinois to contest recent large property tax hikes. The spike in taxes was the result of the Cook County Board of Review's adoption and the county's approval of a plan requiring taxpayers to pay their 1928, 1929, and 1930 real estate taxes, collection of which had been stayed since May 1928 pending completion of a countywide property reassessment, within the next sixteen months. The steep tax increase hit most property owners in Cook County very hard, and many joined ARET. Its members, who hailed mainly from the middle class, numbered around eight thousand in October 1931, and by June 1932 exceeded twenty thousand. Until January 1931, ARET challenged the new assessments and the manner in which the county taxed property through various political channels. When these proved unavailing, ARET and taxpayers affiliated with it began instituting lawsuits to contest the assessments.[1]

Tax resistance metastasized into a tax strike when, in February 1931, ARET began encouraging its members not to pay their property taxes until the courts had rendered final decisions in the lawsuits disputing the taxes. Many property owners, already hard-pressed to pay their taxes, embraced ARET's suggestion, and the tax strike spread quickly. In May 1931, Chicago's treasurer announced that the city had collected just 55 percent of property taxes, the lowest proportion ever, as of the May 15 penalty deadline. Public officials, bankers, Chicago's major newspapers, and others condemned the tax strike in the strongest terms, denouncing strikers as unpatriotic at best and treasonous at worst and characterizing the strike as a step on the road to anarchy. Harsh criticisms did not, however, deter Chicago's tax strikers, for whom the traditional political processes had been ineffectual and who, in their view, had embarked on a tax strike only as a last resort. John J. Mangan, one of ARET's leaders, expressed the overarching rationale for the strike when, in March 1932, he declared that the "only time the politician understands the people mean business is when the money is shut off. So shut the money off!"[2]

When organized taxpayers launched a tax strike in Cook County in 1931, they were taking their cue from labor unions in the United States, which had frequently employed the strike as a tactic in industrial relations during the previous century. Organized labor's experiences in the late nineteenth century had demonstrated the relative inefficacy of legislative and political strategies in promoting workers' interests and had convinced most trade unions to adopt a strategy of voluntarism, which focused on collective action, including work stoppages, in the private sphere. These same dynamics were at play in the genesis and execution of tax strikes in Chicago and elsewhere in the 1930s. Depression-era tax strikers drew on and adapted the voluntarist tradition in the United States and organized labor's own adaptation of that tradition. Moreover, both striking workers and striking taxpayers came to understand the limitations that the American legal order imposed on strikers.

Strikes and the Triumph of Voluntarism in the American Labor Movement

Rapid industrialization and the corresponding proliferation and growth of unions in the decades following the Civil War created the conditions for widespread conflict between organized labor and management. It was an age of adjustment for both employers and employees, who had to navigate their way through a new and ever-changing world of industrial relations in which negotiation, compromise, political and legislative activity, legal action, conflict, and sometimes violence came together. Organized labor became less local, and increasingly regional and national, in its outlook and organization. The American labor movement's experiences between 1865 and 1925 showed its leaders the relative effectiveness and limitations of various strategies and of the tactics available to them, including work stoppages and boycotts, to achieve organized labor's objectives. Organized labor's approach to industrial relations and its long-term strategic aims were forged in the crucible of labor strife in these years.

The 1894 Pullman boycott was a watershed in the history of organized labor in the United States and was representative of how workers' experiences with strikes in this period shaped the American labor movement. It began on May 11, when workers at the Pullman Palace Car Company near Chicago struck to protest a series of painful pay cuts implemented in the wake of the depression that began the previous year. George Pullman simply decided to close the plant and wait out his workforce. As the strike dragged on, support for Pullman employees increased among other unions and the general public. Against the advice of its leadership, the American Railway Union (ARU) voted not to handle any Pullman cars. By the end of June, more than one hundred thousand railway workers had walked off the job, paralyzing traffic on several dozen railroads affecting twenty-seven states. Eugene V. Debs, the ARU's president, counseled moderation, but events soon got out of hand. Mobs comprised mainly of riffraff and criminals began destroying and stealing railroad property and derailing trains, to some of which mail cars were attached. Illinois governor John Peter Altgeld sent state militia to restore order and railway mail traffic.[3]

The U.S. government's response to the interruption of the mail and the growing violence was swift, powerful, and twofold. On July 1, U.S. attorney general Richard Olney authorized the U.S. attorney in Chicago to petition the federal court for injunctive relief against the strikers. The next day the court issued an expansive injunction enjoining the ARU's leaders and "all persons whosoever" from "in any way or manner interfering with, hindering, obstructing or stopping any of the business" of the railroads identified in the court order. In addition, on July 3, President Cleveland ordered two thousand federal troops to Chicago to assist the state militia and U.S. marshals in battling the rioters. For the next week, the violence continued unabated, resulting in at least twenty deaths, many more injuries, and hundreds of thousands of dollars in property damage. The president sent an additional sixteen thousand federal troops, and by mid-July the strike had been broken. Five ARU leaders, including Debs, were arrested and found in contempt for violating the July 2 injunction. The next year, in a landmark decision with profound implications for organized labor, the U.S. Supreme Court upheld the injunction and the contempt convictions of Debs and the others, affirming that the "strong arm of the national government may be put forth to brush away all obstructions to the freedom of interstate commerce or the transportation of the mails."[4]

Strikes and boycotts were not the only context in which the judiciary stymied the efforts of workers to improve their lot. Judges were also a significant impediment to the unions' legislative agendas. From the 1880s through the 1920s, organized labor promoted and secured the passage of legislation regulating the terms of employment and working conditions in nearly every state.

State courts, however, used their power of judicial review to strike down the vast majority of labor statutes, often on liberty of contract grounds. One examination of court rulings on state labor statutes between 1885 and 1900 indicates that judges annulled such statutes in 75 percent of the cases. The U.S. Supreme Court famously endorsed the liberty of contract principal in the *Lochner* decision, in which it declared unconstitutional a New York statute prescribing the hours of bakery employees because the law "necessarily interferes with the right of contract between the employer and the employees." By the time the Supreme Court decided *Lochner* in 1905, many union members had, in William Forbath's words, "concluded that legislation was a distressingly unreliable engine" for refashioning the workplace and industrial relations.[5]

By the turn of the twentieth century, the majority of union leaders viewed the government as more of an adversary than an ally in the contest between labor and capital. The state had used federal troops and marshals, state militia, and local sheriffs and police to break strikes. Courts had proved to be an even more formidable obstacle to organized labor's aspirations, regularly invalidating labor legislation and issuing labor injunctions, enforced by the court's contempt powers, to break general strikes, boycotts, and sympathy strikes. Consequently, unions increasingly abandoned political and legislative strategies and adopted a voluntarist, antistatist approach to industrial relations. Voluntarism, as fashioned by organized labor in the United States, was a political philosophy that minimized politics and instead emphasized action in the private sector and the tactics that had been effective: collective bargaining, contracts, craft unionism, and carefully calibrated strikes when circumstances favored labor success. This pragmatic, private-sector worldview would dominate the American labor movement through the onset of the Great Depression.[6]

In the 1930s, organized taxpayers would draw on the experiences of labor in the United States to meet the challenges that the Great Depression presented to taxpayers. Although legislative and political strategies predominated among taxpayers' organizations, tax strikes and antistatism were important, albeit subordinate, features of Depression-era taxpayer activity. As with organized labor, taxpayers' leagues usually considered voluntarist strategies only when they had lost faith in political reform as a means to their ends.

Tax Strikers and Their Opponents during the Great Depression

The tax strike, in which taxpayers collectively agreed not to pay their property taxes unless and until public officials acceded to taxpayers' demands for spending cuts or other changes in government policy and operation affecting their tax bill, was a radical gambit. Even so, in the early 1930s, taxpayers considered tax strikes, threatened them, and acted on the threat if other avenues of tax relief had been foreclosed. By 1933, tax strikes were common enough for newspapers to report that "organized tax strikes are spreading" and that "'tax strikes' in many parts of the country are indicative of the way the wind is blowing." The *Des Moines Tribune* noted that "evidence has accumulated that sentiment for this sort of protest has grown in many sections of the country." For a few years, tax strikes were a very real possibility.[7]

Tax strikes ranged from brief, isolated episodes to extensive and extended ones. The following incident described in the *National Municipal Review* is typical of spontaneous, short-lived efforts of tax strikers:

> The primitive urge of the tax striker has not yet been completely dissipated, if the recent disturbance in Pottsville, Pa., is any indication. Upwards of a thousand taxpayers . . . stormed the Schuylkill County courthouse, dragged out two of the county commissioners, and read the riot act on tax reduction. Unequal assessments were the cause. The county commissioners promised to hear a taxpayers' grievance committee, and the strikers were appeased.[8]

At the other end of the continuum was the Chicago tax strike, which extended from 1931 to 1933 and was, according to David Beito, "the largest tax strike in the country if not in American history." The strike was organized by the ARET. A large majority of its thirty thousand members in late 1932 hailed from "relatively modest backgrounds" and were small shopkeepers and other small business owners, skilled blue-collar workers, and persons employed in clerical and sales occupations. At the height of the strike in 1932, a majority of real property taxes in Chicago were unpaid, and the city narrowly averted bankruptcy.[9]

The Chicago tax strike had its origins, somewhat incongruously, in a real property tax holiday that Cook County taxpayers had enjoyed from May 1928 to July 1930, while assessing officials conducted a reassessment of all real estate. In the spring of 1930, county officials adopted the new assessment and a payment program that required real estate owners to pay their 1928 taxes by July 1930, their 1929 taxes by February 1931, and their 1930 taxes by November 1931. This accelerated payment schedule, coupled with the substantial tax increases resulting from the new assessment, precipitated the formation of ARET in May 1930.[10]

For the next nine months, these organized taxpayers sought property tax relief through traditional political processes. In the summer and fall, ARET promoted an amendment to the state constitution that aimed to shift the tax burden from owners of real property to owners of stocks, bonds, and other forms of personal property. After voters defeated the amendment in November, ARET petitioned the Illinois Tax Commission to invalidate the 1930 assessment on the grounds that it unlawfully undervalued personal property. On January 5, 1931, the commission rejected ARET's claim. That same month the Cook County Board of Review stopped processing taxpayer appeals of their 1930 property assessments. ARET promptly asked the board to reconsider this decision and resume hearing the forty thousand or more pending appeals, but the board ignored the law requiring it to hear all such appeals and simply provided the county clerk with the 1930 assessments on which to base and issue tax bills.[11]

Having experienced absolutely no success with its initial political strategy, ARET abandoned it and embarked on a two-pronged strategy consisting of litigation and a tax strike. After the Board of Review declined to reopen the tax appeal process in early February 1931, ARET sued the board to compel it to do so. At the same time, it urged its members not to pay their taxes during the pendency of the litigation. ARET prevailed in the trial court, but the Board of Review appealed, and the tax collector proceeded to issue the tax bills for the 1929 tax year. In April 1931, ARET began sending out membership applications declaring that "no taxpayer should pay one dollar of the 1929 tax until the Supreme Court rules on its validity." ARET also instituted a mandamus action and an equity action, both based on its contention that the 1930 assessment unlawfully overassessed real property relative to personal property. ARET's litigation objectives were to shift tax levies from real estate to personal property and to stall the tax sale process so as to give property owners more time to pay their taxes. ARET continued to distribute literature supporting the tax strike. One pamphlet rhetorically asked, "Shall I pay a tax which by general admission is unfair and illegal . . . and which is more than double the amount that would result from a fair, reasonable, legal assessment of the taxable wealth of Cook County?" ARET lost its equity lawsuit but initially prevailed in its mandamus action when, in January 1932, a trial court ruled that $15 million in personal property had been improperly excluded from the 1930 assessment. The previous month in another taxpayers' suit, county judge Edmund Jarecki had invalidated the real estate assessments for the 1928 and 1929 tax years because they underassessed personal property, vacated thousands of tax sales, and enjoined future tax sales.[12]

Public officials, municipal creditors, and Chicago's major newspapers were extremely critical of the tax strikers. The *Chicago Evening Post* argued that for taxpayers to refuse to pay taxes "in the hope that the court will give a reduction is to shirk their responsibilities and duties of citizenship." In a similar vein, Chicago banker Melvin Traylor considered the tax strike "a discredit to any man who carries the badge of citizenship." Chicago's mayor characterized ARET's promotion of the tax strike as "just a scheme to get the taxpayers' money." Organized labor, on the other hand, came to the taxpayers' defense. The Chicago Federation of Labor, many of whose members also belonged to ARET, maintained that ARET was "a legitimate organization of citizens who have recognized the futility of individual protest."[13]

The city of Chicago's response to the steadily diminishing revenue stream resulting from the tax strike included both public relations and fiscal components. In January 1932, Mayor Anton Cermak launched a "Pay Your Taxes" campaign directed at tax delinquents' sense of civic responsibility. Two months later he implemented staff layoffs and other spending cuts. The U.S. Congress declined Cermak's request for financial assistance, and in July he slashed $15 million from the school budget. Between 1930 and 1933, Chicago's municipal budget shrank by more than one-third.[14]

The tide turned quickly against ARET in July 1932, as a result of several developments. First, the Illinois Supreme Court reversed Jarecki's ruling that had struck down the 1928 and 1929 assessments, which meant that the local authorities could again proceed with tax sales of properties for delinquent taxes. In November, after the case had been remanded to the trial court, Jarecki ruled against ARET and sanctioned the tax sale of fifty-six thousand properties. In addition, the city of Chicago received a massive infusion of revenue when the federal government relented, and the Reconstruction Finance Corporation proceeded to lend the state of Illinois a total of $14 million. Public officials increased external pressures on ARET when they convened a grand jury to investigate a criminal conspiracy charge against the organization. The investigation yielded no indictment but nevertheless damaged ARET's reputation. Early 1933 marked the beginning of ARET's demise, when disagreements among its leaders escalated and the organization dissolved into two warring factions, one of which obtained an injunction prohibiting the other from accessing ARET's funds or holding membership meetings. By late 1933, ARET was in receivership.[15]

For Cook County taxpayers, the fiscal consequences of the tax strike were something of a mixed bag. On the plus side, the strike and the related taxpayers' lawsuits had delayed the collection of property taxes on real estate for almost two years. Owners of real property in Chicago also experienced a sizable reduction in their tax payments: annual general property tax collection from 1929 to 1933 averaged less than 75 percent of the 1928 level, whereas elsewhere it averaged 102.3 percent of 1928 payments. After 1932, however,

Chicago's overall tax load increased more than it did in other comparable cities, so some of the "tax savings" were a consequence of shifting more of the tax levies from one class of taxpayers, owners of real estate, to other taxpayers.[16]

Although there were no other Depression-era tax strikes of the magnitude of the Chicago strike, they were seriously considered in many cities and implemented on occasion. Leaders of the Taxpayers' Advisory Council in Milwaukee suggested a tax strike in 1932 but backed off after voters approved a tax limitation measure in the November election. That same year in New York City, the West Side Taxpayers' Association passed a resolution encouraging taxpayers to withhold their taxes, and the Greater Brooklyn Property Owners Association actually initiated a tax strike campaign. The momentum for a tax strike in Brooklyn dissipated, however, as a result of stiff opposition from another taxpayers' organization, the New York Real Estate Board, dissension among the tax strike advocates, and the adoption by Mayor James Walker of a more conciliatory approach on taxation matters.[17] In Atlanta the taxpayers' plight was sufficiently desperate that Hal Steed believed that "an insurrection is brewing" and "that a tax strike was by no means improbable." The moderate wing of the Taxpayers' League of Atlanta and Fulton County succeeded in defusing the situation with a plea for moderation, agreeing that the public officials who were responsible for high taxes and high government debt "should be starved out. But if you try to starve them by refusing to pay your taxes, you will also starve innocent and deserving persons. You will starve policemen, firemen and teachers who are serving us, and, for the most part, had nothing to do with our plight."[18] Most organized taxpayer activity did not target core government functions or essential levels of government services but was aimed at spending that was wasteful or unnecessary, such as that occasioned by redundancy in government services, inefficiency in government operations, and nonessential programs. In contrast, tax strikes, like tax limits, were blunt instruments of tax resistance that dried up municipal revenue streams and forced indiscriminate budget cuts.

The longer the Chicago tax strike dragged on and continued to decimate the city's finances and credit, the more credible and frequent threats of tax strikes became in other communities. One account of tax resistance in Des Moines reported that "speedy enactment of substantial economy measures is intended to head off a large-scale tax strike. . . . There is a definite belief in high places that drastic cuts in the cost of government will squelch the movement once and for all." At a taxpayers' meeting in Johnstown, Pennsylvania, the crowd of a thousand cheered the head of the local "tax reduction committee" as he called for hefty decreases in the tax rate and spending and then vowed that "the taxpayers will go on strike if the demands are not granted."

In Wilkinsburg, a Pittsburgh suburb, representatives of the local taxpayers' association warned councilmen "that a taxpayers' strike is a certainty unless additional heavy slashes" were made to the 1933 budget and that the councilmen would "be responsible for the chaos that will ensue." Taxpayers' groups in Bergenfield, New Jersey, threatened a tax strike to obtain budget cuts. Nearly ten thousand farmers gathered at the Indiana statehouse and promised a "general tax strike . . . unless the present property tax is abolished" and a sales tax enacted. Oregon taxpayers declared that a tax strike was imminent absent immediate property tax relief, and state legislator Frank Lonergan convinced his fellow legislators to enact a sales tax so as to reduce property taxes by arguing that "a tax strike is near in this state and I am not an alarmist." Taxpayers' leagues played the strike threat card with some success in 1933.[19]

When circumstances warranted, organized taxpayers also played the strike card. The taxpayers' league in Hamilton County, Tennessee, launched a tax strike that eventually placed the county's "finances . . . in a terrible condition" and necessitated a reduction in the length of the public school term. Taxpayers in the Wallowa Valley Improvement District in Oregon engaged in "a tax strike for some time" to protest high taxes resulting from the district's excessive debt. In Brisbane, California, a "large percentage of property owners . . . refused to pay utility district tax levies," prompting the local newspaper to predict that "further burdens on the property owner will find a rebellious public." Members of the Sevier County Taxpayers' League in Utah embarked on a "general tax strike," resolving that "we deem it necessary and do jointly and severally refuse to pay any more property taxes until a new and more just tax law is passed." Their efforts to spread the tax strike gospel yielded some converts but not a great awakening of the taxpaying masses: taxpayers in one nearby county voted to participate and those in several counties declined to enlist. Business taxpayers in one sector of the Pennsylvania economy put their own unique spin on the tax strike tactic. When, in late 1933, the commonwealth undertook to levy a tax on all alcoholic beverages exported after the imminent repeal of Prohibition, the operators of all major distilleries closed their facilities and threatened to relocate to other states. Newspapers called the protest a "modern whisky tax strike" reminiscent of the Whiskey Rebellion in the 1790s.[20]

The specter of tax strikes continued to loom over local governments through 1933. At a conference of the American Bankers Association in January, speakers warned that "taxpayers' strikes may result from failure to reduce the cost of government and taxation." Professor H. W. Dodd of Princeton University declared that "taxpayers are in an angry mood," and Massachusetts state senator Samuel H. Wragg insisted that "unless the tax burden is lightened 'there are possibilities of taxpayers' strikes.'"[21] On January 19, 1933, the North Bergen (New Jersey) Taxpayers' and Civic Association threatened a taxpayers' strike unless $180,000 was slashed from the 1933 city budget. Two weeks later the city commission reduced the budget by $119,000.[22] That budgetary concession apparently was not sufficient, because the association still declared a property owners' tax strike to take effect on February 24, 1933. Rudolph J. Welti, the association's president, announced that "all of the 1,000 members of the organization would support the tax-paying holiday and that 5,000 other property owners of the city [of the eight thousand taxpayers] would join the movement." He further explained that the association "was advising the property owners to deposit the amount of their taxes" in an escrow account "pending the outcome of the strike" and that "the strike would continue until the taxpayers' demands for budget reductions were met."[23]

At the annual meeting of the New Jersey Taxpayers' Association in June 1933, there were calls for a tax strike unless the state legislature acceded to the association's demands for reductions in the state budget. Irwin Rubenstein, the attorney for the West New York Taxpayers' Association who was to foil the attempt on his life two years later, proposed a tax strike resolution, but the measure "failed after a sharp debate." The association's president warned that "this is a very controversial question containing a considerable amount of dynamite.... I feel it would be a great mistake to adopt so radical a measure." A director of the association warned that "when respected citizens countenance a tax strike they are undermining the essential services of government.... For this organization to resolve we will stop paying taxes is too radical."[24] These comments belie the stereotype of the taxpayers' organization as a conservative, antigovernment entity. They do not reflect a libertarian mindset but a measured and responsible view of the taxpayers' relationship to government and of their responsibility to pay for essential government services. They also acknowledge the taxpayers' duty to pay taxes, the obligation side of the citizenship coin. Most state taxpayers' associations espoused similar values and adopted a similarly cautious approach to the subject of tax strikes.

In Jersey City, New Jersey, what began as a tax strike in early March 1933 had evolved into a third-party political movement by April. On March 1, the Jersey City Taxpayers' Association declared its intention to call a tax strike unless the Democratic administration of Mayor Frank Hague slashed the city budget by almost 55 percent. The association did not specify the programs or services that it proposed to cut but only the overall level of the requested budget cut. Two other taxpayers' organizations were formed almost immediately to oppose this draconian demand. The association stated that it "has a potential strength of 20,000. We are about to enter upon a tax strike after every effort to come to harmonious and sensible understandings with a headstrong city government has failed." The threat apparently carried little weight, for the city commission adopted the proposed budget without any cuts on March 10. On March 21, the association adopted a resolution urging a tax strike by its members. At about the same time, "resentment over the passage of the Jersey City budget last week without the sharp reductions advocated by the Jersey City Taxpayers' Association led yesterday to the formation of a fusion movement of Republicans and independent Democrats . . . to run against Mayor Frank Hague and the Hague candidates at the city election in May." One of the fusion candidates was Daniel E. C. Somers, an official of the association. Hague was the vice chairman of the Democratic National Committee and had been involved in Jersey City government for seventeen years. Despite winning a position at the top of the ballot, all five fusion candidates were trounced by the Hague administration incumbents. The *New York Times* observed that "it was evident that the defeated Fusion candidates in Jersey City were at a loss to account for the size of the vote rolled up by Mayor Frank Hague and the other incumbent commissioners."[25] This political drubbing stood in stark contrast to the success of the candidates backed by the Newark Taxpayers' Association in the Newark city elections on the same day.[26]

Taxpayers articulated various rationales for participating in tax strikes. The most common was that a tax strike was a final expedient to which taxpayers turned only "after exhausting all peaceful means" of seeking tax relief. Taxpayers espousing this view had concluded that a "tax strike is the only way to bring those in authority to a realization of the fact that the cost of government must be brought down to a level which reduced incomes can support." John Darr, an opinion columnist in Pennsylvania, agreed that the "tax strike seems to be the only alternative left to the taxpayers to get relief from the overwhelming burden of high taxation which has well-nigh broken their backs" because "every legitimate means of protest in the hands of citizens have been exhausted and have availed no particle of relief from" excessive real estate taxes. Darr claimed that all other forms of tax resistance had been tried but "have fallen upon deaf ears or been treated with outright contempt" by the state legislature. He concluded by posing the following question: "Isn't it about time that the taxpayers passed from a state of passive protest to a state of militant action?" A more cynical perspective was that tax moratoriums were inevitable because "the growing mountain of taxes can never be collected" and that when taxing authorities declared a tax holiday "it will be utterly unfair to those who have been straining every nerve to keep their taxes paid up." John Mangan, one of the architects of the Chicago tax strike, contended that the strike had advanced the causes of good government and tax relief in that "this movement has brought about the appointment of a Governor's Committee to study tax relief, a special session of the State Legislature" to consider taxation reform, and "the focusing of public attention on this, the most important political and governmental issue of the present day." Tax strikers consistently characterized the tax strike as a legitimate tool of tax resistance that good citizens could employ when all else failed.[27]

Not surprisingly, both the act and the threat of a tax strike elicited strong opposition on a number of fronts. Such radical action was antithetical to the conservative mindset of business leaders. Businessmen, bankers, municipal bond dealers, and investors in municipal bonds found the notion of tax strikes unsettling and feared that they would cause irrevocable damage to the municipal credit market. Melvin A. Traylor, the president of the First National Bank of Chicago and a leader of the forces that sought to break the Chicago tax strike, maintained in 1932 that the "tax dodger who declines to assume his fair proportion of the cost of government, and the tax striker who refuses to pay taxes levied and assessed against him, constitute the great menace to American governments today." They threatened, he claimed, to cause "the general collapse of municipal credit, which rests solely upon the confidence of the investor in the willingness of the citizen to pay, and the ability of the Government to enforce the collection of revenue sufficient for its needs."[28] The following year Frank H. Morris of Lehman Brothers echoed Traylor, declaring that "if tax strikes become general, we would have in the municipal bond market the equivalent of what happened in 1929 in the stock market."[29]

To the public officials who depended on regular and predictable sources of tax revenues, tax strikes were anathema. Daniel Hoan, the socialist mayor of Milwaukee and a proponent of big government, considered such organized tax resistance a threat to the republic itself. In the *Mr. Taxpayer versus Mr. Taxspender* radio play sponsored by the National Municipal League, Hoan and Luther Gulick, the director of Columbia University's Institute of Public Administration, engaged in a spirited discussion about the "problem of high taxes and tax reduction." Hoan strongly defended the need for active government intervention in the devastated Depression-era economy. "Much as we dislike to pay our tax bills," Hoan declared,

> the fact is that government . . . has stood like the Rock of Gibraltar during this frightful depression to save us the agonies of complete chaos. While banks failed, factories closed, shops went bankrupt, pyramided utilities collapsed, the government was expected to function with more vigor and energy than ever. . . . Is it not high time to call the attention of the citizens of this country to the fact that they are playing with dynamite when they so recklessly undermine and de-

stroy faith in this Republic and all its agencies. . . . The operation of government is as necessary as it is to have a home to live in unless we are to concede that we should slip back to the level of savages. . . . If then, it is true that to have progress we must have efficient public service, it behooves every good citizen to take part in civic and governmental affairs and improve that government and when the time comes to pay the bill, to do so with a sense of civic duty.[30]

Hoan's insistence on the necessity for forceful government action to reduce unemployment, stimulate consumer demand, and provide a bulwark against a deflating economy anticipated the arguments made by British economist John Maynard Keynes three years later in his seminal work, *The General Theory of Employment, Interest, and Money*, and that underpinned much of the discussion about the economic stimulus legislation that the U.S. Congress enacted in February 2009 as the United States slipped into recession and in the spring of 2020 as large segments of the economy shut down during the COVID-19 pandemic.[31] In a 1933 radio forum titled "Secrets of Municipal Credit," New York state comptroller Morris S. Tremaine warned that "a taxpayer strike would double the cost of borrowing" by state government.[32] Tax strikes were a threat to the operation and the very legitimacy of government. Consequently, government officials opposed them vigorously and often reminded taxpayers that a principal obligation of citizenship was paying taxes.

Political scientists and other good government experts and reformers also decried tax strikes. Luther Gulick played the role of the taxpayer in the simulated radio debate with Hoan but nevertheless regarded tax strikers as a threat to the body politic. In a 1932 radio roundtable discussion, he opined that taxpayers' associations could promote economy and efficiency in government in a number of constructive ways but warned that "a taxpayers' strike, or the threat of a strike, is dangerous business. Its first effect is to wreck the credit of the community, jack up the interest rates that must be paid for borrowed money, and perhaps bring on payless pay days for schoolteachers, policemen and firemen."[33] Gulick elaborated on this theme in his discussion with Hoan, questioning the loyalty and patriotism of the tax slacker, "who can, but doesn't pay his taxes cheerfully and promptly [and] is just a plain traitor to his city and town." He quantified the fiscal impact of tax strikes as compared to constructive economy efforts, asserting "that a tax strike costs twenty cents on the dollar on taxes, as over against the normal and legitimate methods open to the citizen of expressing his demands for tax reduction."[34] Public administration professionals frequently emphasized the dire practical consequences and radical nature of tax strikes, and they encouraged taxpayers to engage in more moderate and, in the professionals' view, more effective efforts to reduce their taxes.

The threat posed by tax strikes and tax delinquencies was of sufficient concern to good government experts that in September 1933 the National Municipal League launched "a nation-wide 'Pay Your Taxes' campaign to educate the average citizen throughout the country to the importance of paying his taxes in this critical period if municipal credit is to be preserved and essential local government services continued."[35] The league was a voluntary association of citizens organized in 1894 to promote reform in municipal government.[36] Consequently, it had a direct and vital interest in the threat that tax delinquencies posed to the financial viability of state and local governments. Thomas Reed, a professor of government at the University of Michigan who shared Gulick's dim view of tax strikes and tax limits promoted by organized taxpayers, was selected as the chairman of the National Pay Your Taxes Campaign.[37] The campaign was essentially an intensive, large-scale public relations push designed to make "the taxpayer understand his responsibility for the tone of government" and his civic duty to pay for government. It was backed not only by public employees and good government organizations but also by many in the private sector, to which the financial health of state and local government mattered greatly. An editorial comment in the October 1933 *National Municipal Review* described the campaign's methods in glowing terms:

> The idea of a nation-wide drive against tax delinquency is penetrating businesses and industry clear to the man on the street. In various newspapers, arresting "Pay Your Taxes" advertisements are appearing, sponsored not by the tax gathering powers but by banks and leading industrial institutions. They recall the days of Liberty Loan drives. Telephone, radio, screen appeals in motion picture houses, volunteer house to house campaigns by the unemployed—and by civic employees anxious to avoid this status—all are parts of the unique public movement. More than that, the New York Bureau of Municipal Information reports "sermons given in churches about the Restoration of Faith in Local Government."[38]

The movement gained momentum quickly and produced results in short order. In February 1934, Wade S. Smith, the *National Municipal Review*'s contributing editor for taxation and government, reported that "'Pay Your Taxes' campaigns continued to provide an effective weapon against tax delinquencies in cities with pressing financial difficulties," including Columbus, Ohio;

Houston, Texas; and Tacoma, Washington.[39] The National Municipal League published a campaign manual for use by local Pay Your Taxes campaign committees.[40] Some taxpayers' associations, such as the state taxpayers' organization in New Mexico, supported the campaign.[41] In August 1934, the *National Municipal Review* declared that the "results secured by the campaign during the past year," including the reduction of delinquencies and restoration of municipal credit, "had been highly successful," and it vowed to continue the campaign.[42] A Kentucky newspaper went so far as to claim that when the National Pay Your Taxes Campaign "was launched tax strikes were sweeping the country . . . and the credit of many cities seriously threatened" but that "tax strikes are now virtually eliminated."[43]

By late 1934, tax strikes had waned for a number of reasons. First, and perhaps most important, the tax strike was an extreme measure with destructive potential that most Americans were not prepared to embrace. Moreover, actual tax strikes had not proven all that effective and often resulted in considerable public backlash. As noted earlier, the New Deal's HOLC loan program reduced support for tax strikes among the many homeowners who participated in the program after the HOLC opened for business in June 1933. Finally, the National Municipal League's National Pay Your Taxes Campaign succeeded to a large extent in diverting the energies of tax resisters into more constructive and more cooperative channels for advancing their agendas. By September 1934, the *National Municipal Review* was reporting that tax protesters throughout the nation "seem definitely to have lost their old tax strike enthusiasm."[44]

The overall inefficacy of tax strikes in the 1930s contrasts sharply with the relative success that organized labor had with work stoppages during the New Deal. Several things account for this disparity. Most important is the fact that tax strikes were illegal, whereas most forms of labor strikes were lawful. Consequently, tax strikes evoked swift and strong responses from the state and considerable opprobrium from the public. In contrast, federal government policy became more supportive of organized labor under Roosevelt, as did the public's attitude toward unionization. Moreover, the Wagner National Labor Relations Act of 1935 shifted the balance of power between labor and management in favor of the former. Among other things, the act banned company unions as well as numerous employers' unfair labor practices, including blacklisting, discriminatory termination of employees, and unfair propaganda. Historians have noted that the National Labor Relations Act "threw the weight of government behind the right of labor to bargain collectively, and compelled employers to accede peacefully to the unionization of their plants" and that the act and "changing government policy" toward labor made "a tangible contribution to labour gains in the 1930s."[45] Tax strikers, on the other hand, had the weight of the government and the public thrown against them.

When confronted with painful contractions in the economy and their incomes, taxpayers in the early 1930s drew on the experiences of organized labor with work stoppages to experiment with tax stoppages. Strikes represented an urgent, direct, and confrontational assertion of rights: for workers, the rights to have a greater say in the terms and conditions of their employment and to enhance their status and power vis-à-vis their employers, and for taxpayers, the rights to have a greater say in the reach, structure, and priorities of local government, in how much tax they paid, and in how their tax dollars were spent. Both organized labor and organized taxpayers engaged in strikes to defend, construct, and expand their rights and to achieve their goals.

Some of the tax strikes or threats thereof during the Great Depression were more successful than others, but the degree to which they were or were not effective in particular circumstances does not determine their importance. On this issue, labor historian Herbert G. Gutman's observation about striking railway workers in Pennsylvania in the early 1870s applies with equal force to the striking taxpayers in the 1930s: "the significance of the strikes lay not in their success or failure but rather in the readiness of the strikers to express their grievances in a dramatic, direct and frequently telling manner."[46] Tax strikes elicited prompt and strong opposition from powerful stakeholders and from the general public, and in most cases, taxpayers were ready to employ the most militant tactic available to them only when they were utterly frustrated with state and local legislative, political, and administrative remedies. Tax strikes were often symptomatic of a breakdown in the political processes that normally provided a viable forum for dialogue, compromise, and accommodation among conflicting interests.

The fact that tax strikes were drastic actions of last resort makes their spontaneity all the more remarkable. Depression-era tax strikes were not the product of long-range strategic planning on the part of organized taxpayers. Instead, like the formation of taxpayers' associations in this period, they were relatively spontaneous responses to rapidly evolving and pressing circumstances. Although ARET had alluded to the possibility of withholding taxes in November 1930, it did not threaten a tax strike until after the Illinois Tax Commission ruled against it on January 5, 1931, and it called on its members not to pay their taxes almost immediately after the Board of Review refused to hear pending tax assessment appeals in early February. Likewise, the Greater Brooklyn Property Owners Association first considered the tax strike option at a meeting in late March 1932 and decided to meet again less than a month later to call for a strike beginning May 1 if it did not reach an accommodation with the Walker administration.[47]

Though not political activities as such, tax strikes nevertheless had political overtones. Tax strikes manifested a voluntarist, antistatist current in American political culture that remained potent and served as a counterpoint to New Deal statism. As historian F. Alan Coombs has argued, even the economic catastrophe of the Great Depression "could hardly eliminate" among some "the old Jeffersonian feeling that government was best which governs least." In pursuing their legislative strategies, which comprised the lion's share of organized taxpayer activities in this period, taxpayers' organizations endeavored to work with state and local governments to achieve tax relief and economy and efficiency in government. Tax strikes, in contrast, were fundamentally assaults on the state. Milwaukee mayor Daniel Hoan, admittedly no fan of taxpayers' leagues, argued that such efforts to starve the public sector were "misguided and destructive," undermined "faith in government," and seriously threatened the ability of municipalities to provide basic, essential services. Tax strikes represented organized taxpayers' most radical turn toward voluntarism.[48]

The Chicago tax strike was the most serious challenge to municipal solvency by organized taxpayers in these years. It was notable for its scope and duration, its devastating impact on Cook County's finances, and its galvanizing effect on a broad, diverse array of tax strike opponents. ARET's unwavering reliance solely on litigation once its leaders had decided on a strike was among the strike's most salient features. By invoking the coercive power of the law and the courts to further its agenda, however, ARET was not breaking new ground but was tapping into a long-standing legal instrumentalist tradition in the United States. For decades ordinary Americans had turned to the courts to protect and promote their interests. In the 1930s, taxpayers seeking relief from the fiscal demands of local government invoked a particular form of legal action, the taxpayers' lawsuit, to advance theirs.

6

Taxpayers' Litigation in the Great Depression

Protecting the Taxpayers' "Hard Earned Money"

A taxpayer's July 1931 letter to the editor, published in the *Middlesboro Daily News* in Middlesboro, Kentucky, touched on many of the salient aspects of organized taxpayer activity in the United States. The writer praised the recently formed Taxpayers' League of Bell County, declaring that "we have a few unselfish citizens in our towns and county who have organized a Taxpayers' League for the purpose of protecting the hard earned money the taxpayers pay into the cities' and county's treasuries." The writer argued that such a taxpayers' organization was essential for several reasons. First, history had shown numerous "irregularities and misapplication[s]" of public funds by officials, as a result of which there were then pending thirty-seven suits against public officials to recover those funds. Moreover, because local officials "do not have full and complete audits made of their records so that the taxpayers may know how their tax money is being spent, . . . we need a Taxpayers' League to compel such audits to be made." Finally, the writer maintained, the "Taxpayers' League is the only unselfish friend the taxpayer has—the only friend that will go out into the open and into the courts and fight for the rights of the taxpayer." The letter concluded with a ringing indictment of opponents of the league, declaring that any "man that hates and abuses the Taxpayers' League . . . is not a first-class citizen of the country in which he lives."[1]

The anonymous letter is hardly an objective assessment of taxpayers' associations but, rather, a partisan paean to them. It does, however, illustrate how taxpayers applied conceptions of citizenship and called on the law and the courts to promote their interests. The writer grounded the very origins of the taxpayers' league in notions of citizenship, equated good citizenship with participation in organized taxpayer activity, and questioned the citizenship status of the organization's opponents. The overarching purpose of the league was to protect taxpayers' dollars. To this end, these Kentucky taxpayers regularly resorted to the courts and there invoked the coercive power of the law to enforce the rights of citizen taxpayers and to hold public officials accountable. The letter thus reflects organized taxpayer activity as a realm of action in which Americans relied heavily on the law and legal institutions to achieve their goals.

Taxpayers' litigation was the fourth and final class of weapons in the Depression-era taxpayers' association's arsenal. Taxpayers' suits are commonly defined as "proceedings in which one or more taxpayers, representing an entire class of taxpayers, seek a remedy for illegal acts injurious to their interests as taxpayers through misuse, disuse, or spoliation of public funds or property."[2] Taxpayers employed this remedy when they deemed it necessary to safeguard the public purse and to enforce economy and efficiency in local government. Taxpayers brought such lawsuits most often to restrain the unauthorized expenditure of public funds, to require the return of taxpayer dollars already improperly paid out, and to enjoin other unlawful municipal acts such as the unlawful issuance of municipal bonds. When taxpayers believed that town, city, and county governments were not adhering to constitutional and statutory provisions regarding local government finance and operation, they turned to the courts to force compliance.

Because the reported information regarding taxpayers' actions is so diffuse, it is impossible to measure with precision the number of such lawsuits brought annually in the 1930s compared to the 1920s.[3] For several reasons, though, we can be sure the number of taxpayers' suits instituted during the 1930s increased sharply. First, this type of litigation was expensive, so it was most often undertaken or sponsored by organized groups, which multiplied exponentially between 1931 and 1935. Second, the information gleaned from the Decennial Digests, rough and imprecise though it is, suggests that there was a surge in taxpayers' actions in the 1930s. For example, in the five-year period between 1923 and 1927, there were 105 reported taxpayers' suits, whereas in the five-year period between 1933 and 1937, there were 146, a 39 percent increase.[4] Third, a revived interest in taxpayers' actions among legal commentators during the Great Depression suggests an increase in the frequency and importance of these suits. In 1937, the *Harvard Law Review* took a positive view of taxpayers' lawsuits. It observed that "recent attempts to enjoin governmental expenditures have brought into renewed prominence the problem of defining the scope of suits by taxpayers against officials mismanaging public property or funds." It concluded that

> the taxpayers' suit must then be understood as not only a means of vindicating individual rights but as a governmental device to safeguard the legal restrictions on state and local governments, which, if not subjected to the careful scrutiny of the individual taxpayer, might well become dead letters. . . . The overwhelming acceptance of such suits is in keeping with the distrust of the executive and administrative self-restraint in the use of the spending power and with the readiness to allow the courts to assume the role of arbiter in the governmental scheme.[5]

In contrast, the Iowa Supreme Court's 1933 decision in *Wertz v. Shane*, holding that a taxpayer was authorized to prosecute suits "to recover back" on behalf of "the state funds wrongfully expended if the proper officials refuse to act," elicited criticism from the *Illinois Law Review* because "such suits might be employed merely to discredit honest officials. Individuals or factions could contest the execution of an administrative policy which appeared odious to them, and unduly hamper officials whom a majority had elected."[6] The commentators' differing perspectives of taxpayers' actions show the spectrum of opinion about the desirability of these lawsuits. The first commentator also reflects the view of consensus legal historians that courts acted as honest arbiters of citizens' disputes with their governments.

Taxpayers' reliance on litigation to promote their interests in the 1930s was rooted in two elements of the American legal order that had emerged in the preceding century. The first was the recognition by courts and legislatures of the right, or standing, of taxpayers to bring taxpayers' suits against local governments and public officials and the development of the legal principles defining and governing those rights. The second was the increasingly widespread acceptance of an instrumentalist view of the law.

"Where Justice Requires a Remedy": The Evolution of Taxpayers' Suits

In July 1895, Land, Log & Lumber Company and other taxpayers of Vilas County, Wisconsin, appeared before the county board of supervisors with what they likely considered a relatively straightforward request. They asked the board to institute suit against F. W. McIntyre, the former chairman of the board, to recover moneys that the taxpayers alleged had been "corruptly drawn by him" from the county treasury. The taxpayers informed the board that between April 1894 and April 1895, while he was chairman of the board of supervisors, McIntyre had submitted, and had the county treasurer pay, fraudulent bills for excessive and "pretended services" and for "constructing a so-called county road that had no existence in fact." To the surprise and chagrin of the taxpayers, the county board refused to pursue the matter. The taxpayers, on behalf of themselves and all other county taxpayers, then filed suit against McIntyre to require him to account for and repay the money that he had illegally obtained. McIntyre argued that only the county could bring such an action and that, therefore, the taxpayers had no right to relief. The Wisconsin Supreme Court emphatically rejected this contention, stating that if

> a county or other corporation has a plain cause of action for an injury done to it, that should be enforced for the protection of its members, and its governing body refuses to perform its plain duty . . . , our system of jurisprudence is by no means so weak that justice can thereby be defeated. . . . It certainly would be a strange situation if unfaithful officials could plunder a county . . . and be free from danger of being compelled to return their ill-gotten gains, or make good the injury caused by their corrupt conduct, because they had retired from office and the corporation, through its proper officers, unjustly refused to prosecute them.

The court declared that the "powers of courts of equity are broad and absolute enough to fit all situations where justice requires a remedy" and ruled that the taxpayers were entitled to maintain their taxpayers' action.[7]

Though largely ignored by historians, taxpayers' lawsuits, by providing an effective legal mechanism by which taxpaying citizens of all backgrounds could hold officeholders to account, eliminate corruption, and promote reform in local government, have profoundly influenced politics and the public sector in the United States. In the twentieth century, there are hundreds of reported cases in which taxpayers prevailed in such actions, preventing or righting a host of wrongs.[8] Specific, tangible benefits accrued to local communities as a result of these court rulings. The cumulative impact of these decisions, which have acted as a leaven in the American political system to foster the honest and healthy functioning of local government, has been significant. Moreover, taxpayers' suits have provided a means by which citizens could lawfully and constructively express political discontent. Admittedly, not all taxpayers' actions have been prompted by lofty motivations or had salutary effects. Some cases have involved disgruntled cheapskates and gadflies who sued to delay or derail the political process or to frustrate or circumvent the will of the majority.⁹ Nevertheless, the overall impact of taxpayers' suits on the American political order generally has been positive.

Taxpayers' litigation is not, however, only a twentieth-century phenomenon. The foundation for this legal edifice was established during the sixty years before World War I. During the late nineteenth and early twentieth centuries, courts of equity in most states came to recognize the standing of taxpayers to bring actions to enjoin illegal or corrupt acts by municipal and county officials. In those states in which the courts did not do so, such as New York, legislatures authorized taxpayers' actions in order to create a judicial remedy for malfeasance in local government. By the eve of the First World War, American courts had developed a mature body of law regarding taxpayers' lawsuits and had applied that law to a variety of taxpayers' claims.

Nineteenth-century taxpayers instituted actions against local government officials for reasons as numerous as the universe of official misdeeds. In most cases taxpayers filed lawsuits in courts of equity to obtain injunctive relief—that is, a court order requiring a public official either to do or to refrain from doing something. The most common suits were those to obtain injunctions restraining the expenditure or misappropriation of public funds through the lawless acts of local officials.[10] Taxpayers also sought to enjoin other allegedly unlawful municipal actions, ranging from the illegal issuance of municipal bonds to the unauthorized extension of a waterworks franchise.[11] If municipal officials had already improperly paid out public funds, as in an Illinois case in which officials had donated moneys to pay the debts of a private company, taxpayers brought lawsuits to compel the return of the moneys paid.[12] Finally, taxpayers initiated proceedings to enforce municipal causes of action where the public officers wrongfully declined to do so.[13] In short, taxpayers turned to courts of equity for relief in a wide range of circumstances, in which they maintained that they had suffered or would suffer damage as taxpayers as a result of the acts of local government that violated the law.

The recognition and expansion of taxpayers' rights to bring such actions in the nineteenth century was not, however, a tale of uninterrupted progress. Courts of equity in a number of states refused to entertain taxpayers' suits. In Massachusetts, the Supreme Judicial Court consistently ruled that, unless conferred by statute, courts of equity in that state did not have jurisdiction to hear actions by taxpayers to enjoin wrongful acts of municipalities.[14] Courts of equity in New York also denied taxpayers a remedy. In an 1822 decision, a New York chancery court judge rejected a taxpayer's request to restrain a town from collecting moneys to pay bounties for the destruction of wolves, stating that "I cannot find, by any statute, or precedent, or practice, that it belongs to the jurisdiction of chancery, as a Court of equity, to [grant the requested injunction] . . . and in the whole history of the English Court of Chancery, there is no instance of the assertion of such jurisdiction as is now contended for."[15] Although some early lower-court decisions in New York did allow taxpayers' lawsuits and some did not, in 1858, New York's highest court settled the matter, ruling that a taxpayer had no right to bring an action against municipal officials to restrain the waste of public funds or illegal acts unless the taxpayer would sustain some particular injury not common to all taxpayers.[16] Unlike courts in most states, the New York Court of Appeals declared that "no private person or number of persons can assume to be the champions of the community, and in its behalf challenge the public officers to meet them in the courts of justice to defend their official acts."[17] Courts in Kansas and Michigan adopted the New York common law rule.[18]

In most states, though, courts of equity were prepared to afford taxpayers the right to bring taxpayers' suits for the public benefit and to craft appropriate relief to address citizens' complaints. The willingness of nineteenth-century judges to jump into the breach and devise equitable relief for taxpayers is reflected in the Wisconsin Supreme Court's bold assertion of the equity powers of the courts in its 1898 decision in *Land, Log & Lumber Company v. McIntyre*, in which it declared,

> If for conduct such as detailed in the complaint, there is no remedy . . . the taxpayers are at the mercy of dishonest officials and must stand by and see the public treasury plundered. . . . The idea is simply preposterous, and that is all that need be said about it. While guided by precedents, equity is not bound by them, but may meet new situations as they arise, so that in the race between it and the ingenuity of unfaithful officials, the former will generally prevail.[19]

In an 1882 taxpayers' suit to require a judge and two county commissioners to repay to the county funds that they, through fraud and collusion, had obtained, the Oregon Supreme Court likewise held that a "taxpayer has an equity which entitles him to claim, through a court of equity, that he shall not be subjected to the payment of additional sums of taxes on account of the fraudulent and illegal disposal of the public funds and property by public officers."[20] In so ruling, the court expressly rejected the New York rule denying taxpayers such a remedy, observing that the "effect of these decisions in New York was to leave the inhabitants of a municipal corporation without remedy where its officers made a fraudulent disposition of its revenues."[21] These sentiments reflected the views of judges in the vast majority of states on the subject of taxpayers' actions. Most nineteenth-century courts were prepared to expand the rights of taxpayers to provide more effective protection against the unlawful acts of local government officials.

By 1900, courts in almost all states recognized the standing of taxpayers to bring taxpayers' suits against local officials. The conceptual basis for such actions that most courts articulated was that public property was held in trust by public officials for the benefit of the body of taxpayers, analogizing the situation to the relationship between corporate officers and stockholders. In 1897, the Georgia Supreme Court ruled that a taxpayer was entitled to an injunction restraining a city from operating a plumbing business that competed with the taxpayer's plumbing business on the grounds that the city's actions were unauthorized and hence illegal. The court offered this justification for taxpayers' suits:

> Following out the theory which regards the municipal corporation as a trustee for the inhabitants, it is almost, if not quite universally, conceded by the courts in the United States that . . . any . . . municipal taxpayer may resort to equity to prevent municipal corporations or officials from exceeding their lawful powers or neglecting or violating their legal duties, under any circumstances where the taxpayer's interest will be injuriously affected. . . . In private corporations, it is well settled that if the directors will not protect the rights of the creditors and stockholders, then the latter may and should attend to their own interests. There is no reason whatever why a different rule should be applied to municipal corporations, in which the taxpayers are the beneficiaries upon whose shoulders will ultimately fall the loss and expense which is caused by illegal, fraudulent, or tortious acts.[22]

In a similar vein, the Wisconsin Supreme Court observed that the

> philosophy of the taxpayer's action . . . is that the taxpayer is a member of a municipal corporation who, by virtue of his contributions to the funds of the municipality, has an interest in its funds and property of the same general quality as the interest of a stockholder in the funds of a business corporation, and hence when corporate officers are about to illegally use or squander its funds or property he may appeal to a court of equity on behalf of himself and his fellow stockholders (i.e., taxpayers) to conserve and protect the corporate interests and property from spoliation by its own officers.[23]

Courts explicitly acknowledged that public officials held a position of trust with respect to public property and funds and that taxpaying citizens had a substantial and legally enforceable interest in ensuring that local officers did not violate that trust.

These rationales highlight several important features of the American judiciary in the late nineteenth century. It is not surprising that common law judges, at a time when business and corporation law were evolving into their modern forms and when business and economic issues occupied such a prominent place in American jurisprudence, would utilize business analogies in evaluating taxpayers' claims. Moreover, judges in this period were notably protective of private property rights and vigorous in shielding private interests from government intrusion.[24] Taxpayers' suits represented a clash between public and private rights in which most courts were prepared to intervene to protect taxpayers from the transgressions of public officials.

Taxpayers' actions shared at least two characteristics. First, in every case one or more taxpayers filed suit because they were in some way dissatisfied with how government officials were spending their tax dollars. In this sense the taxpayers' suit was a legal manifestation of what historian Meg Jacobs has called "pocketbook politics."[25] Second, in each case taxpaying citizens turned to the courts in order to bypass and, they hoped, overrule political processes that were not working to their advantage.[26] Some of these lawsuits did not involve issues of great public import but were filed by obstructionists who simply disagreed with the wisdom of a particular government action or policy and sought to frustrate the will of the majority through protracted litigation.[27] Most taxpayers' actions, however, were brought by those in the political minority who lacked access to or influence in the local political machinery in order to promote reform and combat corruption in government.[28] Taxpayers' suits gave political outsiders an effective and much-needed weapon.

Nineteenth-century judges developed two principal limitations on a taxpayer's right to obtain relief. First, the taxpayer must have a pecuniary interest in the matter; that is, he must be able to demonstrate that the municipal action he was challenging would increase his tax bill. For example, in *Patten v. Chattanooga* taxpayers in Chattanooga, Tennessee, who asked the court to declare void a franchise that the city had granted to a utility company were denied relief because the ordinance in question "cannot affect their tax burden."[29] Second, courts generally would not grant relief with respect to acts within the authorized, lawful discretion of public officials because such actions, even mistaken ones, were "beyond legal redress."[30] This meant that taxpayers could not second-guess or micromanage the lawful decisions of public officials or obtain relief for their mistakes and poor judgment. In those circumstances, taxpayers were left to their political remedies, including voting such unwise officials out of office. As the Michigan Supreme Court observed in 1885,

> there has been an idea in some places . . . that courts of equity can always stand between citizens and municipal authorities, to shield them from abuses and extravagant action. This is not one of the functions of courts. It is one of the incidents of popular government that the people must bear the consequences of the mistakes of their representatives. No court can save them from this experience. It is one of the means of teaching the necessity of choosing proper servants.[31]

In applying the first restriction, judges were essentially adopting a "no harm, no foul" rule. In applying the second, they were giving appropriate deference to the political (nonjudicial) branches of government and demonstrating a pragmatic approach to the limits of judicial authority in political matters.

Several factors account for the increasing frequency with which taxpayers' suits were instituted in the decades following the Civil War. Perhaps most important, the rapid industrialization and urbanization of the United States in this era dramatically expanded the public sector and public spending and, as a consequence, multiplied the potential scope, magnitude, and incidence of official misconduct. Conversely, the extension of local government institutions into the unsettled frontier regions also threatened the interests of taxpayers. In his study of the Wisconsin lumber industry in the nineteenth century, James Willard Hurst identified the reasons why the lumber industry and large taxpayers in that state generally opposed the creation of new local government units. They were concerned that the "temptations inherent in the spending that would go with setting up a whole new county machinery" would "tend to increase the burden of taxation." Furthermore, the establishment of new town and county governments conduced to public corruption because "in the newer, thinly settled counties . . . it was peculiarly hard for local officials to withstand private importunities and peculiarly difficult to staff the public offices with men of probity and detachment from personal fortune."[32] Indeed, one of these newly created counties was Vilas County, the source of the *Land, Log, & Lumber Company* litigation, in which a county official was alleged to have, among other things, billed the county for constructing a "pretended county highway" that did not exist.[33] Finally, the absence of central supervision of local government by state legislatures in many states contributed to the rise in taxpayers' litigation. As Hurst noted, "Legislative initiative for policing or invigorating local government was rare, episodic, and marked by that relative indifference to adequate implementation that stamped most nineteenth-century statute law."[34]

In those few states in which the judiciary did not afford taxpayers the right to maintain taxpayers' suits, the other two branches of government, responding to political pressure, came to the rescue. In Massachusetts, where the courts had refused to provide taxpayers with a judicial remedy for alleged abuse of authority by municipal officials, the legislature in 1847 gave the state supreme judicial court jurisdiction, upon the petition of ten or more taxable residents of a town, to restrain the unlawful expenditure of public funds.[35] In 1905, the legislature in Kansas, in which the courts had followed the New York rule denying taxpayers the right to enjoin the illegal acts of public officials, enacted a statute affording taxpayers that remedy.[36] In some states in which the judges had already established the right of taxpayers to challenge local government actions in court, the legislatures expanded those rights. An 1881 statute in Indiana, for example, authorized county taxpayers to appeal certain actions of county commissioners.[37]

Perhaps the state in which taxpayers were most in need of a judicial remedy for illegal acts of government officials, though, was New York. As the New York Court of Appeals observed decades later, the "need for legislation upon this subject was made very apparent in the litigation growing out of the frauds of [William 'Boss'] Tweed and his associates."[38] Accordingly, in 1872, the New York legislature passed "an act for the protection of taxpayers against fraud, embezzlement and wrongful acts of public officers and agents." The 1872 statute authorized a taxpayers' suit "to prevent waste or injury to any property, funds or estate" of any county, town, or municipal corporation.[39] The legislature amended the 1872 taxpayers' statute on several occasions and eventually incorporated it in section 1925 of the New York Code of Civil Procedure.[40]

In 1881, the New York legislature passed a second, broader "act for the protection of taxpayers" to provide more effective restraints on official misconduct. Not only did this statute authorize a taxpayer to bring suit to prevent "waste or injury" to public property, as had the 1872 law, but it also authorized taxpayers' actions to "compel the restitution of such property" and to "prevent any illegal official act." This statute was amended in 1887 and again in 1892, and it was eventually codified in section 51 of the General Municipal Law.[41]

By the turn of the twentieth century, the United States had undergone something of a taxpayer's legal revolution. The taxpayers' suit, almost unheard of a half century earlier, had become firmly ensconced in the jurisprudence of every state, through the efforts of either courts or state legislatures. Over the course of these decades, Americans had articulated and constructed a taxpayer's right to hold local government officials accountable for conduct affecting the people's tax burden and had developed a form of legal action to enforce that right.

The taxpayers' lawsuits of the nineteenth century are significant because of what they tell us about Americans' evolving notions of citizenship. Taxpayers viewed themselves as political actors; they saw paying taxes as a source of political legitimacy and empowerment and as a badge of citizenship. The connection between paying taxes and citizenship was most often made by Americans when considering the right to vote. In the colonial era and the early republic, the right to vote was extended only to those who owned property and paid taxes. Suffragists likewise understood tax paying and voting as inextricably intertwined, anchoring one indication of citizenship, the right to vote, on another, the obligation to pay taxes.[42] Nineteenth-century judges explicitly acknowledged the connection between paying taxes and citizenship, variously identifying the persons bringing lawsuits as "taxpayers and citizens," "citizens and taxpayers," and "citizens who pay taxes."[43] The obligation to pay taxes was an incident of citizenship on which Americans grounded a right as citizens to take legal action to ensure that public officials did not violate the trust that citizens had reposed in them.

The development of the law regarding taxpayers' lawsuits also served an important political function. By empowering the judiciary to entertain taxpayers' actions and afford relief in appropriate cases, courts and legislatures provided a means by which citizens could lawfully, and within the bounds of civil society, achieve legitimate goals, require public officials to answer for their actions, and encourage good government. As a consequence, the law and the legal order gave citizens an outlet through which they could release political steam, a constructive way in which to vent and to obtain a public benefit for themselves and their fellow citizens. This aspect of taxpayers' suits served the United States well in the late nineteenth and early twentieth centuries as the growth of cities increased the size and scope of municipal government and the taxes of property owners.

In taxpayers' litigation we see, among other things, a fusion of legal activism and political activism. Time and again, citizens resorted to the courts in the pursuit of political objectives that they had been unable to attain through traditional politics. When Wisconsin taxpayers were unable to convince the county board of supervisors to file suit against a former county official to recover funds that he had plundered from the county treasury, they called on the law, as did New Yorkers when they, through the usual administrative and political channels, failed to prevent city officials from turning a public theater into a fire trap.[44] Taxpayers' litigation proved a reliable means by which political outsiders could combat corruption, challenge unlawful acts of public officials, and make local government more transparent.

The evolution of the taxpayers' lawsuit was itself representative of another salient feature of the nineteenth-century American legal order: the emergence of an instrumental conception of the law. By "instrumentalism," I mean generally the notion that the law and legal institutions may be employed as tools or instruments to obtain desired ends. Scholars of U.S. legal history have identified two principal aspects of this instrumentalist view of the law. Critical legal studies (CLS) scholars focus on the manner and extent to which American elites have used the law to promote their interests. The CLS interpretation emphasizes the substantial centrifugal flow of influence from the legal order and the common law courts to society, in the form of concrete and durable social change.[45] In contrast, consensus historians such as James Willard Hurst look at how ordinary Americans invoked the law for their own purposes and to shape their environment. This interpretation stresses the agency of ordinary people and the subordination of law to them as their instrument.[46] In contrast to the CLS school, the pluralist consensus view posits that the law "has functioned as an honest broker through which conflicting interests have sought to achieve their own ends" in the United States and has resulted in widespread prosperity and the development of a large middle class.[47]

Taxpayers' lawsuits partake of elements of both the CLS conception of instrumentalism and the pluralist consensus view. As to the former, they reflected the expansion of judicial review and judicial intervention in American life.[48] Nineteenth-century judges understood that they were breaking new ground in recognizing taxpayers' actions, noting that "the precedents for suits of this nature are of modern origin."[49] For the most part, judges were unwilling to see justice want for lack of a remedy when confronted with waste, injury to public property, or illegal acts by government officials. They adapted the law, addressed citizens' complaints, and devised such equitable remedies as the situation demanded in order to promote integrity and accountability in government. Judicial rulings in favor of taxpayers generally restrained, modified, or compelled specific actions of local officials. In granting such relief, judges shaped and affected the operation of government and the course of public policy. Throughout the nineteenth century, both courts and legislatures refashioned the law to accommodate the needs of a growing and urbanizing society, in which the public sector and public spending played increasingly important roles.

The widespread use of taxpayers' suits by Americans from all walks of life also demonstrates the significant degree to which they believed that they "could by law measurably shape environment to [their] ends." Nineteenth-century taxpayers "wanted the law's help positively to bring things about" and employed the law in general and the taxpayers' action in particular as instruments to that end. At its most fundamental level, the taxpayers' suit is about bringing the coercive power of the law to bear in order to force public officials to do, or refrain from doing, specific things. Such lawsuits were among the many ways in which ordinary citizens "made considerable use of legal compulsion to meet the challenges of [their] environment." Taxpayers' willingness to entrust these disputes to the courts indicates that they did indeed view the courts as honest brokers for the resolution of competing claims and interests.[50]

The taxpayers' action, then, was itself a manifestation of a common instrumentalist view of the law that characterized the U.S. legal order by 1900. Drawing on this nineteenth-century legal heritage, taxpayers during the Great Depression employed taxpayers' suits with increasing frequency to lighten their tax loads, promote good government, and hold public officials to account.

Depression-Era Taxpayers' Litigation

By 1930, the common law and the statutory law concerning taxpayers' lawsuits was well established. The taxpayers' action was judicially recognized in most states. In other states, legislatures not only had authorized taxpayers to bring suits to enjoin or otherwise redress unlawful or unauthorized acts of local governments but also had enhanced and extended taxpayers' rights. Taxpayers brought most of these lawsuits for one of three purposes: to restrain acts of local governments, to recover moneys that county or municipal governments had improperly paid to public officials or third parties, and to enforce causes of action where public officials wrongfully failed to do so.[51]

Taxpayers most frequently brought suits to prevent public officials from doing something that taxpayers considered detrimental to the interests of the taxpaying public. Reducing, or at least containing, the cost of government was the overarching and perennial objective of taxpayers. In many lawsuits taxpayers sought to limit wages, salaries, and expense reimbursements of municipal personnel or third parties contracting with local governments.

A taxpayers' suit in Houston reflects the municipal financial dynamics and the crisis in taxation that fueled much Depression-era taxpayers' litigation.

The local taxpayers' organization instituted suit to restrain the Houston school district from restoring cuts it had made to teachers' salaries during the 1932–1935 school years "due to a prevalent economic depression" and to enjoin it from expending $37,500 to construct twenty-three temporary school buildings. In 1932, the school board had implemented a 10 percent reduction for the 1932–1933 period and a 17 percent reduction for the 1934–1935 scholastic year. These wage cuts "were not only expressly made as emergency measures, but also upon the distinct recognition of that fact on both sides and the mutual agreement between the board and the employees that such reductions thereby made were only temporary . . . and if and when possible would be restored." By February 1935, the school district's finances had improved: it found itself with an unexpected $121,000 cash balance left over from the 1934 budget and almost $250,000 more in anticipated revenues than it had estimated. Accordingly, the school board voted to restore a portion of the wage cuts and to award contracts to construct temporary school buildings. The taxpayers' association filed suit to enjoin both expenditures.[52]

The Texas Civil Court of Appeals upheld the trial court's denial of a temporary injunction on several grounds, including that the school board's actions violated neither the state budget act nor the state constitution and that the school board was authorized to expend these sums. In rejecting the taxpayers' claim concerning the partial restoration of the wage reductions, the court observed that the "prevailing salary schedules and the contracts from which they proceeded had never been abrogated, but instead, due to financial stringency" that had prompted the wage cuts, "had merely been temporarily suspended as an emergency measure . . . due to the prevailing financial depression." The court further noted that "the depression had been lifted by the previous unanticipated inflow of nearly double the estimated amount of delinquent taxes, thereby giving" the school board "ample revenues for the restoration," and that the board "violated no provision of any of the laws invoked against it in doing so."[53] Two years later this taxpayers' league was also unsuccessful in a lawsuit to prevent the enforcement of two municipal ordinances setting minimum salaries for various municipal employees.[54]

In Baltimore, however, taxpayers prevailed in a taxpayers' suit to enjoin the implementation of a city order adopting a wage scale for municipal contracts. The taxpayers alleged that the enforcement of the pay scale would increase the cost of municipal work and thereby increase their taxes. The Maryland Court of Appeals ruled that the statute on which the city based its order did not, in fact, authorize it to establish such a wage scale and that, therefore, the city's action was illegal, and the taxpayers were entitled to an injunction preventing the enforcement of the wage scale.[55]

These lawsuits in which taxpayers challenged local government spending decisions captured the essence of the "Mr. Taxpayer versus Mr. Taxspender" dynamic and the ongoing tension between public officials charged with spending tax dollars responsibly and taxpayers concerned about their tax bills. Officeholders had a duty to provide adequate public services and faced very real challenges in fulfilling that charge as tax revenues declined, especially in the early 1930s. Taxpayers needed and generally expected these municipal services but felt they simply could not afford them. They litigated these issues with government officials because, as Hal Steed had learned, taxes had become a problem.

Taxpayers' suits aimed to stop a wide range of other local government actions. Bond issues were a common target, since they often involved large sums that had a significant impact on local tax rates. The Taxpayers' League of Wayne County, Nebraska, filed suit to enjoin the sale of a bond issue to repair and enlarge a local school, but the Nebraska Supreme Court rejected the taxpayers' claim that the election at which voters had approved the bond offering was void because of fraud or failure to muster the requisite number of votes.[56] Taxpayers were successful, however, in taxpayers' lawsuits to prevent public officials from appointing election officials in violation of civil service laws, to restrain New York City from constructing and operating an electric power plant, and to enjoin the city of Kennett, Missouri, from borrowing money from the federal government and using the loan proceeds to build a municipal power plant.[57] In each of the power plant cases, the courts ruled that the municipalities had no legal authority to undertake the proposed actions and expenditures.

In addition to enjoining public spending and other acts of local governments, taxpayers also employed the taxpayers' suit in order to compel public officials or third parties to repay moneys that local governments had unlawfully paid to them. A Wyoming lawsuit is illustrative of this class of taxpayers' litigation. In 1935, the Taxpayers' League of Carbon County brought suit against the former sheriff, John McPherson, and deputy sheriff to recover approximately $3,200 that the county had paid to them for travel reimbursement in excess of the amounts to which they were legally entitled. McPherson had been elected to a two-year term as sheriff in November 1930 and reelected in November 1932. At the time he commenced serving his first term in January 1931, the statutory travel reimbursement rate was $0.15 per mile. The Wyoming legislature thereafter reduced the rate to $0.10 per mile effective February 18, 1931. Two years later the legislature reduced the mileage rate to $0.08 per mile, effective February 15, 1933. From February 1931 to December 1932, McPherson and his deputies charged the county at the rate of $0.10 a mile, and thereafter at the rate of $0.08 a mile until February 1934. In April 1934, however, they submitted to the county claims for an additional $0.02 per mile on the miles each had traveled from February 1933 to February 1934, and in December 1934, each presented claims for an additional $0.05 a mile on the miles each had traveled in 1931 and 1932. In December 1934, McPherson and the deputy also billed the county for travel expenses from March to December 1934, at the rate of $0.10 per mile, not the $0.08 per mile rate then in effect under the 1933 statute. The county paid all of these supplemental claims.[58]

The taxpayers' league sued McPherson and the insurance company that had issued his surety bond to recoup the moneys paid to the sheriff and his deputy exceeding the applicable statutory mileage rates. The $3,200 amount in dispute was substantial for the time, especially given that the sheriff's annual salary was only $2,000. McPherson defended his actions, arguing that his travel reimbursements constituted "emoluments" that could not, under the state constitution, be decreased after his election and that, consequently, he was entitled to be reimbursed at the earlier, higher mileage rates. The Wyoming Supreme Court rejected his contention, ruling that "the expenses of public officers incurred in the performance of their official duties" are "neither salary nor an emolument" within the meaning of the constitutional prohibition and that the legislature had the power "to reduce the mileage rate . . . regardless of an officer's term." As a result, the Wyoming taxpayers' organization was able to recover funds for the county treasury and compel public officials' compliance with the law.[59]

A taxpayers' lawsuit in New Hampshire is representative of the third class of taxpayers' actions, in which taxpayers filed suit to enforce a claim or cause of action belonging to a municipality or county where officeholders wrongly failed to perform that duty. The litigation was precipitated by municipal graft and corruption. After a local bank in Berlin, the fourth largest city in the state, collapsed in 1931, city officials learned that the tax collector, John Labrie, had deposited city funds in the amount of $75,000 into his own account at the failed bank. Mayor Corbin and the city council instructed the city solicitor to bring suit against Labrie and Fidelity and Deposit Company of Maryland to enforce the city's claim against the $35,000 surety bond that Fidelity had issued to secure the city's liability for embezzlement by the tax collector. Corbin, however, did not seek reelection, and in April 1932, the new mayor, Ovide Coulombe, and the city council voted to dismiss the suit against the bonding company and to release Labrie from liability. Coulombe then reappointed Labrie as city tax collector. Infuriated by this course of events, a group of citizens organized the Berlin Taxpayers' Association and went to court to obtain justice.[60]

In 1933, the Taxpayers' Association filed a petition in the superior court requesting

> leave to prosecute an action at law, originally begun by the City of Berlin against the Fidelity and Deposit Company of Maryland, to recover upon its bond given as surety for John A. Labrie, tax collector of Berlin, which the petitioners allege the City of Berlin illegally, unlawfully, and fraudulently, without right, by vote duly recorded, voted to drop.[61]

The city's response alleged that those involved with bringing the petition were

> political enemies of the present administration, who are opponents because of personal, fancied grievances; and that said petition brought by them was not brought in good faith but for political purposes to try to discredit the administration.[62]

The superior court ruled in favor of the taxpayers' association, resulting in a settlement agreement with the bond company and Labrie's resignation.[63]

The subsequent criminal prosecution of Labrie highlights the remedial function that taxpayers' lawsuits often served. In October 1934, the state indicted him on twelve counts of embezzlement by a public official. Labrie pleaded guilty to all the charges and was sentenced to four years in the state prison. The taxpayers' litigation had brought Labrie's embezzlements to the public's attention and had resulted in his prosecution. The suit had proved an effective tool in combating corruption in local government and in holding public officials accountable.[64]

Not all taxpayers' actions were brought by taxpayers' organizations. In some cases, individual taxpayers filed suit on behalf of taxpayers' associations with which they were affiliated.[65] In others, they brought suit as individuals but to further the interests of taxpayers generally.[66] In yet others, taxpayers' lawsuits instituted by individual taxpayers served to advance their own private rights and those of the taxpaying public.[67] Business taxpayers also engaged in taxpayers' litigation to protect their commercial interests. For example, a number of taxpayers' suits in the 1930s were brought by power companies seeking to prohibit cities from operating municipal utilities that would compete with the private sector.[68] There was a fair amount of support for public ownership of utilities in the Great Depression, which provoked corresponding opposition from private utilities, among others.[69]

Nevertheless, taxpayers' litigation was an important component of the programs of many taxpayers' leagues. Some, such as the Harris County, Texas, Taxpayers' Association, litigated more than one taxpayers' lawsuit. At least one local taxpayers' organization engaged in a concerted taxpayers' litigation program that was central to obtaining its objectives of promoting economy, efficiency, integrity, and transparency in local government finances and administration.

The taxpayers' organization in Bell County, Kentucky, embraced such a litigation strategy and provides an interesting case study of the litigation activities of taxpayers' associations during the Great Depression. Established by the state legislature in 1867, Bell County is in southern Kentucky in the region of the Cumberland Gap and the Cumberland River. It abuts the far southwestern corner of Virginia and Tennessee's northern border. In the 1930s, the principal cities of Bell County were Middlesboro and Pineville.[70]

The Taxpayers' League of Bell County was formed in 1930 "by a number of businessmen to correct the abuses attending in the administration of Bell County's financial affairs and the illegal expenditures of the taxpayers' monies and want[ed] every taxpayer in the county to become a member."[71] Those abuses included the misappropriation of public funds by officials, the refusal by public officials to allow regular audits of government financial records, and what taxpayers considered wasteful or excessive expenditures of tax dollars for employee salaries and other things.[72] In an "Open Letter to Taxpayers" in the *Middlesboro Daily News*, the league urged all county taxpayers to join because "it will show that you still have the interest of the county and its citizens and good government at heart."[73] It "built up an extensive membership of taxpayers" in the county. The league's stated objectives were

> to curb unlawful and injudicious expenditures of public funds and to take such legal steps as in its judgment appeared necessary to protect the monies raised by taxation for public purposes; to audit or have audited public records of Bell County, and to publish reports of the same; to employ such agencies, including the engagement of legal talent, as might be necessary to promote the end sought; and generally to do all things leading to the ultimate purpose of the organization, such as would tend to elevate the government to a higher plane.[74]

It promised "to see that when money is collected from the taxpayers it will be spent for the purposes for which it was levied."[75]

Taxpayers' litigation was the centerpiece of the league's agenda and the taxpayers' action its main weapon. In its March 1931 "Open Letter to Taxpayers," the league boasted that it had "been instrumental in having some suits brought against former officials to recover" public funds and that "eight suits are now pending to recover about $60,000.00, and every citizen should be interested in these matters."[76] At its May 25, 1931, meeting, the league adopted a resolution declaring that one of the league's main objectives was to ensure that public officials "honestly and faithfully perform their duties, regardless of politics and political pressure," and that investigations by the league had revealed "that many of the officers are not complying with their legal duties." The resolution went on to "unhesitatingly condemn these practices" and instructed the league's attorneys "to prepare and file such actions as may be necessary to compel the proper performance by the public officials of Bell County of the duties imposed upon them by law."[77] Some taxpayers' lawsuits were thereafter brought by the league itself, while others were instituted by officers of the league on its behalf.[78] In all these cases, the plaintiffs were represented by attorney Martin T. Kelly, a central figure in the league's taxpayers' litigation program.[79]

One of the league's earliest taxpayer cases was initiated by James Hoskins and other members of the league's executive committee in December 1930, against James Helton, the former Bell County sheriff, to recover moneys wrongfully withheld by Helton. The taxpayers claimed that Helton had refused to remit to the county and the board of education approximately $42,000 in taxes he had collected as sheriff, that the taxpayers had demanded that county and school officials institute suit to recover the funds, and that these public officials had not only declined to take such action but "had been hostile to the efforts of the taxpayers of Bell County to compel the sheriff to comply with the law." The trial court dismissed the taxpayers' petition on the ground that they lacked the legal capacity to prosecute such an action. The Kentucky Court of Appeals reversed, ruling that the taxpayers had a right to maintain the lawsuit since the petition alleged that "the sheriff is retaining money that he should have paid over, and that the fiscal court has failed and refused to correct the matter and is averse to doing so." The court declared that the "taxpayers should not be left without remedy, for they are the real parties in interest, and they have a right to demand that the account be settled and judgment entered for the county for the amount due."[80] In so ruling, Kentucky's highest court reiterated the settled principle that taxpayers were entitled to enforce causes of actions belonging to local government where officeholders wrongfully refused to do so.

In 1931, the league, through several of its members, brought a taxpayers' suit against the city of Middlesboro, its mayor, and its commissioners to force them to allow the plaintiffs and their accountant to inspect and audit the city's financial records. An audit the previous year by the city's auditor had revealed that a number of the county officers "were short in their accounts," and the league had vowed to push for "a thorough investigation to the end." The trial judge denied the taxpayers' petition on the ground that "inasmuch as the city had had an audit made . . . that it should be sufficient." The taxpayers appealed, and the Kentucky Court of Appeals reversed, holding that, "subject to . . . reasonable rules and regulations, . . . the taxpayers have the right at any time to inspect the records of the city with a view of making an audit and discovering the truth as to its financial affairs and the manner in which the public business is conducted."[81] Such lawsuits promoted transparency in government and accountability of public officials, two chief objectives of proponents of a business model of government since the Progressive Era.

The following year representatives of the taxpayers' league filed a taxpayers' action against the Middlesboro board of commissioners to recover for the city treasury excess salaries paid to the commissioners. In 1922, the voters of Middlesboro had adopted a commission plan of government. The city charter for which they voted also provided that each member of the board of commissioners would receive an annual salary of $900. In 1929, the commissioners enacted an ordinance increasing their compensation, which prompted the taxpayers' suit. The Bell County Circuit Court dismissed the petition, but the court of appeals reversed, ruling that the electorate had fixed the commissioners' compensation in the city charter, that therefore "the city commissioners did not have the power to increase their compensation, however much it may have been deserved," and that the plaintiffs were entitled to recover for the use and benefit of the city the illegal excess salaries paid to the officials. The court grounded its decision on "the supremacy of the voice of the people," declaring that "the will of the electorate . . . must be given full force and effect. . . . Municipal councils . . . are but the servants of the people and when the people register their will in respect to things directly submitted to them, that will is controlling." As the court observed, the case presented "a novel and important question with respect to the limitations on the power of the board of commissioners . . . by reason of the referendum under which that method of government was adopted."[82]

It would appear that nepotism in county government prompted the taxpayers' league's next lawsuit. In 1930, George Vanbeber, the county judge, had appointed Ed Vanbeber clerk to the county judge. The league brought suit against both Vanbebers and the Bell County fiscal court to recover moneys paid to Ed Vanbeber as clerk and to enjoin further payment of his salary, alleging that he had not attended to his duties as clerk and had only been present a total of fifteen days. In this action the league's efforts were unavailing. The court of appeals affirmed the trial court's dismissal of the petition, ruling that a citizen and a taxpayer could not maintain an equitable action for injunctive relief where, as in Vanbeber's case, there were specific remedies at law available.[83] It is unclear what those other remedies were or whether the taxpayers thereafter pursued them through litigation.

The taxpayers' league had better luck the next year, again putting a stop to an attempt to increase a public official's salary. In February 1931, the Bell County fiscal court voted to increase the fiscal court clerk's salary from $60 monthly to $100 monthly, pursuant to which the clerk, J. M. Pursifull, was paid $100 per month in 1931, 1932, and 1933. The league filed a taxpayers' suit challenging the fiscal court's order. The Kentucky Court of Appeals affirmed the trial court's order awarding the league "judgment for the use and benefit of the county for the excess of $40 a month" because the state constitution prohibited such a change in the clerk's compensation.[84]

The Bell County group's taxpayers' litigation program was highly effective. It prosecuted taxpayers' actions in a coordinated and vigorous manner. In the *Hoskins* case, the league elicited a reminder from Kentucky's highest court that "taxpayers should not be left without remedy," a premise underlying taxpayers' actions since their inception almost a century earlier. In a libel action that the league brought against Sun Publishing Company, the publisher of *The Pineville Sun*, the court of appeals called attention to "the very commendable things which [the league] had undertaken, and to some degree accomplished." The taxpayers' league's clout is evidenced by the fact that in 1933 the county attorney of Bell County felt obliged to seek the league's approval of a proposal by the county fiscal court to borrow funds to pay county expenses that had accrued the previous year.[85] Organized taxpayers in Bell County, like those throughout the nation, were ready, willing, and able to go to court when they believed that doing so was necessary to protect taxpayers' rights and to require public officials to adhere to the law.

The litigation activities of Depression-era taxpayers' associations served as an enforcement mechanism for their legislative programs and for the business model of government those legislative programs aimed to implement. Their taxpayers' suits were fundamentally about compelling compliance with structural reforms and other good government measures that had been enacted but that local public officials were ignoring or evading. Putting good government reforms in place did little good if public officials were able to work around their constraints. The creation of a merit-based civil service system fell short of the mark if government officials could ignore their requirements and make appointments or promotions on the basis of personal and political considerations. Likewise, the adoption of transparent and scientific systems of public finance was a hollow victory for organized taxpayers if local government units were able to spend taxpayers' dollars unlawfully and then resist audits that would bring such conduct to the public's attention. The taxpayers' action provided a means by which citizen taxpayers could force municipal and county officers "to perform the duties imposed upon them by the laws of the state, honestly and faithfully."[86] Such coercive remedies helped to ensure that good government reforms were realized and not merely words on paper.

Most taxpayers' associations only occasionally invoked the taxpayers' lawsuit to supplement and effectuate their extensive legislative and political activities. In Bell County, however, the taxpayers' league employed the taxpayers' action in furtherance of a concerted litigation strategy. Its litigation campaign was an early manifestation of a feature of the American legal order that, in the twenty-first century, Americans take for granted: the use by organized interest groups of litigation as a strategy to advance political and institutional reform or to enforce their rights. Since the mid-1960s, organizations advocating women's rights have turned to the courts to facilitate legal change regarding reproductive rights, workplace equality, and women's rights generally. During the same period, environmental activists sought to refashion environmental law and public policy through litigation. In the mid-1930s, the National Association for the Advancement of Colored People embarked on a coordinated litigation strategy targeting segregation in public schools that spanned four decades. When organized interest groups in present-day United States find legislatures unreceptive to their causes or traditional political processes unavailing, they frequently seek judicial intervention. The coordinated litigation campaign is now among the panoply of recognized tactics available to associations of citizens to further their interests and foster change in the public sphere. In the 1930s, though, it was still an inchoate phenomenon.

Organized taxpayer litigation during the Great Depression reflected the two interpretations of instrumentalism and the reciprocal flow of influence between American society and its legal order. On one hand, these taxpayers' suits demonstrated the significant extent to which citizen taxpayers relied on the law and the courts to promote their interests and shape their environment to their purposes. Taxpayers' lawsuits represented the taxpayers' "demand for positive help from the law" and evinced their expectation that the law would "help positively to bring things about" in the realm of local government.[87] The fact that taxpayers were willing to submit these issues to the courts shows their confidence that the judiciary would, for the most part, fairly and impartially decide, according to the rule of law, important matters concerning the conduct of public officials. Taxpayers may not have believed that politics never informed judicial decisions, but they trusted the courts as an institution that generally would serve as an honest intermediary of disputes between citizens and their government.

Conversely, the taxpayers' organizations' litigation programs attest to the profound impact of the law and legal institutions in the United States. The courts' decisions in these cases determined how local government units within the jurisdiction of those courts conducted business and how much tax their taxpayers paid. One sees in these rulings the "radiating effects of courts" and the centrifugal flow of influence from the courts to the parties in these lawsuits and to the wider society beyond.[88] These taxpayers' suits also highlight broad features of the American legal order. Because, as Tocqueville observed, "scarcely any question arises in the United States which does not become, sooner or later, a subject of judicial debate," Americans "are obligated to borrow the ideas, and even the language usual in judicial proceedings, in their daily controversies. . . . The language of the law thus becomes, in some measure, a vulgar tongue; the spirit of the law . . . gradually penetrates . . . into the bosom of society."[89] Americans' conceptions of legality in general, and the jurisprudence regarding taxpayers' actions that evolved between 1860 and 1930 in particular, both framed the disputes between taxpaying citizens and government units and determined their outcomes. In this regard, the law was, as Christopher Tomlins has hypothesized, "a mode of operation, a structure, a discourse in itself" that "informed and helped constitute" the discourse of power.[90] Moreover, the issues that taxpayers' lawsuits presented and resolved—the specifics of how tax dollars were to be spent and how local government was to be operated—were acutely political ones. Consequently, taxpayers' litigation manifests the dynamic relationship between law and politics, the alliance of legal and political activism, and the taxpayer as political and legal actor. In doing so, they reflect the "complex interrelationship between law and politics" articulated by critical legal studies scholars.[91]

Taxpayers' lawsuits in the Great Depression thus evidence the centrality of law and the complex, reciprocal relationship between law and society in the United States. Through the instrument of taxpayers' litigation, ordinary Americans made affirmative use of the law and of conceptions of legality for their own purposes in order to advance their interests, arbitrate their controversies with local government officials, and influence the conduct of government. That same instrument simultaneously served as a conduit for a substantial centrifugal flow of influence from the legal order and the courts throughout the nation.

Conclusion

An assessment of the taxpayers' association movement involves, at a minimum, an examination of its impacts and its importance. The question of impact is mainly one of efficacy. To what extent did Depression-era taxpayers' organizations succeed in promoting economy and efficiency in government and in reducing their members' taxes in the short term? To what extent did they act as a long-term positive force in the cause of good government by facilitating enduring structural changes in the institutions and operations of local and state government? The question of importance is essentially a historical one. What insights may be gained from organized taxpayer activity in this period regarding American political development, political and civic institutions, and political and civic culture? What does the taxpayers' association movement tell us about the nature and development of American law and the American legal order?

How one evaluates the impacts and effectiveness of taxpayers' leagues during the Great Depression depends to some extent on how, and from whose perspective, one measures and defines effectiveness. If success is measured by the degree to which organized taxpayers attained their goals of making government cheaper and more efficient and of lightening their tax load, then taxpayers' groups were relatively effectual. In 1931, the New England Council had already concluded that "local taxpayers' associations have been found the most effective means in dealing with" the fiscal demands of government.¹ In late 1933, George L. Leffler, a professor of finance at the University of Toledo, examined "the burden of taxation" in six states (New York, Michigan, Illinois, Wisconsin, Ohio, and Indiana) and found, among other things, that "the influence of strong, well-organized taxpayers' associations have forced economy in 92 percent of the taxing units of" Indiana. He predicted that, in these states, "the burden of taxation will be much reduced in 1933" and concluded that "the campaign for reduced taxation has made marked progress during 1933 toward its goal. Reduced budgets and tax limiting laws are the order of the day."² That same year Claude Tharp found that taxpayers' associations had made important contributions to the cause of efficient and less costly government.³

As one might expect, taxpayers' organizations regularly touted the accomplishments of their policies and programs. The Worcester Taxpayers' Association reported that its third year of work, 1934, "saw a reduction in property taxes in Worcester for the second successive year," from approximately $11.4 million in 1932 to $9.7 million in 1934. In 1935, the Association of Omaha Taxpayers asserted that it had "been instrumental in securing the adoption of several important reform measures," including a county manager plan of government. The Taxpayers' Research League of Delaware likewise claimed that it had a hand in "important and constructive measures enacted by the legislature." The local taxpayers' organization in New Haven, Connecticut, quantified the value of its research activities, claiming that "every dollar spent in research by this agency resulted in the formulation of definite recommendations for saving about $30 annually in a normal year in the operation of city services."⁴ Although such reports are admittedly self-serving, they appear to be mostly accurate. Many state taxpayers' associations played an important part in the enactment by their state legislatures of worthy reforms concerning government operations and finance.

At the end of the decade, three journalists who reported on taxpayers' leagues had decidedly favorable views of them. In 1939, John Elting examined the gamut of organized taxpayer activity at the municipal level, from "militant taxpayers' groups" to "fact-finding research organizations," from those "mix[ing] actively in politics" to those "working quietly as a 'pressure group.'" His findings convinced him that there was no need to "tolerate high taxes . . . when the real facts prove that *taxes can be cut!*" Elting was equally effusive about state and county taxpayers' associations: "Can taxes be cut? The answer is a ringing YES—if the methods are right." Economist and journalist Sylvia Porter, who considered the "growing burden of taxes [to be] one of the gravest problems confronting the next administration," was "convinced that we Americans at last are thoroughly aroused about" reducing taxes and eradicating government waste, duplication, and inefficiency. She praised the strides that taxpayers' associations had made in reining in taxes and spending, noting that taxpayers' groups in Massachusetts had helped to slash municipal debt "from a 1931 peak of $316,000,000 to $287,000,000"; that the Nebraska Federation of County Taxpayers' Leagues had saved taxpayers $140 million in general tax levies in the past decade; that in 1939 the taxpayers' organization in Westchester County, New York, had prevented a 22 percent tax increase in county taxes and pared $1 million off the county budget; and that the taxpayers' league in South Bend, Indiana, had cut taxes by 38 percent in six years. Porter hailed organized taxpayers as a powerful new constituency in American politics, declaring, "You can't ignore a movement that is gaining strength against political power and public apathy, that is attracting tens of thousands from every state, from all classes. It's a revolt of the masses." Gordon Gaskill also viewed the rise of organized taxpayer activity as a positive development in American civic life. In early 1941, he reported that local and state taxpayers' associations were "lopping sizeable chunks off" budgets and producing significant tax savings by exposing and combating carelessness, "graft, extravagance, and inefficiency" in state and local government. He commended "the hard-pressed American taxpayer [for] band[ing] together with fellow victims to form vigilante committees against waste" of taxpayer dollars.[5]

Public officials, bankers, and, to a lesser extent, experts on government took a less sanguine view of the impact of taxpayers' organizations. Milwaukee mayor Daniel Hoan rarely missed an opportunity to deride "the 'cut cost of government' leagues in this country." Based on his experience in that city, he considered the demands of taxpayers' associations for economy and budget cuts as unreasonable and unrealistic. He maintained that such reductions in public spending would impair the ability of government to "furnish . . . community services that we can't get along without" and believed that "our citizens have thoughtlessly rallied to the cry that if taxes can be drastically cut somehow their troubles will be solved."[6] Frederick L. Bird, the director of municipal research for Dun & Bradstreet, rued the negative effects that tax limitation measures had on municipal credit.[7] *National Municipal Review* editor Wade S. Smith contended in January 1934 that although recent legislation enacted in a number of states forgiving interest and penalties on past-due taxes had been adopted at the urging of taxpayers "to induce the tax defaulter to pay up, in nearly every instance they have had just the opposite effect and have encouraged further tax delinquency."[8] Sidney Demers, the manager of the Buffalo Municipal Research Bureau, had "no quarrel with those taxpayers' associations whose work is based on research" but condemned any type of "militancy" by organized taxpayers, insisting that the "claim of any group less than that of the people themselves to dictate to the elected officials their course of action, under threat or duress of any kind, is outside the constitution and the laws, and is nothing less than mob rule."[9] Political scientist Thomas Reed similarly approved of those taxpayers' groups organized "for the purpose of finding the facts and passing reasonable judgments on them" but warned that the more extreme tax reduction and tax limitation efforts would wreak havoc on state and local governments.[10]

Most experts in public administration saw in taxpayers' associations the potential for both good and evil but concluded that their promise outweighed any peril they posed. For good government professionals, the question was whether organized taxpayers would devote their energies to constructive or destructive ends.[11] While he was president of the National Municipal League, Murray Seasongood framed the issue as follows:

> There can be no doubt of the strength and sincerity of taxpayer sentiment for economy.... The question is, shall this sentiment be mobilized and directed toward an intelligent and discriminating economy which preserves the good while eliminating the bad, separates the essential from the non-essential service, and actually makes government better, or shall it be left under uninformed and fanatical leaders in the newly-discovered cause of economy to pass away in empty vaporings or to disrupt administration, destroy essential services, and bring government itself into contempt.[12]

Seasongood and other authorities on government generally regarded the collaborative activities of taxpayers' leagues, especially their research and legislative programs, as forms of constructive economy but maligned tax strikes and tax limits as species of destructive economy.

Others also emphasized the importance of intelligent and informed taxpayer action and found great potential in such efforts directed at working with, not against, government officials. Luther Gulick of Columbia University opined that "if a taxpayers' or civic organization is willing to get at the facts painstakingly and think intelligently about their government, such an association can be of tremendous value."[13] National Municipal League secretary Howard P. Jones saw in the emerging taxpayers' association movement "an opportunity before those interested in local government that has never existed before and may never come again.... There is at present citizen interest, energy and enthusiasm regarding problems of local government which, directed into intelligent channels, may work wonders" by generating the public support necessary to modernize and refashion the structures and operations of state and local governments throughout the nation.[14] Edmond M. Barrows, recognizing that taxpayers' associations "provide at once menace and opportunity," was encouraged by their increasing embrace of intelligent and balanced legislative, research, and other constructive economy programs. He urged organized taxpayers to obtain relevant information and assistance "from their better trained co-workers in the field of civic advance"—that is, good government experts. He concluded that taxpayers' leagues "are allies . . . for the advocates of governmental reconstruction" and that they "are after simplicity, sound financing, and centralized responsibility in local government. In these efforts they are on solid ground."[15] By and large, good government experts in the 1930s assessed taxpayers' associations favorably, most likely because the lion's share of organized taxpayer activity was of the constructive economy type.

Many tax spenders also concluded that taxpayers' organizations were not driven as much by antipathy toward big government as they had feared. Of course, there was an undercurrent of such sentiment in the taxpayers' association movement. Some of its supporters in the business community, like *Nation's Business* editor Merle Thorpe, whom Beito described as representing "the dwindling hard-core anti-big-government wing of the organized business community," were truly of a libertarian ilk.[16] At the grassroots level, many shared the desire of the Iowa farmer who "would also like to buy less government" and the belief of the West Virginia Taxpayers' Association that "the price of government should undergo the same measure of deflation as every other branch of human activity."[17] Although these opinions reflected some degree of preference for smaller government, they were fundamentally about the cost, not the size and scope, of government. The vast majority of organized taxpayers simply wanted some relief from their onerous tax burdens. As one leader of a county taxpayers' association in Minnesota put it, "The tax burden will always be with us, but we must learn to control it."[18] To this end they sought to eliminate unnecessary services and wasteful spending and to make government more economical. The activities of taxpayers' organizations like Hal Steed's Taxpayers' League of Atlanta and Fulton County were devoted to constructive economy measures, not destructive ones. For the most part, taxpayers' leagues responsibly balanced their right to press for lower taxes against their obligation to pay their fair share of the cost of a reasonable level of government services. The National Pay Your Taxes Campaign was so successful because most organized taxpayers were not individualist ideologues. Small-government sentiment was a minor component of the taxpayers' association movement, not a major one.

The same cannot be said of the free enterprise antistatist vision of government that conservatives in the 1930s were fashioning and on which conservatives in post-1960s United States would draw for political gain. Free enterprisers' aversion to taxes was fundamentally ideological; taxpayers' groups' opposition to taxes was practical and mundane. Uncompromising antistatists opposed taxation because they feared that an activist state and its attendant increasing tax burdens would inexorably lead to the creation of a totalitarian state organized on principles of collectivism and would destroy American capitalism and Americans' liberty.[19] Organized taxpayers at the local and state levels engaged in tax resistance because they could no longer afford to pay their rising tax bills. Had they been able to pay their taxes, then, like Hal Steed and his fellow Atlanta taxpayers in the 1920s, it is very likely they would have continued to do so and not organized nationwide. Even in the few instances in which taxpayers' leagues resorted to tax strikes, admittedly an antistatist tactic, it was out of desperation and only after they had exhausted all alternatives, not in furtherance of some antistatist mission to diminish government and protect the liberties of businesses and individuals. The overall tenor of the taxpayers' association movement in the 1930s was, like that of the New Deal, pragmatic, not dogmatic.

With the benefit of two generations of hindsight, taxpayers' associations during the Great Depression may properly be seen as largely effective and as having exerted a significant influence on both American political institutions and culture and on the fabric of American civic life. Tax strikes were a dangerous and radical option, and that is why they were rarely employed. Tax limitation measures were crude instruments of tax relief policy, but in scores of states and localities they did in fact achieve the goal of reducing property taxes. Taxpayers' organizations also promoted better and less costly government through taxpayers' lawsuits and an array of traditional political activities.

Many taxpayers' associations did not rely on a single strategy but experimented with multiple programs, each of which often facilitated and paved the way for other efforts. The frequent interplay of the tactics that organized taxpayers employed served to enhance the efficacy of taxpayers' leagues. They applied political pressure or turned to the courts to require public officials to implement and adhere to budgetary, borrowing, and administrative reforms that their constructive economy activities had helped to put in place. In Duluth, Minnesota, the Taxpayers' League of St. Louis County participated in a lawsuit to enforce a statutory tax limit against a local school district. ARET's litigation strategy enabled it to maintain the tax strike in Chicago for as long as it did. Calls for a tax strike in Jersey City metamorphosed into a fusion political movement directed at ousting the Democratic machine headed by Mayor Frank Hague. In New Hampshire, the taxpayers' suit brought by the Berlin Taxpayers' Association began a chain of events that led to the formation of the Berlin Farmer-Labor Party. The energies released by these aggressive efforts of taxpayers' groups in both cities generated the requisite critical political mass for the creation of a third-party political movement. There was a considerable degree of interaction between the various tactics of taxpayers' organizations, and each reinforced others to some extent.

The programs of taxpayers' organizations that had the most significant and enduring impact, though, were their extensive legislative and research efforts. Through these activities organized taxpayers in every state and in hundreds of communities transformed the manner in which state and local governments were organized, operated, and financed. They influenced thousands of decisions and actions by state and local legislative and executive bodies. Their campaigns for institutional reform resulted in the enactment of innumerable measures affecting the organization and administrative structures of government and the means and methods of public finance and public administration. The cumulative impact of taxpayers' groups was enormous.

Prior to the Great Depression, the institutions of state and local government evolved largely in an ad hoc manner, without much forethought from a public administration perspective. County governments were formed when population density attained a certain level. Government departments and bureaucracies were created by elected officials to meet a specific, usually acute, need or to advance a particular agenda, not on the basis of long-term planning or the application of business management principles to public entities. The 1930s was a watershed decade in this regard. For the first time the influence of the business model of government extended widely and powerfully beyond the halls of academia, the National Municipal League, and other nongovernmental professional associations to state and local governments across the nation. Henceforth, the structures of state and local government developed and operated to a lesser degree on an ad hoc basis and to a greater degree as a result of thoughtful planning informed by professional expertise.

This is not to say that taxpayers' associations are entitled to all the credit for such reforms. Good government reformers, business leaders, and public officials themselves made important contributions. Still, taxpayers' organizations played a crucial and indispensable part in the process of refashioning state and local government in the United States in these years. In doing so, they fulfilled their promise, envisioned by Barrows and other good government reformers, of being not only advocates of government reconstruction but also agents of such change.

One of the recurring themes in American political history is the engagement, and often conflict, between taxpayers and tax spenders. As Julian Zelizer has observed, "hostility toward taxation [is] an age-old tradition" in the United States, in which tax revolts are a time-honored practice. Zelizer's contention that "questions of taxation and broad-based antistatism . . . have continually shaped American political culture" is borne out by events in the 1930s, when antitax agitation erupted in every state. Historically, tax spenders have been concerned mainly with maintaining what they regard as a reasonable and necessary level of government activity, whereas taxpayers care more about the cost of doing so. Speaking for the tax spenders in the 1933 *Mr. Taxpayer versus Mr. Taxspender* radio play, Daniel Hoan rhetorically asked, "Do we really want the cheapest kind of government?" He maintained that it was the taxpayer's civic duty to fund the proper cost of government—that is, "the actual cost of necessary services to promote the public welfare." Luther Gulick, representing the beleaguered taxpayer, instead focused on public frustration with government spending and the "problem of high taxes and tax reduction," summarizing taxpayer sentiment as follows: "They don't get any more out of me. I'm going to stop paying taxes." Conflict over whether and how to spend tax dollars has been a central feature of taxpayer–tax spender engagement.[20]

The programs and activities of Depression-era taxpayers' associations represented various manifestations of, in historian Meg Jacobs's formulation, "pocketbook politics." Almost all taxpayers were consumers of government services, and all helped to pay for those services with their taxes. The taxpayers' association movement, at its most fundamental level, was a protest by consumers of government services against the escalating cost of the services as evidenced by their escalating tax burdens. Each of the programs of taxpayers' organizations, directly or indirectly, aimed in some way to lighten that load. Organized taxpayers brought these concerns to their legislative bodies, to the polls, and to the courts in order to advance economy and efficiency in government and to reduce or at least limit their taxes. Like the Progressives who, according to Jacobs, "transformed their agenda of mass purchasing power into a program of national recovery and reform during the Great Depression of the 1930s, pushing it from the margins to the center of political debate," so too did taxpayers' groups in the 1930s force their agenda of government reconstruction and tax reduction from the periphery to the hub of political debate throughout the United States.[21]

Organized taxpayer activity highlights the role of the taxpayer as reformer. The Founders declared independence pursuant to "the right of the people," articulated in the Declaration of Independence, "to alter or . . . abolish . . . any form of government" when that government "becomes destructive" of the ends for which governments are established. A little more than 150 years later, the *National Municipal Review* concluded that an urgent desire to reform and reconstruct the institutions of government was the impetus behind Depression-era taxpayer activity. It commended the "widespread citizen interest in ways and means of achieving governmental economy" and made the following observation:

> Disillusioned and cynical taxpayers are being beaten by economic necessity into the realization that waste and extravagance and inefficiency and corruption are not necessary attributes of government and that if they themselves will give to public affairs some of the time and thought—not to say money—they have wasted on the stock market, the returns will be proportionately greater, individually and socially. For government, which seems to flow on inevitably like a river, is too readily dammed by those who would irrigate their own pastures at the expense of their fellows downstream.[22]

Nearly all the efforts of organized taxpayers in the 1930s evinced a similar motivation. Taxpayers' associations served as important instruments through which taxpaying citizens in the United States have fulfilled the function and realized the status of reformer.

In addition, organized tax resistance enabled taxpayers to realize their status as political and legal actors. Taxpayers' leagues acted as conduits of both political influence and legal influence, conveying to public officials the will of the taxpaying people and transmitting the constitutive power of the law and legal institutions to shape the structures of government and to decide specific taxpayer–tax spender disputes affecting the cost of government. For 150 years, taxpayers' organizations have embodied a vital fusion of political and legal activism.

Taxpayers' associations demonstrate the importance of local institutions and the "persistence of localism" in the nation's politics. Taxpayers' leagues were local civic-political organizations directed at local taxes and local problems. The strategies that organized taxpayers adopted were likewise a function of localism. As John Elting observed, which of the methods that taxpayers "used to attack the tax citadel . . . is best depends on local conditions." The same was true of collective tax resistance at the state level, as taxpayers' groups tailored their objectives and programs to the prevailing circumstances in each state. The goals and tactics that made sense in a rural, sparsely populated state with low demand for government services were ill-suited to a populous industrial state whose residents expected more from government. Localism persisted and predominated in the taxpayers' association movement of the Great Depression, which, although national in scope, was nevertheless local in its impetus and its character. Taxpayers' associations and taxpayers have been among "the subnational political institutions and actors" that have shaped public policy at the state and local levels.[23]

Americans' evolving notions of citizenship have actuated much organized taxpayer activity. Taxpayers have invoked the citizens' freedom of association to organize taxpayers' associations through which they might advance their interests. They used their obligation to pay taxes as a rationale to assert and construct a corresponding right to hold government officials accountable for how they expended public funds and operated government. When Daniel Hoan declared that "it behooves every good citizen to take part in civic and governmental affairs and improve that government and when the time comes to pay the [tax] bill," he hit on the essential connection between being a citizen, paying taxes, and promoting political reform.[24]

Taxpaying citizens sought to enforce their right to good government through political, legislative, and research efforts, and through litigation. The growth of organized taxpayer activity in the twentieth century paralleled and was fueled by the evolution of a rights-based conception of citizenship and of a legal culture emphasizing individual rights. The emergence of a citizenship of rights and of a legal culture of rights after 1930 are complementary and mutually reinforcing developments.

Conversely, the taxpayers' association movement had long-term impacts on American civic life and views of citizenship. For one thing, Americans became far more knowledgeable about and involved in their government. Americans had always interacted with public officials and the institutions of government, but before the Great Depression such interaction tended to be sporadic and superficial, usually provoked by and limited to particular issues and problems. As a result of the crisis of the Great Depression, however, citizens engaged (usually constructively, occasionally destructively) their state and local governments and public officials to a far greater extent. Not all Americans did so, for many had all they could do to put food on the table, much less agitate for better and less costly government. There was, though, an increasing level of citizen–government engagement and, consequently, of citizens' understanding of how their governments did function and should function. This process in turn informed Americans' notions of citizenship, both by further integrating ordinary citizens into the fabric of American public life and by promoting a more rights-based vision of citizenship in the United States.

The necessity for constructive engagement with local government on the part of taxpaying citizens was apparent to contemporary observers of the taxpayers' association movement and to taxpayers' organizations. In 1933, Clyde L. King of the Agricultural Adjustment Administration insisted that a "better informed citizen" was among the "prerequisites to that wholesome and responsive government we call democracy" and to battling political patronage and corruption in government.[25] Howard P. Jones considered citizen organizations essential to achieving progress in county government, declaring that

> most important of all . . . is the increased citizen interest in public affairs resulting generally from the depression and specifically from the desire to reduce taxes. . . . In America nothing can be accomplished without citizen interest. Organization follows interest, action follows organization, and gradually, slowly, cumbersomely . . . the bit of leaven leavens the whole lump.[26]

A 1935 editorial in the *National Municipal Review* exhorted citizens to organize and campaign for good government, arguing that it "is idle to think good government can be protected by the spontaneous desire of each individual citizen acting alone" and that "the only way . . . to make the average citizen feel he has a part in local government is through organization."[27] Later that year Thomas Reed seconded that emotion, contending that "without citizen organization, permanent citizen organization, good government is impossible."[28]

Taxpayers' leagues expressed similar views about the duty and the right of citizens to engage public officials constructively in order to improve public administration. Paul Reynolds, the director of the Wisconsin Taxpayers' Alliance, wrote that the motto of the alliance could be "We will never have good government until the people take an active interest in government affairs."[29] The local taxpayers' league in Duluth, Minnesota, maintained that "a democratic form of government requires that every citizen should spend the maximum time possible in doing his part to ensure that his government does the best job possible."[30] Americans' ideas about citizenship were energized and reshaped by organized taxpayer activity in the 1930s.

Collective action by taxpayers also illuminates the intimate connection between law and citizenship. Being subject to, and able to derive the benefit and protection of, the rule of law is a defining characteristic of citizenship. Simone Weil, citing Montesquieu and Rousseau, argued that "the difference between a slave and a citizen is that a slave is subject to his master and a citizen to the laws. It may happen that the master is very gentle and the laws very harsh: that changes nothing. Everything lies in the distance between caprice and rule."[31] The relationship between citizenship and the law is fundamental; law is inextricably bound to citizenship and citizenship to the law. As Weil observes, the very concept of citizenship is defined with reference to the rule of law. Hence, it is not surprising that law and litigation have played such a crucial part in organized taxpayer political activism.

Litigation, specifically the taxpayers' action, was a principal tactic used by organized taxpayers to reform the institutions and administration of local and state government and to lighten their tax burdens. In the last half of the nineteenth century, taxpayers convinced courts and legislatures to develop a body of jurisprudence that defined the nature and scope of the taxpayer's right to sue public officials and restrain official actions. The Bell County Taxpayers' League and the Berlin Taxpayers' Association relied heavily on taxpayers' litigation to accomplish their political reform and tax reduction objectives. Other taxpayers' associations during the Great Depression similarly used the taxpayers' suit to facilitate economy and efficiency, and to fight corruption, in local government.

The extent to which taxpayers resorted to the courts was an essentially positive development. The notion of litigiousness has a negative connotation, and people can and do bring frivolous lawsuits. Notwithstanding such abuses, most taxpayers' litigation in the 1930s was not frivolous. The ability and the willingness of citizens to call on the law to enforce their rights and on the courts to serve as arbiters of their disputes is a measure of the influence of law in a society and of the confidence of its citizens in the rule of law and in the courts as honest brokers. Thus, the degree of litigiousness in a society is a barometer of an energized and vital legal culture.

Organized taxpayer activity has embodied the civic, economic, and legal dimensions of citizenship. Taxpayers expressed the economic element of citizenship by engaging in pocketbook politics. They exhibited its civic component by organizing in voluntary associations to further their interests and to influence government. They reflected citizenship's legal aspect by relying on the rule of law and by invoking law and legal institutions in their reform and tax resistance efforts.

Taxpayers' associations provide a rich setting in which the historian may, in legal historian James Willard Hurst's words, seek better "to understand the law . . . as it had meaning for workaday people and was shaped by them to their wants and visions."[32] Through their research, legislative, litigation, and political programs, taxpayers' organizations exercised significant influence on the law and, in doing so, on the structures of government and on American public life. Organized taxpayers regularly made "affirmative use of the law" in an effort to "materially control their environment" and their destinies.[33]

One also sees in the taxpayers' organizations of the 1930s the dynamic relationship between law and society in the United States. The vast majority of organized taxpayers' programs somehow implicated and invoked the law. Taxpayers petitioned, persuaded, and otherwise agitated to procure the passage of dozens of tax limits nationwide. They instituted scores of taxpayers' lawsuits in order to bring the coercive power of the law to bear on public officials and require them to comply with laws relating to state and local government finance and administration. The research and legislative programs of taxpayers' associations were instrumental in producing a large body of new legislation that, for the most part, improved the quality and efficiency of government. Time and again taxpaying citizens successfully resorted to the law to refashion state and local governments and thereby appreciably shape their environment to their ends. Conversely, the law substantially framed and shaped the interactions between taxpayers and public officials. The formative and constitutive power of the law is demonstrated by the very fact that citizens were required to rely on it so often to achieve their objectives. The Depression-era taxpayers' association movement evidences the reciprocal flow of influence between law and society, between legal institutions and ideas and civic institutions and ideas.

Taxpayers' organizations continued to proliferate through the 1930s, but at a slower pace after 1933. By 1939, for example, the number of taxpayers' leagues in Massachusetts had increased from 140 to 150. In the last half of the decade, as the tax crisis abated to some extent, more taxpayers' associations dissolved than were established. This trend accelerated after 1940, when the United States began transitioning to a burgeoning war economy. Moreover, many of the local groups were small and relatively transitory, ones that "spring up overnight and speedily pass out of existence," according to the Tax Policy League. In a 1938 survey, the Tax Policy League identified 1,159 taxpayers' associations in the nation, of which 1,032 were local, 110 were statewide, and 17 were national in scope. Two years later Sylvia Porter characterized the formation of taxpayers' groups as a "spontaneous, nationwide movement" that "every week adds new units to this army of more than 1,200 militant taxpayer organizations." Gordon Gaskill, writing in *American Magazine* in 1941, found that there were then 27 state taxpayers' leagues and approximately 1,500 local ones. Although the raw number of taxpayers' groups had diminished since the mid-1930s, Gaskill was still impressed by the "amazing growth of these taxpayers' leagues," which he described as "moving full speed ahead."[34]

The number of taxpayers' associations decreased somewhat after the 1930s, but they have remained numerous and a significant presence in American public life. One study identified forty taxpayers' organizations in Massachusetts alone in the mid-1960s, almost as many as there were in the entire nation forty years earlier.[35] Many Depression-era taxpayers' leagues are still hard at work in their states and communities. In California, the Kern County Taxpayers Association, founded in 1939, calls itself the "guard dog protecting the interests of . . . taxpayers," and the California Taxpayers Association continues to "advocate for sound tax policy and government efficiency" by providing a "voice for taxpayers" in "legislative proceedings, courtrooms, elections and discussions with tax agency leaders." The Iowa Taxpayers Association, established in 1935, is a "network of tax policy experts, educators and advocates for sound fiscal policy" that provides "state policymakers with objective, nonpartisan research about the impact of specific tax and spending policies." For decades the Nevada Taxpayers Association, chartered in 1922, the Utah Taxpayers Association (1923), the Taxpayers Association of Central Iowa (1921), and the Taxpayers Association of Vigo County, Indiana (1936), have prosecuted their missions to "promote the cause of the taxpayers, for responsible government at a reasonable price," through "research, education, advocacy and community leadership."[36]

In addition, taxpayers have organized new advocacy groups since the Great Depression. Shortly after attaining statehood, Hawaiian taxpayers formed the Tax Foundation of Hawaii, and in the 1990s Floridians founded Florida TaxWatch.[37] Other post-1930s taxpayers' associations include the Associated Taxpayers of Idaho, formed in 1946, the Taxpayers Association of Cape May, New Jersey (1948), the Taxpayers' Association of Indian River County in Florida (1957), the Taxpayers League of Minnesota (1997), the Taxpayer Association of Oregon (1997), and the Pennsylvania Coalition of Taxpayer Associations (2006). This last group describes itself as "an alliance of eighty-six nonpartisan grassroots Pennsylvania taxpayer advocacy groups that span the entire Commonwealth and represent tens of thousands of taxpayers," and it is a single-issue organization, advocating for "legislation that will abolish school property taxes in Pennsylvania and will equitably replace a broken education finance system." The mission of most post-Depression taxpayers' leagues, however, is the same as that of organized taxpayers in the 1930s: to "promote efficiency and economy in government . . . toward the end of reducing taxes without impairment of the benefits received." Present-day taxpayers' organizations typically take a constructive economy approach to tax reduction, cooperating with public officials, "develop[ing] mutual understanding between entities and taxpayers," conducting "in-depth studies . . . of significant public issues," and presenting their findings and recommendations to government decision-makers.[38] Since 1940, taxpayers have continued to resist taxes and to press for reformation of state and local governments through taxpayers' associations.

A tradition of tax resistance harks back to the nation's founding. The intensity and scope of tax resistance and organized taxpayer activity in the twenty-first century reflect the continuing vitality of a powerful antitax sentiment in the United States. News reports of taxpayers' opposition to taxes in March 2009, in the midst of the credit-market crisis, sound very much like those one reads in the newspapers of the 1930s, perhaps because the nation was then confronting its most serious economic crisis since the Great Depression. On March 9, 2009, the day before the annual town meetings in New Hampshire, the Associated Press reported that "keeping property taxes in check is taking precedence" over all other matters with New Hampshire voters.[39] Three days later the *New Hampshire Union Leader* declared that "town meeting voters this year have turned a skeptical eye toward anything that looks like unnecessary spending" and that, like the Iowa farmer quoted in the *National Municipal Review* in 1933, they were looking to buy less government.[40] In Polk County, Iowa, officials were "bracing for an onslaught of [property tax] protests" because "everybody wants a reduction right now."[41] Organized taxpayers in Chapel Hill, North Carolina, and Hoboken, New Jersey, participated in large-scale property tax protests.[42] In West New York, the site of much organized taxpayer activity during the 1930s, hundreds of taxpayers rallied on two occasions to protest "soaring property taxes" and to demand a spending freeze.[43]

Taxpayers' groups are active across the United States in 2020. The numerous state taxpayers' associations conduct extensive research projects, hold annual conferences, publish regular newsletters and voter education material, evaluate and rank state legislators on their taxpayer-friendly credentials, and work with state and local legislative bodies. The eighteen statewide organizations that belong to the National Taxpayers Conference engage in a wide array of traditional constructive economy activities.[44] The stated missions and philosophies of these entities reflect the collaborative approach and good government objectives that predominated in Depression-era taxpayers' associations. Representative is the Tax Foundation of Hawaii, which "works with public officials, private organizations, and individuals in an effort to improve the methods, systems, and procedures of public administration." Many have professional staffs. Research and education of the public and public officials continue to be core tandem functions. The New Mexico Tax Research Institute, for example, emphasizes that it does "not advocate any agenda for or against taxation" but seeks "only to study, inform and educate the public and tax policy makers concerning the pressing issues of taxation facing our state."

Others are more involved in shaping tax and spending decisions and legislation, testifying before legislative committees, analyzing budgets and proposed tax legislation, and "advocat[ing] for sound tax policy."[45] The National Taxpayers Conference and its member organizations pursue constructive economy in state and local government in a way that would be familiar to both Progressive Era government research bureaus and organized taxpayers in the 1930s.

Local taxpayers' leagues have engaged in politics and taxpayers' litigation. The San Diego County Taxpayers Association created a "nonpartisan voters guide to help voters make informed decisions" about measures on the March 2020 ballot, and its president discussed several of the measures on a local morning news program. Atlantic City taxpayers' associations came out in opposition to proposed changes in local government that would eliminate ward councilmen and abolish the initiative and the referendum, the effect of which would be to make city government less representative and less responsive to the voters. The Howard Jarvis Taxpayers Association challenged the CalSavers Retirement Savings Program in federal court, arguing that California's defined contribution plan for private-sector workers who do not have an employer-sponsored retirement plan is unlawfully spending taxpayer funds. In Green Bay, the Brown County Taxpayers Association litigated the validity of a sales tax that the county adopted to fund capital improvements, contending that Wisconsin statutes authorize county sales taxes "only for the purpose of directly reducing the property tax levy."[46]

Depression-era taxpayers' groups and these traditional taxpayers' organizations that carry on their work today differ in significant ways from most other tax resistance movements in the past fifty years. The taxpayers' association movement and modern tax resistance do have a few things in common. The stagflation and economic malaise of the 1970s, combined with rising tax burdens, precipitated the tax revolts of the 1970s that produced Proposition 13 in California and Proposition 2½ in Massachusetts at the end of the decade, and the 2008–2009 recession and housing market collapse prepared the way for the Tea Party, as the Great Depression had spurred taxpayers to organize and resist taxes. The tax revolts of the 1970s, like the taxpayers' association movement, were mainly grassroots, populist phenomena.[47] That, however, is where the similarities between organized taxpayer activity in the 1930s and most modern tax resistance largely end.

Much of the tax resistance of the past fifty years springs from the conservative strains in American politics that served as counterpoints to the New Deal and is closely aligned with modern conservatism. Opposition to taxes since the 1970s has concentrated more on vindicating the rights of taxpayers than on reducing their tax bills.[48] It has been driven by ideology and partisanship to a much greater degree than Depression-era tax resistance, and, consequently, modern antitax movements have been about far more than taxes. Various elements of post-1960s conservatism—ranging from traditional small government conservatives to the Religious Right, to free enterprisers and Tea Partiers—have appropriated populist tax resistance and attached to it their thick-centered conservative ideologies to advance political, social, and religious agendas.[49]

The free enterprise antitax movement that helped to put Ronald Reagan in the White House and whose vision of government the Reagan administration sought to implement bears little resemblance to the taxpayers' association movement. In his 1981 inaugural address, Reagan set the tone for his time in office by declaring that "in this present crisis, government is not the solution to our problems; government is the problem." For many taxpayers in the 1930s, however, government, in the form of the New Deal, was indeed a solution to their personal tax problems and to the economic crisis. The hardline antistatism that the 1980s iteration of free enterprise manifested was not merely opposed to the activist state but, in antitax activist Grover Norquist's words, aimed to reduce government "to the size where I can . . . drown it in the bathtub."[50] Depression-era taxpayers' groups worked for government that was better and less expensive, not government that was so small and feeble that it could barely govern. In the Reagan era it was conservative elites and interest groups, not the public, that were the driving forces behind proposals to slash spending and taxes; in the 1930s, it was ordinary taxpayers at the state and local levels who worked to cut taxes.[51] Supply-side economic ideology, which emphasized the importance of the private, rather than the public, sector in promoting economic growth, has underpinned antistatist tax resistance since the 1970s.[52] As such, modern tax resisters have pressed for and secured tax cuts for corporations and the wealthy, from the substantial (though short-lived) Reagan tax cuts in 1981 to those that Congress enacted during the Trump administration.[53] Taxpayers and taxpayers' leagues in the Depression widely favored tax increases on business firms and the rich based on ability to pay.

Many of the same features of the Tea Party movement distinguish it from the tax revolt of the 1930s. Grassroots activists were not the sole impetus for the creation of the Tea Party; a "panoply of national funders and ultra-free market advocacy groups" as well as conservative media elites were also driving forces.[54] A considerable amount of Tea Partiers' antistatist-antitax energies are directed at federal government spending and taxation, not the local and state taxes on which taxpayers' associations in the 1930s focused. Tea Partiers, like Reagan-era tax resisters, oppose wealth distribution.[55] Their goals go well beyond the financial one—lower taxes—that was the urgent objective of Depression-era organized taxpayers. Tea Partiers proclaim that they are fighting for "a culture of life," "religious freedom," and "our Constitution." Indeed, in their examination of the Tea Party, Theda Skocpol and Vanessa Williamson found that "Tea Party members rarely stressed economic concerns to us."[56] The taxpayers' association movement was impelled by and entirely about taxpayers' economic concerns.

The taxpayers' association movement was a tax revolt to reduce taxes. Opposition to taxes in the past half century has been so much more than a "tax revolt." For modern tax resisters, tax reduction is not the journey's end. Tax resistance is the means to broader ends, a wagon to which conservatives have hitched their ideologies and agendas in order to realize them and reach their destinations.

Spikes in organized taxpayer activity tend to coincide with economic downturns that place financial pressure on taxpayers and on local and state governments. As such, the COVID-19 pandemic may well produce a recrudescence of widespread tax resistance in the United States. The dramatic contraction of the economy and the loss of tens of millions of jobs in the second quarter of 2020 made it a challenge for many Americans to meet their tax and other financial obligations. During the same period, state tax revenues were estimated to decline by $150 billion, a reduction that "is larger in nominal terms than during the [2007–2009] Great Recession, when state tax revenues fell by $100 bn from peak to trough in three years." In June 2020, experts predicted that the gap between state revenues and spending would range from $75 billion to $120 billion in fiscal 2020, $125 billion to $315 billion in 2021, and $180 billion in 2022.[57] The confluence of these circumstances may create a crisis in taxation to rival that of the 1930s. However Americans navigate this economic maelstrom, taxes will be firmly situated at or near the center of American politics in the coming decades, and the taxpayers' association will continue to be a principal institution through which taxpayers and tax spenders contest the citizens' tax burden, the fiscal constraints on the state, and the size and role of government in the United States.

Notes

INTRODUCTION

1. Hal Steed, "Adventures of a Tax Leaguer," *Saturday Evening Post* 206, no. 19 (November 4, 1933): 16; *Atlanta Constitution*, April 9, 1933, 28.

2. Steed, "Adventures of a Tax Leaguer, November 4, 1933." Years later Steed identified Atlanta as the city in which his adventures had occurred. David T. Beito, *Taxpayers in Revolt: Tax Resistance during the Great Depression* (Chapel Hill: University of North Carolina Press, 1989), 16.

3. Steed, "Adventures of a Tax Leaguer," November 4, 1933.

4. *Atlanta Constitution*, April 13, 1932, 4.

5. Steed, "Adventures of a Tax Leaguer," *Saturday Evening Post* 206, no. 20 (November 11, 1933): 29–30, 90–91.

6. Beito, *Taxpayers in Revolt*, 15.

7. Edward M. Barrows, "A Challenge to Reform," *National Municipal Review* (hereafter *NMR*) 22, no. 5 (May 1933): 223.

8. Howard P. Jones, "Unrest in County Government," *NMR* 21, no. 8 (August 1932): 469, 470.

9. "Mr. Taxpayer versus Mr. Taxspender," *NMR* 22, no. 8 (August 1933): 359; Daniel W. Hoan, *City Government: The Record of the Milwaukee Experiment* (New York: Harcourt, Brace, 1936), 19, 159.

10. Tax Policy League, "Taxpayers' Organizations in the United States," *Tax Policy* 5 (September 1938): 1; "Taxpayers' Organizations: Supplement," *Tax Policy* 6 (March 1939): 1.

11. John Elting, "The Tax Fight," *Forbes*, February 15, 1939, 12–14, 36–37; John Elting, "You CAN Cut Taxes," *Forbes*, March 1, 1939, 10–11, 27; S. F. Porter, "Taxpayers on the Warpath," *American Magazine* 130 (October 1940): 50–52, 162; Gordon Gaskill, "Caviar on Your Tax Bill," *American Magazine* 131 (April 1941): 116–119.

12. Beito, *Taxpayers in Revolt*, xii.

13. Thomas H. Reed, "Organizing to Save Our Communities," *NMR* 22, no. 7 (July 1933): 310.

14. Steed, "Adventures of a Tax Leaguer," November 11, 1933.

15. James Ring Adams, *Secrets of the Tax Revolt* (San Diego: Harcourt Brace Jovanovich, 1984), 39, 276.

16. Only a few taxpayers' organizations (e.g., the Lowell [Massachusetts] Taxpayers' Association) included federal government activities in their remit.

17. "The Collection of Real Property Taxes," *Law and Contemporary Problems* 3, no. 3 (June 1936): 335–461.

18. W. Elliot Brownlee, *Federal Taxation in America: A History*, 3rd ed. (New York: Cambridge University Press, 2016), 117–119; Arthur M. Schlesinger Jr., *The Age of Roosevelt: The Crisis of the Old Order, 1919–1933* (New York: Bookspan, 2002), 231–234, 240–241; Anthony J. Badger, *The New Deal: The Depression Years, 1933–1940* (Chicago: Ivan R. Dee, 1989), 41–54.

19. Molly C. Michelmore, *Tax and Spend: The Welfare State, Tax Politics, and the Limits of American Liberalism* (Philadelphia: University of Pennsylvania Press, 2012), 7; Badger, *The New Deal*, 154; William E. Leuchtenburg, *Franklin D. Roosevelt and the New Deal* (New York: HarperCollins, 2009), 23–24, 51.

20. "Mr. Taxpayer versus Mr. Taxspender," 359.

21. Julian E. Zelizer, "The Uneasy Relationship: Democracy, Taxation and State Building since the New Deal," in *The Democratic Experiment: New Directions in American Political History*, edited by Meg Jacobs, William J. Novak, and Julian E. Zelizer (Princeton, NJ: Princeton University Press, 2003), 277.

22. Ira Katznelson, "The Possibilities of Analytical Political History," in *The Democratic Experiment*, 381–400; Meg Jacobs and Julian Zelizer, "The Democratic Experiment: New Directions in American Political History," in *The Democratic Experiment*, 1–19.

23. Essays that examine these facets of American political history include William J. Novak, "The Legal Transformation of Citizenship in Nineteenth-Century America," in *The Democratic Experiment*, 85–119, which traces the evolution of the American conception of citizenship from one grounded in the local polity to a modern, national citizenship status; Brian Balogh, "'Mirrors of Desires': Interest Groups, Elections, and the Targeted Style in Twentieth-Century America," in *The Democratic Experiment*, 222–249, which explores how "interest groups played a key role in linking voters to public officials" from 1900 to 1970 and "served as crucial conduits of the democratic will"; Zelizer, "The Uneasy Relationship," in *The Democratic Experiment*, 276–300, which treats taxation as central to political development in the United States and endeavors to meet "the important challenge facing the next generation of political historians" by "grappling with antistatism in modern America, as expressed through resistance to taxation and in other incarnations"; and Thomas J. Sugrue, "All Politics Is Local: The Persistence of Localism in Twentieth-Century America," in *The Democratic Experiment*, 301–326, which argues that scholars of American political development have given short shrift to local political institutions and looks at how local actors and institutions have influenced and informed national policy.

24. Badger, *The New Deal*, 157–159, 193–196, 209–211, 306–307. The Tennessee Valley Authority provides a notable illustration of localism's potency. According to historian Arthur Schlesinger, "Instead of reconstructing life in the Valley, TVA seemed to be accommodating itself to the strongest local interests," as reflected in its decisions to exclude "Negro agricultural colleges" from its fertilizer program and to prioritize the needs of large farmers at the expense of tenant farmers in the administration of its agricultural program. Arthur M. Schlesinger Jr., *The Age of Roosevelt: The Politics of Upheaval, 1935–1936* (Boston: Houghton Mifflin, 2003), 371–372.

25. James Willard Hurst, *Law and the Conditions of Freedom in the Nineteenth-Century United States* (Madison: University of Wisconsin Press, 1956), 33, 107.

26. For discussions of the constitutive power of American law and its role in influencing society and policy, see Christopher Tomlins, *Law, Labor and Ideology in the Early American Republic* (Cambridge: Cambridge University Press, 1993); Morton J. Horowitz, *The Transformation of American Law, 1780–1860* (New York: Oxford University Press, 1992); and William E. Forbath, *Law and the Shaping of the American Labor Movement* (Cambridge, MA: Harvard University Press, 1991).

27. Sugrue, "All Politics Is Local," in *The Democratic Experiment*, 301–326.

28. See, for example, Badger, *The New Deal*, 56–57; William C. Harris, *The Day of the Carpetbagger: Republican Reconstruction in Mississippi* (Baton Rouge: Louisiana State University Press, 1979), 624–631; Eric Foner, *Reconstruction: America's Unfinished Revolution, 1863–1877* (New York: HarperCollins, 2005), 415–416, 498.

29. Beito, *Taxpayers in Revolt*, 8–21; Mark H. Leff, *The American Historical Review* 95, no. 5 (December 1990): 1648.

30. Thomas H. Reed, ed., *Government in a Depression: Constructive Economy in State and Local Government* (Chicago: University of Chicago Press, 1933).

31. See Claude R. Tharp, *Control of Local Finance through Taxpayers' Associations and Centralized Administrations* (Indianapolis: M. Ford Publishing Company, 1933) for an examination of such taxpayers' associations' programs at the state level.

32. Adams, *Secrets of the Tax Revolt*, 39, 276.

33. Martin J. Schiesl, *The Politics of Efficiency: Municipal Administration and Reform in America, 1880–1920* (Berkeley: University of California Press, 1977); Kenneth Feingold, *Experts and Politicians: Reform Challenges to Machine Politics in New York, Cleveland and Chicago* (Princeton, NJ: Princeton University Press, 1995); Mordicai Lee, *Bureaus of Efficiency: Reforming Local Government in the Progressive Era* (Milwaukee: Marquette University Press, 2008); John Louis Recchiuti, *Civic Engagement: Social Science and Progressive-Era Reform in New York City* (Philadelphia: University of Pennsylvania Press, 2007).

34. Badger, *The New Deal*, 290–297; Alan Brinkley, *Voices of Protest: Huey Long, Father Coughlin and the Great Depression* (New York: Vintage Books, 1983); Schlesinger, *The Politics of Upheaval*, 16–68, 242–252, 556–561.

35. Forbath, *Law and the Shaping of the American Labor Movement*.

36. Hurst, *Law and the Conditions of Freedom*, 32.

37. Kermit L. Hall, *The Magic Mirror: Law in American History* (New York: Oxford University Press, 1989), 7; Hurst, *Law and the Conditions of Freedom*, 33, 107.

38. *The Economist*, August 17, 2013, 32.

39. Badger, *The New Deal*, 56.

CHAPTER 1

1. *San Jose (CA) Mercury News*, published as *The Evening News*, October 10, 1899, 5.

2. Sven Beckert, "Democracy in the Age of Capital: Contesting Suffrage Rights in Gilded Age New York," in *The Democratic Experiment*, 146–174; Foner, *Reconstruction: America's Unfinished Revolution*, 415–417, 498.

3. *New York Herald*, December 6, 1858, 3; November 1, 1860, 2, 3.

4. Ibid., November 27, 1861, 4.

5. *San Francisco Bulletin*, January 7, 1862, 3; August 15, 1862, 2.

6. *New York Herald*, November 27, 1861, 4; *Wilkes-Barre (PA) Times Leader*, August 7, 1915, 8; *Philadelphia Inquirer*, August 18, 1905, 3; *New North* (Rhinelander, WI), August 23, 1917, 16; *San Jose (CA) Mercury News*, October 10, 1899, 5.

7. Jason Kaufman, "Three Views of Associationalism in 19th-Century America: An Empirical Examination," *American Journal of Sociology* 104, no. 5 (March 1999): 1296, 1301. Kaufman examines three conceptions of associationalism in the United States: a neo-Toquevillian perspective in which individuals associate to pursue common interests and goals and, in doing so, "gain a new sense of their responsibility to the community and at the same time perform services that would otherwise be required of the state"; a social movements theory that treats associations as special interest groups mobilized to advance their members' specific goals; and a social capital model that emphasizes the ability of associations to foster interpersonal connections that allow individuals to prosecute common objectives, resulting in "greater civic commitment, trust, and collective engagement." Taxpayers' leagues reflect all three conceptions, though the social movements one is the strongest.

8. Linda Kerber, *No Constitutional Right to Be Ladies: Women and the Obligations of Citizenship* (New York: Hill & Wang, 1998), 36, 304.

9. Alexis de Tocqueville, *Democracy in America* (New York: Schocken Books, 1961), Vol. 1, 216, 220, 221.

10. Tocqueville, *Democracy in America*, Vol. 2, 142, 128.

11. Christopher Capozzola, *Uncle Sam Wants You: World War I and the Making of the Modern American Citizen* (Oxford: Oxford University Press, 2008), 8, 11.

12. Ibid., 6, 14, 213–214.

13. Meg Jacobs, *Pocketbook Politics: Economic Citizenship in Twentieth-Century America* (Princeton, NJ: Princeton University Press, 2005), 2, 265.

14. William J. Novak, "The Legal Transformation of Citizenship in Nineteenth-Century America," in *The Democratic Experiment*, 86, 109–112.

15. *Philadelphia Inquirer*, July 20, 1875, 3.

16. Ibid., August 31, 1875, 3; July 20, 1875, 3; January 31, 1876, 3; September 4, 1876, 7.

17. Ibid., October 8, 1878, 3; February 8, 1879, 3.

18. *New York Times* (hereafter *NYT*), February 18, 1870, 2; January 11, 1872, 8; November 28, 1875, 2; May 11, 1893, 6; February 18, 1894, 12; March 12, 1894, 9; February 25, 1894, 12.

19. *Baltimore Sun*, August 6, 1874, 4; *Inter Ocean* (Chicago, IL), July 12, 1874, 1; *Baltimore Sun*, July 29, 1874, 1; August 6, 1874, 4; September 9, 1876, 1; July 17, 1880, 1; March 3, 1878, 1.

20. Beckert, "Democracy in the Age of Capital," in *The Democratic Experiment*, 146–174.

21. Robin L. Einhorn, *American Taxation, American Slavery* (Chicago: University of Chicago Press, 2006), 3–8, 231, 239, 242, 244–251; *McCulloch v. Maryland*, 17 U.S. (4 Wheat.) 316 (1819).

22. Foner, *Reconstruction: America's Unfinished Revolution*, 588.

23. Quoted in Ibid., 424, 590.

24. Ibid. 415–416, 498; Harris, *The Day of the Carpetbagger*, 624–631.

25. Nicholas Lemann, *Redemption: The Last Battle of the Civil War* (New York: Farrar, Straus, and Giroux, 2006), 82–83; Foner, *Reconstruction: America's Unfinished Revolution*, 416.

26. Quoted in Sven Beckert, *The Monied Metropolis: New York City and the Consolidation of the American Bourgeoisie, 1856–1896* (Cambridge: Cambridge University Press, 2001), 227.

27. *Memphis (TN) Daily Avalanche*, January 27, 1869, 3.

28. *Macon (GA) Weekly Telegraph*, March 19, 1872, 1.

29. Ibid., May 22, 1874, 2.

30. *N. C. Winston et als. v. Tennessee & Pacific R.R. Co., County Court of Smith County and Justices of Said County*, 60 Tenn. 60, 1 Baxt. 60 (1873).

31. Beckert, "Democracy in the Age of Capital," in *The Democratic Experiment*, 160.

32. *NYT*, January 3, 1875, 1; *Inter Ocean* (Chicago, IL), December 12, 1874, 9; Harris, *The Day of the Carpetbagger*, 645–649; *Inter Ocean* (Chicago, IL), December 13, 1874, 1; Lemann, *Redemption*, 82–86: Foner, *Reconstruction: America's Unfinished Revolution*, 550–551, 554, 558.

33. Foner, *Reconstruction: America's Unfinished Revolution*, 416, 498; Beckert, "Democracy in the Age of Capital," in *The Democratic Experiment*, 160–163.

34. Foner, *Reconstruction: America's Unfinished Revolution*, 588.

35. Beito, *Taxpayers in Revolt*, 15.

36. Fernand Braudel, *The Structures of Everyday Life: The Limits of the Possible* (New York: Harper & Row, 1985).

CHAPTER 2

1. *Lowell (MA) Sun*, August 1, 1935, 1; U.S. Bureau of the Census, Fourteenth Census, 1920; U.S. Bureau of the Census, Fifteenth Census, 1930; U.S. Bureau of the Census, Sixteenth Census, 1940.

2. *Lowell (MA) Sun*, July 18, 1932, 2.

3. Newspaper Archive, 1920–1928, http://www.newspaperarchive.com (accessed November 16, 2008).

4. Ibid. See numerous articles in the *Fresno (CA) Bee*.

5. *Dallas Morning News*, October 14, 1905, 9.

6. *Philadelphia Inquirer*, August 18, 1905, 3.

7. *Daily Herald* (Natchez, MS), June 7, 1921, 5.

8. *Sheboygan (WI) Press*, January 12, 1925, 1.

9. United States Bureau of Labor Statistics, "Unemployment Rate since 1929"; United States Department of Labor, "Employment and Earnings, Table C-1," 7, no. 2 (August 1960).

10. Badger, *The New Deal*, 15.

11. William B. Munro, "Taxation Nears a Crisis," *Current History* 37, no. 6 (March 1933): 656, 661–662.

12. *Lincoln (NE) Star*, January 22, 1933, 52.

13. Melvin A. Traylor, "What Can Be Done about Taxes: An Address by Melvin A. Traylor" (University of North Carolina at Chapel Hill, North Carolina Collection, 1932).

14. "Retrenching in State and Local Expenditures: A General View," in Reed, *Government in a Depression*.

15. "Redrawing the Boundaries of Local Government," in Reed, *Government in a Depression*.

16. "Reorganizing County Government," in Reed, *Government in a Depression*.

17. Murray Seasongood, "Getting Our Bearings," *NMR* 22, no. 12 (December 1933): 585–586.

18. Tharp, *Control of Local Finance*, v, 3.

19. F. Robertson Jones, "Taxing Misfortune" (Washington, DC: American Taxpayers League, 1933).

20. *Lowell (MA) Sun*, October 8, 1931, 5.

21. Ibid., July 18, 1932, 1–2.

22. Ibid., March 21, 1933, 2.

23. *Mountain Eagle* (Whitesburg, KY), March 9, 1933, 1.

24. *St. Cloud (MN) Times*, September 17, 1934, 9.

25. Beito, *Taxpayers in Revolt*, 141; Merle Thorpe, "In Behalf of the Delinquent Taxpayer—Present and Prospective" (n.p., 1932).

26. Paige, "Governmental Research Association Notes," *NMR* 22, no. 12 (December 1933): 623.

27. Beito, *Taxpayers in Revolt*, 80–86.

28. Steed, "Adventures of a Tax Leaguer," November 4, 1933.

29. Barrows, "A Challenge to Reform," 223.

30. Governmental Research Association, "The Search for Facts in Government," *Supplement to the National Municipal Review* 22, no. 6 (June 1933): 305, 301, 302.

31. "Constructive Economy in State and Local Government," in Reed, *Government in a Depression*, 9.

32. National Municipal League, Committee on Citizens' Councils for Constructive Economy, "A Citizens' Council, Why and How?" (New York, 1933), 1.

33. "The Collection of Real Property Taxes," *Law and Contemporary Problems* 3, no. 3 (June 1936): 335.

34. Hoan, *City Government*, 158; Jones, "Unrest in County Government," 469; Barrows, "A Challenge to Reform," 223, 226, 230; "Constructive Economy in State and Local Government," 3–4; "Reorganizing County Government," 1–2.

35. "Retrenching in State and Local Expenditures," 1.

36. "Reorganizing County Government," 2.

37. *Lowell (MA) Sun*, October 8, 1931, 5.

38. Tharp, *Control of Local Finance*, 7–8; A. E. Holcomb, "Thomas Sewall Adams, 1873–1933," *Bulletin of the National Tax Association* 18, no. 7 (April 1933): 194–201.

39. Barrows, "A Challenge to Reform," 226, 230.
40. "Reorganizing County Government," 2.
41. Barrows, "A Challenge to Reform," 226.
42. Tharp, *Control of Local Finance*, 6, 30–31.
43. Ibid., 2.
44. *Lowell (MA) Sun*, July 18, 1932, 2.
45. Ibid., March 21, 1933, 2.
46. Robert M. Paige, "Governmental Research Association Notes," *NMR* 22, no. 11 (November 1933): 567, and 22, no. 10 (October 1933): 529.
47. Ibid., 23, no. 5 (May 1934): 276.
48. Ibid., 24, no. 12 (December 1935): 712.
49. Tharp, *Control of Local Finance*, 23.
50. Paige, "Governmental Research Association Notes," *NMR* 25, no. 12 (December 1936): 751–752; *Central New Jersey Home News*, October 17, 1934, 3.
51. Tharp, *Control of Local Finance*, 24–25.
52. Ibid., 27.
53. Newspaper Archive, 1901–1936, http://www.newspaperarchive.com (accessed November 30, 2008).
54. Wheeler McMillan, "The Farmer Buys Less Government," *NMR* 22, no. 1 (January 1933): 7.
55. Ibid.
56. *Lowell (MA) Sun*, October 8, 1931, 5.
57. Tharp, *Control of Local Finance*, 1, 10.
58. Paige, "Governmental Research Association Notes," *NMR* 23, no. 9 (September 1934): 489.
59. *Lowell (MA) Sun*, July 18, 1932, 2.
60. Ibid., March 21, 1933, 2.
61. Rudolph Kuchler, "Reports of Western Taxpayers Associations," *Tax Digest* (November 1932): 401, quoted in Tharp, *Control of Local Finance*, 11.
62. Tharp, *Control of Local Finance*, 17.
63. *NYT*, June 10, 1933, 25–26.
64. Teaneck Taxpayers' League, "Teaneck's Most Progressive 12 Years, 1929–1941," pamphlet, Teaneck Collection at Teaneck Public Library, Teaneck New Jersey.
65. Paige, "Government Research Association Notes," *NMR* 25, no. 7 (July 1936): 434.
66. Badger, *The New Deal*, 56.
67. *Atlanta Constitution*, February 21, 1932, 10.
68. *Boston Globe*, August 30, 1932, 1; *Chadron (NE) Record*, March 23, 1932, 7, March 25, 1932, 4, July 21, 1933, 4; *Reno (NV) Gazette-Journal*, July 6, 1932, 14.
69. *Mount Carmel (PA) Item*, March 5, 1935, 4.
70. *Ashbury Park (NJ) Press*, February 5, 1934, 15, September 26, 1934, 3; *Daily Record* (Long Branch, NJ), February 17, 1934, 1, April 3, 1934, 1; *Currier News* (Bridgewater, NJ), February 14, 1934, 6, June 4, 1934, 6. Interestingly, much of the newspaper coverage of women's taxpayers' groups appeared in the "Social News" sections of newspapers, suggesting that reporters viewed collective tax resistance by women differently than organized taxpayer activity by men, which generally was reported in the politics or business sections of newspapers.

71. Ronnie L. Podolefsky, "Illusion of Suffrage: Female Voting Rights and the Women's Poll Tax Repeal Movement after the Nineteenth Amendment," *Notre Dame Law Review* 73 (1998): 839–888.

72. Thorpe, "In Behalf of the Delinquent Taxpayer," 26.

73. Jacobs, *Pocketbook Politics*, 7.

74. Jones, "Unrest in County Government," 470–471.

75. Barrows, "A Challenge to Reform," 223; "Retrenching in State and Local Expenditures," 1.

76. Barrows, "A Challenge to Reform," 223.

77. Elting, "The Tax Fight," 13.

78. Tharp, *Control of Local Finance*, 16–17.

79. *American Taxpayers' Quarterly* 1, no. 1 (November 1931): 5.

80. Tax Policy League, "Taxpayers' Organizations in the United States," *Tax Policy* 5, no. 10 (September 1938): 1.

81. *Hartford (CT) Courant*, January 30, 1933, 3.

82. Schlesinger, *The Crisis of the Old Order*, 231–234, 240–241; Badger, *The New Deal*, 41–52; Brownlee, *Federal Taxation in America*, 117–119.

83. Depression-era taxpayers from the middle classes generally agreed with the proposition that taxation should be based on ability to pay and, therefore, supported increasing taxes on the wealthy and corporations, as most Americans still do. Badger, *The New Deal*, 102–104; Brownlee, *Federal Taxation in America*, 126, 135; Ajay K. Mehrotra, *Making the Modern American Fiscal State: Law, Politics and the Rise of Progressive Taxation* (New York: Cambridge University Press, 2013), 416.

84. Molly Michelmore, *Tax and Spend*, 4–11; Brownlee, *Federal Taxation in America*, 120–135; Schlesinger, *The Politics of Upheaval*, 325–328.

85. Badger, *The New Deal*, 14–16; Leuchtenburg, *Franklin D. Roosevelt and the New Deal*, 23–24.

86. Badger, *The New Deal*, 15, 147–169; Leuchtenburg, *Franklin D. Roosevelt and the New Deal*, 52, 193.

87. Badger, *The New Deal*, 239; Leuchtenburg, *Franklin D. Roosevelt and the New Deal*, 53, 193; Hoan, *City Government*, 172–173; Beito, *Taxpayers in Revolt*, 144–145.

88. Leuchtenburg, *Franklin D. Roosevelt and the New Deal*, 124–126, 133–134; Badger, *The New Deal*, 74, 79, 81–83, 190–200; Brownlee, *Federal Taxation in America*, 135–136.

89. Leuchtenburg, *Franklin D. Roosevelt and the New Deal*, 193.

90. Keith L. Bryant Jr., "Oklahoma and the New Deal," in *The New Deal: The State and Local Levels*, edited by John Braeman, Robert H. Bremner, and David Brody (Columbus: Ohio State University Press, 1975), 192; Michael P. Malone, "The Montana New Dealers," in *The New Deal: The State and Local Levels*, 262–263.

91. Brownlee, *Federal Taxation in America*, 128–135; Michelmore, *Tax and Spend*, 6–8, 10–12.

92. Beito, *Taxpayers in Revolt*, 142–146. Despite the overall popularity of PWA projects, taxpayers in some communities, including Worcester, Massachusetts, and Roanoke, Virginia, opposed them because local governments had to incur debt to be able to fund the locality's share of the construction costs.

93. Kerber, *No Constitutional Right to Be Ladies*, xx, xxii.
94. Thorpe, "In Behalf of the Delinquent Taxpayer," 43, 68.
95. Teaneck Taxpayers' League, "Teaneck's Most Progressive 12 Years."
96. Capozzola, *Uncle Sam Wants You*, 14, 17.
97. Barrows, "A Challenge to Reform," 223.
98. Steed, "Adventures of a Tax Leaguer," November 11, 1933.
99. *NMR* 21, no. 2 (February 1932): 77.
100. Editorial Comment, "Citizens' Councils for Constructive Economy," *NMR* 22, no. 4 (April 1933): 157; "Citizens Councils for Constructive Economy," *Journal of Health, Physical Education, Recreation* 4, no. 4 (April 1933): 44–45.
101. Beito, *Taxpayers in Revolt*, xiv.
102. Zelizer, "The Uneasy Relationship," 276, 281.
103. West Virginia Taxpayers' Association, *The Tax Burden in West Virginia* (Charleston, 1932), quoted in Beito, *Taxpayers in Revolt*, 18.
104. Thorpe, "In Behalf of the Delinquent Taxpayer," 9–14, 32.
105. Sterling E. Edmonds, *The Federal Octopus in 1933: A Survey of the Destruction of Constitutional Government and of Civil and Economic Liberty in the United States and the Rise of an All-Embracing Federal Bureaucratic Despotism*, 3rd ed. (Charlottesville, VA: Michie, 1933).
106. Lawrence Glickman, *Free Enterprise: An American History* (New Haven, CT: Yale University Press, 2019), 4, 16–17, 80.
107. Ibid., 5–6, 8, 44, 76–77, 81, 84, 90.
108. Ibid., 75, 229–233.
109. Ibid., 75–77, 90, 152–153.
110. Reprinted in *The New Deal: A Documentary History*, edited by William E. Leuchtenburg (New York: Harper & Row, 1968), 193–197, 203–205.
111. James Holt, "The New Deal and the American Anti-Statist Tradition," in *The New Deal: The National Level*, edited by John Braeman, Robert H. Bremner, and David Brody (Columbus: Ohio State University Press, 1975), 46–47 (concluding that "anti-statist individualism survived the New Deal as a popular political credo" and that "despite the New Deal, life in post-depression America remained essentially competitive and individualistic"); Robert F. Hunter, "Virginia and the New Deal," in *The New Deal: The State and Local Levels*, 133 (finding that in Virginia, "to a much greater extent, the New Deal was remembered as a time when the federal government engaged in deficit spending for dubious purposes with too little restraint, and when it became involved in matters outside its legitimate concern"); F. Alan Coombs, "The Impact of the New Deal on Wyoming Politics," in *The New Deal: The State and Local Levels*, 233–235 (noting that the New Deal did not "alter the basic voting habits and partisan allegiances of great numbers of voters" in Wyoming's "predominantly rural political culture"). Even William Leuchtenburg, an admirer of the New Deal who emphasized the extent to which the New Deal reshaped the public's view of the federal government and the welfare state, acknowledged that the "more successful the New Deal was" and the "more prosperous the country became, the more people returned to the only values they knew, those associated with an individualistic, success-oriented society." Leuchtenburg, *Franklin D. Roosevelt and the New Deal*, 273.

112. "Why a Farmer-Labor Party in New Hampshire?" leaflet (Berlin, NH: Ruemely Press, 1936), in the records of the Farmer-Labor Party of New Hampshire, New Hampshire Historical Society, Concord, New Hampshire.

113. *Mountain Eagle* (Whitesburg, KY), March 9, 1933, 1.

CHAPTER 3

1. November 17, 1932, Press Release, California Taxpayers' Association, *The Tax Digest*, Franklin Hichborn Papers, University of California, Los Angeles, Charles E. Young Research Library, Department of Special Collections (hereafter UCLA/DSC).

2. *Mountain Eagle* (Whitesburg, KY), March 9, 1933, 1.

3. "Constructive Economy in State and Local Government," 12–13; "Retrenching in State and Local Expenditures," 6–7.

4. "Reorganizing County Government," 2–3.

5. Edmond Kelly, City Club of New York Records, 1896–1925, Manuscripts and Archives Division, Humanities and Social Science Library, The New York Public Library (hereafter HSSL/NYPL); Richard Welling to Henry Curran, February 1, 1928, Richard Welling Papers, 1881–1941, HSSL/NYPL; *The City Club, A Brief History, 1950*, Albert Bard Papers, HSSL/NYPL; *The City Club of New York: Constitution, Bylaws, and House Rules, Officers, Committees, and Members*, May 15, 1908, Stanley Turkel Collection of City Club Memorabilia, 1908–1997, HSSL/NYPL; Henry H. Curran, *The City Club of New York*, 1935, Richard Welling Papers, HSSL/NYPL; Reminiscences of William Jay Schieffelin (1949), 23–24, Oral History Research Office Collection of the Columbia University Libraries (hereafter OHRO/CUL); Reminiscences of Lawrence Arnold Tanzer (1949), 14, 17, OHRO/CUL; Augustus Cerillo Jr., "The Reform of Municipal Government in New York City: From Seth Low to John Purroy Mitchel," *New York Historical Society Quarterly* 57, no. 1 (1973): 51–56; Recchiuti, *Civic Engagement*, 98–100; James J. Connolly, *An Elusive Unity: Urban Democracy and Machine Politics in Industrializing America* (Ithaca, NY: Cornell University Press, 2010), 193–194.

6. Martin J. Schiesl, *The Politics of Efficiency: Municipal Administration and Reform in America, 1880–1920* (Berkeley: University of California Press, 1977), 3–5, 73–77, 189–198; Michael Willrich, *City of Courts: Socializing Justice in Progressive Era Chicago* (Cambridge: Cambridge University Press, 2003), xxxviii–xxxix, 31–32; Recchiuti, *Civic Engagement*, 1–2, 98–124; Mordecai Lee, *Bureaus of Efficiency: Reforming Local Government in the Progressive Era* (Milwaukee: Marquette University Press, 2008), 17–18; Kenneth Fox, *Better City Government: Innovation in American Urban Politics, 1850–1937* (Philadelphia: Temple University Press, 1977), xiv–xix, 63–89; Kenneth Finegold, *Experts and Politicians: Reform Challenges to Machine Politics in New York, Cleveland and Chicago* (Princeton: Princeton University Press, 1995); Cerillo, "The Reform of Municipal Government," 51–71. For additional discussions of municipal reform in this period, see Jon C. Teaford, *The Unheralded Triumph: City Government in America, 1870–1900* (Baltimore: John Hopkins University Press, 1984), and Clifton K. Yearley, *The Money Machines: The Breakdown and Reform of Governmental and Party Finance in the North, 1860–1920* (Albany: State University of New York Press, 1970).

7. Fox, *Better City Government*, xvii–xix, 63, 70–74; Rebecca Menes, "Limiting the Reach of the Grabbing Hand: Graft and Growth in American Cities, 1880 to 1930," in *Corruption and Reform: Lessons from America's Economic History*, edited by Edward L. Glaeser and Claudia Goldin (Chicago: University of Chicago Press, 2006), 85–89.

8. New York Civil Service Reform Association, *Purposes of the Civil Service Reform Association* (New York, 1881), 13; Schiesl, *Politics of Efficiency*, 31–45; Teaford, *The Unheralded Triumph*, 132; Lee, *Bureaus of Efficiency*, 17; Fox, *Better City Government*, xv, 42–43.

9. Fox, *Better City Government*, 68–70, 74–75, 77–78, 91; Recchiuti, *Civic Engagement*, 103–104; Cerillo, "The Reform of Municipal Government," 60–62.

10. Recchiuti, *Civic Engagement*, 104; Cerillo, "The Reform of Municipal Government," 60–62, 65–66, 68; Fox, *Better City Government*, 68–71, 74–80.

11. Cerillo, "The Reform of Municipal Government," 69, 71; Lee, *Bureaus of Efficiency*, 17–18, 98–99; Fox, *Better City Government*, 63, 72–73, 82–83; Finegold, *Experts and Politicians*, 22–26.

12. Lee, *Bureaus of Efficiency*, 15–26, 158–171, 196; Cerillo, "The Reform of Municipal Government," 57–63; Finegold, *Experts and Politicians*, 29–34, 154–156.

13. Fox, *Better City Government*, xviii, 77, 92–93, 114; Lee, *Bureaus of Efficiency*, 198; Menes, "Limiting the Reach of the Grabbing Hand," 90; Finegold, *Experts and Politicians*.

14. Gerald Kurland, "The Amateur in Politics: The Citizens Union and the Greater New York Mayoral Campaign of 1897," *New York Historical Society Quarterly* 53, no. 4 (1969): 356; Robert Muccigrosso, "The City Reform Club: A Study in Late Nineteenth-Century Reform," *New York Historical Society Quarterly* 52 (1968): 240–242; Rechiutti, *Civic Engagement*, 98–99; Lee, *Bureaus of Efficiency*, 17, 68–73, 117, 256; Yearley, *The Money Machines*, 100–104; Beckert, *The Monied Metropolis*, 317–322; David C. Hammack, *Power and Society; Greater New York at the Turn of the Century* (New York: Russell Sage Foundation, 1982), xix, 140–142.

15. Reed, ed., *Government in a Depression: Constructive Economy in State and Local Government*.

16. Tharp, *Control of Local Finance*, 6, 11–28.

17. Ibid., 18–26.

18. Ibid., 24–25.

19. A. C. Rees, "Reports of Western Taxpayers' Associations," *Tax Digest* (November 1932): 406, quoted in Tharp, *Control of Local Finance*, 26.

20. Harry Miesse, "The Functions of an Association of Taxpayers in Connection with the Control of Public Expenditures," Address before the Twenty-Fourth National Tax Conference, 1931, 254, quoted in Tharp, *Control of Local Finance*, 10.

21. Rees, "The Functions and Progress of Taxpayers' Associations, with Suggestions for Their Organization Activities," National Tax Association, 1928, New York City, 11, quoted in Tharp, *Control of Local Finance*, 15.

22. Miesse, "The Functions of an Association of Taxpayers," 256, quoted in Tharp, *Control of Local Finance*, 16.

23. Tharp, *Control of Local Finance*, 17–18, 22–25.

24. Other publications included *The Taxpayers' Magazine*, the monthly publication of the Arizona Taxpayers' Association, and the Taxpayers' Association of New

Mexico's bimonthly *New Mexico Tax Bulletin*; Tharp, *Control of Local Finance*, 12–14; Paige, "Governmental Research Association Notes," *NMR* 23, no. 4 (April 1934): 230.

25. *Mountain Eagle* (Whitesburg, KY), March 9, 1933, 1.

26. Paige, "Governmental Research Association Notes," *NMR* 22, no. 12 (December 1933): 622–623; Paul W. Wager, "County and Township Government," *NMR* 23, no. 5 (May 1934): 281–281; Paige, "Governmental Research Association Notes," *NMR* 22, no. 11 (November 1933): 569; *NMR* 22, no. 8 (August 1933): 398; *NMR* 22, no. 5 (May 1933): 252; *NMR* 22, no. 8 (August 1933): 399, 400; *NMR* 22, no. 9 (September 1933): 459, 460; *NMR* 22, no. 11 (November 1933): 566.

27. *NMR* 23, no. 1 (January 1934): 37.

28. *NMR* 23, no. 3 (March 1933): 182; 23, no. 7 (July 1934): 402.

29. *NMR* 23, no. 6 (June 1934): 335.

30. *NMR* 24, no. 1 (January 1935): 54–55.

31. *NMR* 24, no. 2 (February 1935): 131–132.

32. *NMR* 23, no. 10 (October 1934): 557.

33. *NMR* 23, no. 11 (November 1934): 635.

34. *NMR* 23, no. 12 (December 1934): 707.

35. *NMR* 23, no. 1 (January 1934): 37; no. 2 (February 1934): 126; no. 4 (April 1934): 230; no. 12 (December 1934): 708; 24, no. 5 (May 1935): 283–284.

36. *NMR* 24, no. 1 (January 1935): 56.

37. *NMR* 24, no. 3 (March 1935): 186–187; 24, no. 7 (July 1935): 409–410.

38. *NMR* 24, no. 10 (October 1935): 546–548.

39. *NMR* 24, no. 2 (February 1935): 131; no. 3 (March 1935): 187; no. 4 (April 1935): 237–239; no. 5 (May 1935): 283; no. 7 (July 1935): 412; no. 10 (October 1935): 549; no. 11 (November 1935): 655; no. 12 (December 1935): 710.

40. *NMR* 25, no. 5 (May 1936): 304.

41. *NMR* 25, no. 6 (June 1936): 381.

42. *NMR* 26, no. 6 (June 1937): 325.

43. *NMR* 25, no. 9 (September 1936): 549; no. 10 (October 1936): 631; no. 11 (November 1936): 683–684.

44. *NMR* 26, no. 6 (June 1937): 325.

45. *NMR* 22 no. 12 (December 1933): 623; *NMR* 24, no. 2 (February 1935): 130–131; Paul Wager, "County and Township Government," *NMR* 23, no. 5 (May 1934): 281–282; Paige, "Governmental Research Association Notes," *NMR* 25, no. 5 (May 1936): 302.

46. Paige, "Governmental Research Association Notes," *NMR* 24, no. 4 (April 1935): 239; Wager, "County Township and Government," *NMR* 23, no. 5 (May 1934): 281.

47. Paige, "Governmental Research Association Notes," *NMR* 22 no. 8 (August 1933): 398; 24, no. 10 (October 1935): 546–547; *NMR* 25, no. 2 (February 1936): 113; *NMR* 25, no. 10 (October 1936): 631.

48. Cerillo, "The Reform of Municipal Government," 63, 61.

49. *NMR* 24, no. 11 (November 1935): 654; *NMR* 23, no. 5 (May 1934): 275; Editorial Comment, *NMR* 24, no. 1 (January 1935): 4.

50. *NMR* 22, no. 10 (October 1933): 490.

51. *Asbury Park (NJ) Press*, April 10, 1934, 2.

52. *NMR* 25, no. 7 (July 1936): 434; 23, no. 6 (June 1934): 334.
53. *NMR* 25, no. 7 (July 1936): 434–435.
54. *NMR* 24, no. 6 (June 1935): 361; 25, no. 11 (November 1936): 683; 24, no. 9 (September 1935): 486; 23, no. 1 (January 1934): 37.
55. *NMR* 23, no. 12 (December 1934): 707; 25, no. 12 (December 1936): 751.
56. *NMR* 25, no. 7 (July 1936): 435; 24, no. 5 (May 1935): 283–284; 26, no. 11 (November 1937): 552.
57. *NMR* 24, no. 3 (March 1935): 187–188; 25, no. 6 (June 1936): 382–383.
58. *NMR* 22 no. 10 (October 1933): 529; 22 no. 7 (July 1933): 348; 23, no. 1 (January 1934): 35; 23, no. 9 (September 1934): 489; 23, no. 10 (October 1934): 557; 24, no. 10 (October 1935): 549; 25, no. 9 (September 1936): 548; 5, no. 10 (October 1936): 630; 25, no. 11 (November 1936): 680; 26, no. 1 (January 1937): 46; 26, no. 4 (April 1937): 208; 26, no. 7 (July 1937): 373; 26, no. 12 (December 1937): 614.
59. Elting, "The Tax Fight," 12–14, 36–37.
60. Elting, "You CAN Cut Taxes," 10–11, 27.
61. Porter, "Taxpayers on the Warpath," 50–52, 162. When Porter began writing articles on finance in various periodicals in 1932, her employers did not want to disclose her gender, so she used the byline "S. F. Porter." Although she became the *Post*'s financial editor and began writing a daily column in 1938, the *Post* did not change her byline to "Sylvia F. Porter" until July 15, 1942, when it concluded that her gender was not a liability. Porter later remarked, "On that day I became a woman." The disclosure of Porter's gender actually increased her popularity and the demand for her columns. Porter wrote numerous books on personal finance and income tax for the general public that were widely read and included a *New York Times* best seller in 1975. At the height of her popularity in the 1970s, her column, published five times a week, was available to forty million readers through 450 newspapers across the globe. See Peggy K. Pearlstein, "Sylvia Field Porter," *Jewish Women: A Comprehensive Historical Encyclopedia*, February 27, 2009, Jewish Women's Archive (viewed on March 20, 2021), https://jwa.org/encyclopedia/article/porter-sylvia-field; Tracy Lucht, *Sylvia Porter: America's Original Personal Finance Columnist* (Syracuse, NY: Syracuse University Press, 2013).
62. "Organization of California Taxpayers' Association Is Outstanding Event," *California Tax Digest* 2, no. 8 (March 1926): 72–76, Hichborn Papers, UCLA/DSC; "We Pass the Information On," *Escalon (CA) Times*, June 9, 1927, 2–3, Hichborn Papers, UCLA/DSC; Franklin Hichborn, "Camouflage Organizations," pamphlet, 1926, Hichborn Papers, UCLA/DSC.
63. California Taxpayers' Association, "Your Business," pamphlet, c. 1930, Hichborn Papers, UCLA/DSC; Rolland A. Vandegrift, "The State Tax System of California," pamphlet, reprinted from *Tax Digest* (October 1927): 12, Hichborn Papers, UCLA/DSC; William B. Munro, "Taxation Nears a Crisis," *Current History* 37, no. 6 (March 1933): 656.
64. James E. Hartley, Steven M. Sheffrin, and David Vasche, "Reform during Crisis: The Transformation of California's Fiscal System during the Great Depression," *Journal of Economic History* 56, no. 3 (September 1996): 657, 659–660; Vandegrift, "The State Tax System of California," 3–4.
65. Hartley et al., "Reform during Crisis," 660.
66. "Organization of California Taxpayers' Association Is Outstanding Event," 72–73.

67. Paige, "Government Research Association Notes," *NMR* 25, no. 7 (July 1936): 434.

68. Elmer H. Stafflebach, "California Tax Crisis: 1933," reprinted from *Sierra Educational News*, February 1933, 12, John Randolph Haynes Papers, UCLA/DSC.

69. Franklin Hichborn, "Aims and Influences Moving the Taxpayers' Association," reprinted from *Sacramento (CA) Bee*, December 21, 1927, Hichborn Papers, UCLA/DSC; Franklin Hichborn to Rudolph Spreckles, August 18, 1925, Hichborn Papers, UCLA/DSC; Franklin Hichborn, "The Significance of the California Tax Problem," February 8, 1936, radio address, Hichborn Papers, UCLA/DSC. A short biography of Hichborn appears at the end of his article "How Minorities Dictate to the Majority and Development of Their Power," Hichborn Papers, UCLA/DSC.

70. Tharp, *Control of Local Finance*, 9, 18, 27–28.

71. Elting, "You CAN Cut Taxes," 10–11.

72. Hartley et al., "Reform during Crisis," 659–660; Vandegrift, "The State Tax System of California," 3–8.

73. Vandegrift, "The State Tax System of California," 3.

74. Hartley et al., "Reform during Crisis," 660–661, 668–669.

75. Ibid., 668, 676–677.

76. Ibid., 666–669, 672.

77. Hichborn, "The Significance of the California Tax Problem."

78. California Taxpayers' Association, "Your Business," 2–5; California Taxpayers' Association, "The Government of San Diego County," 1931, Hichborn Papers, UCLA/DSC.

79. Tharp, *Control of Local Finance*, 18–19.

80. Paige, "Governmental Research Association Notes," *NMR* 23, no. 6 (June 1934): 333–334.

81. Tharp, *Control of Local Finance*, 18–19.

82. Paige, "Governmental Research Association Notes," *NMR* 23, no. 6 (June 1934): 334; 25, no. 7 (July 1936): 434.

83. The sole exception was the merit-based civil service system, because it was already widespread at the state level and in large and midsize cities by 1930.

84. Paige, "Governmental Research Association Notes," *NMR* 22, no. 12 (December 1933): 622–623; 26, no. 6 (June 1937): 325; 25, no. 11 (November 1936): 683–684.

85. "Editorial Comment: Citizens Councils for Constructive Economy," *NMR* 22, no. 4 (April 1933): 157–158, 194–196; "Citizens' Councils for Constructive Economy," *Journal of Health, Physical Education, Recreation* 4, no. 4 (April 1933): 44–45; Beito, *Taxpayers in Revolt*, 106–110, 157–158.

86. Steed, "Adventures of a Tax Leaguer," November 4, 1933.

87. Elting, "The Tax Fight," 14.

CHAPTER 4

1. *Coos (NH) Guardian*, February 1, 1934, 2, February 8, 1934, 1, February 15, 1934, 1, February 22, 1934, 2, March 1, 1934, 1, March 8, 1934, 2, University of New Hampshire, Milne Special Collections; Linda Upham-Bornstein, "Citizens with a 'Just Cause': The New Hampshire Farmer-Labor Party in Depression-Era Berlin," *Historical New Hampshire* 62, no. 2 (Fall 2008): 117, 121, 124–130.

2. Cas Mudde and Cristobal Rovira Kaltwasser, *Populism: A Very Short Introduction* (Oxford: Oxford University Press, 2017), 2–6; Benjamin Moffitt, *The Global Rise of Populism: Performance, Political Style, and Representation* (Stanford, CA: Stanford University Press, 2016), 12–27: Paul Taggart, *Populism* (Buckingham, UK: Open University Press, 2000), 1–2. Cas Mudde has characterized the task as "defining the undefinable." Mudde, "The Populist Zeitgeist," *Government and Opposition* 39, no. 4 (Oxford: Blackwell Publishing, 2004), 541–563. I make no attempt to do so, but merely identify some of the descriptions and characteristics of populism that are manifested in Depression-era taxpayer political activity. For those interested in examining the various interpretations of populism and the extensive scholarly literature on the subject, Moffitt undertakes a thorough historiographical survey of that literature.

3. Michael Kazin, *The Populist Persuasion: An American History* (Ithaca, NY: Cornell University Press, 1998), 1–5; Mudde, "The Populist Zeitgeist," 543–544; Mudde and Kaltwasser, *Populism*, 5–20; Lawrence Goodwyn, *The Populist Moment: A Short History of the Agrarian Revolt in America* (Oxford: Oxford University Press, 1978).

4. Mudde, "The Populist Zeitgeist," 546; Taggert, *Populism*, 1; John D. Hicks, *The Populist Revolt: A History of the Farmers' Alliance and the People's Party* (Lincoln: University of Nebraska Press, 1931), 324; Jan-Werner Müller, *What Is Populism?* (Philadelphia: University of Pennsylvania Press, 2016), 1, 11; Mudde and Kaltwasser, *Populism*, 22.

5. Taggart, *Populism*, 1–2; Mudde, "The Populist Zeitgeist," 563; Kazin, *The Populist Persuasion*, 1–25, 46; Richard Hofstadter, *The Age of Reform: From Bryan to F.D.R.* (New York: Vintage Books, 1955), 4–5, 58–59.

6. There were, of course, numerous other manifestations of populism, especially at the local or regional levels. See, for example, Theodore Saloutos and John D. Hicks, *Twentieth Century Populism: Agricultural Discontent in the Middle West, 1900–1939* (Lincoln: University of Nebraska Press, 1951).

7. Saul Cornell, *The Other Founders: Anti-Federalism and the Dissenting Tradition in America* (Chapel Hill: University of North Carolina, 1999), 200; Thomas P. Slaughter, *The Whiskey Rebellion: Frontier Epilogue to the American Revolution* (New York: Oxford University Press, 1986); William Hogeland, *The Whiskey Rebellion: George Washington, Alexander Hamilton, and the Frontier Rebels Who Challenged America's Newfound Sovereignty* (New York: Scribner, 2006).

8. Peter S. Onuf, *Jefferson's Empire: The Language of American Nationhood* (Charlottesville: University Press of Virginia, 2000), 14–15, 69–71, 161–163; Hofstadter, *The Age of Reform*, 23–36; Arthur M. Schlesinger Jr., *The Age of Jackson* (Boston: Little, Brown, 1945), 308–314.

9. Onuf, *Jefferson's Empire*, 68–72, 89–90; Cornell, *The Other Founders*, 176–178, 185–186, 211.

10. Tomlins, *Law, Labor, and Ideology*, 1–8; Kazin, *The Populist Persuasion*, 13–18; Cornell, *The Other Founders*, 185–186, 216, 249–253.

11. Henry L. Watson, *Liberty and Power: The Politics of Jacksonian America* (New York: Hill & Wang, 1990), 83, 91; Linda Upham-Bornstein, "'Men of Families': The Intersection of Labor Conflict and Race in the Norfolk Dry Dock Affair, 1829–1831," *Labor: Studies in Working Class History* 4, no. 1 (Spring 2007): 68; Henry Watson, *Jacksonian Politics and Community Conflict* (Baton Rouge: Louisiana State University Press,

1981), 119; Robert B. Remini, *Andrew Jackson and the Course of American Freedom, 1822–1832* (New York: Harper & Row, 1981), 148; Charles Sellers, *The Market Revolution: Jacksonian America, 1815–1846* (New York: Oxford University Press, 1991), 270.

12. Upham-Bornstein, "Men of Families," 75; Watson, *Liberty and Power*, 91, 238; Schlesinger, *The Age of Jackson*, 163–164, 168–172, 180–185, 306–307, 318–319; Kazin, *The Populist Persuasion*, 19.

13. Hall, *American Legal History*, 167–168; Urofsky, *A March of Liberty*, 284–286; Schlesinger, *The Age of Jackson*, 89–92; Watson, *Liberty and Power*, 143–148.

14. Hicks, *The Populist Revolt*, 324, 428, 436–437, 440–442; "The Omaha Platform," reprinted in Hicks, *The Populist Revolt*, 439–444; Hofstadter, *The Age of Reform*, 62–67, 70–77; Kazin, *The Populist Persuasion*, 28, 30–32, 37, 41; Robert C. McMath Jr., *American Populism: A Social History, 1877–1898* (New York: Hill & Wang, 1993), 7, 51–53, 72–73, 121, 167–169.

15. Badger, *The New Deal*, 78, 293–296; Brinkley, *Voices of Protest*, 40–41, 71–74, 143–168; Schlesinger, *The Politics of Upheaval*, 42–68.

16. Brinkley, *Voices of Protest*, 89–97, 110–114; Kazin, *The Populist Persuasion*, 113–123; Father Charles E. Coughlin, "A Third Party," Vital Speeches II (1936), 613–616, reprinted in William E. Leuchtenberg, ed, *The New Deal; A Documentary History* (New York: Harper & Row, 1968), 186–190; Schlesinger, *The Politics of Upheaval*, 16–28.

17. Brinkley, *Voices of Protest*, 222–224; Badger, *The New Deal*, 230, 234, 292; Schlesinger, *The Politics of Upheaval*, 29–41.

18. Badger, *The New Deal*, 296–297; Kazin, *The Populist Persuasion*, 123–127; Brinkley, *Voices of Protest*, 224–226, 251–257; Schlesinger, *The Politics of Upheaval*, 550–561, 626–630.

19. Badger, *The New Deal*, 94, 103, 201, 290; Schlesinger, *The Politics of Upheaval*, 385–408.

20. Badger, *The New Deal*, 294–295, Brinkley, *Voices of Protest*, 144–146, 161–168.

21. Tharp, *Control of Local Finance*, 11, 9.

22. Reese, "The Functions and Progress of Taxpayers' Associations," 11, quoted in Tharp, *Control of Local Finance*, 15.

23. Miesse, "The Functions of an Association of Taxpayers," 255, quoted in Tharp, *Control of Local Finance*, 15.

24. Teaneck, New Jersey, Taxpayers' League, "Teaneck's Most Progressive 12 Years." Taxpayers' groups' claims of being nonpartisan and nonpolitical did not equate to being apolitical. Taxation is inherently political: it is fundamental to the citizen-state relationship and the state's ability to govern. When taxpayers' organizations insisted on the necessity of maintaining a nonpartisan stance, they meant that they should avoid affiliation with a particular political party and instead work constructively with all public officials and support candidates—of whatever political party and regardless of party affiliation—who pledged to represent the views and advance the agendas of organized taxpayers.

25. *Mountain Eagle* (Whitesburg, KY), March 9, 1933, 1.

26. *St. Cloud (MN) Times*, September 17, 1934, 9; *Central New Jersey Home News*, October 17, 1934, 3; *Asbury Park (NJ) Press*, April 10, 1934, 2.

27. Paige, "Governmental Association Research Notes," *NMR* 23, no. 5 (May 1934): 276; 25, no. 11 (November 1936): 683; *Central New Jersey Home News*, October 17, 1934, 3.

28. Paige, "Governmental Association Research Notes," *NMR* 25, no. 6 (June 1936): 382.

29. *NYT*, May 24, 1934, 20.

30. *St. Cloud (MN) Times*, September 17, 1934, 9.

31. Porter, "Taxpayers on the Warpath," 52.

32. Gaskill, "Caviar on Your Tax Bill," 116–119; *Mountain Eagle* (Whitesburg, KY), March 9, 1933, 1.

33. Elting, "You CAN Cut Taxes," 10, 27; Porter, "Taxpayers on the Warpath," 51; *Lincoln (NB) Star*, January 22, 1933, 52.

34. Gaskill, "Caviar on Your Tax Bill," 116–119; Porter, "Taxpayers on the Warpath," 52, 162.

35. United States Bureau of Labor Statistics, "Unemployment Rate since 1929"; United States Department of Labor, "Employment and Earnings, Table C-1," 7, no. 2 (August 1960).

36. *NYT*, May 10, 1933, 4.

37. *NYT*, October 12, 1933, 22; November 8, 1933, 9.

38. *NYT*, March 21, 1933, 4, 7; April 27, 1933, 4; May 9, 1933, 13; May 10, 1933, 4; May 11, 1933, 4.

39. *NYT*, April 18, 1935, 2; April 19, 1935, 16; May 15, 1935, 10.

40. Steed, "Adventures of a Tax Leaguer," November 4, 1933; November 11, 1933.

41. Elting, "The Tax Fight," 12–14, 37.

42. *Hartford (CT) Courant*, January 30, 1933, 3.

43. *Berlin Taxpayers Association v. The Mayor and City Council of Berlin and the Fidelity and Deposit Company of Maryland*, Coos County Superior Court, October term, 1933; Upham-Bornstein, "Citizens with a 'Just Cause,'" 117, 124–126.

44. *Coos (NH) Guardian*, February 1, 1934, 2, February 22, 1934, 2, March 1, 1934, 3, July 12, 1934, 2.

45. *Coos (NH) Guardian*, March 1, 1934, 1, 3; Farmer-Labor Platform, fall election, 1934, in Records of the Farmer-Labor Party of New Hampshire, New Hampshire Historical Society, Concord, New Hampshire; Upham-Bornstein, "Citizens with a 'Just Cause,'" 128.

46. Upham-Bornstein, "Citizens with a 'Just Cause,'" 127, 129–130; *Coos (NH) Guardian*, March 22, 1934, 3, quoting the *Boston Sunday Globe*.

47. Berlin City Reports, Journal no. 13, January 1932 to December 1934, May and June 1934; Berlin City Reports, Journal no. 14, January 1935 to December 1936; "Brown Company Financial History," Research and Development Papers, Berlin and Coos County Historical Society, Berlin, New Hampshire; Upham-Bornstein, "Citizens with a 'Just Cause,'" 125–127, 129–130; *Political News, Farmer-Labor Party*, March 1937, a copy of which is in the Party Records.

48. Upham-Bornstein, "Citizens with a 'Just Cause,'" 130–133; Philip Glasson, retired Brown Company research librarian, interviewed by E. John Allen, November 15, 1983, audiotape and transcript, in "Reflections of Berlin: Transcripts of Interviews," at

the New Hampshire Historical Society, Concord, NH. Excerpts from this interview were published in Allen, *Reflections of Berlin* (Berlin, NH: Berlin City Bank, 1985), 60–65.

49. *Coos (NH) Guardian*, February 1, 1934; July 12, 1934; Upham-Bornstein, "Citizens with a 'Just Cause,'" 132.

50. Upham-Bornstein, "Citizens with a 'Just Cause,'" 126, 128.

51. Ibid., 133.

52. S. J. Barrick, "Ohio Learns a Second Lesson," *NMR* 24, no. 11 (November 1935): 616; Adams, *Secrets of the Tax Revolt*, 276.

53. Tharp, *Control of Local Finances*, 33–35; Adams, *Secrets of the Tax Revolt*, 276–277; Jens P. Jensen, "Legislative Proposals Last Year and This," *NMR* 24, no. 11 (November 1935): 631–634; John F. Sly, "The By-products of Tax Limitation in West Virginia," *NMR* 24, no. 11: 611–615; Barrick, "Ohio Learns a Second Lesson," *NMR* 24, no. 11: 616–620; Joseph P. Harris, "Taxpayers Strike in Washington," *NMR* 22, no. 1 (January 1933): 27, 39–40.

54. Mabel L. Walker, "Overhauling State Revenue Systems," *NMR* 23, no. 8 (August 1934): 424; Wade S. Smith, "Taxation and Government," *NMR* 23, no. 12 (December 1934): 700–702; Barrick, "Ohio Learns a Second Lesson," 617; Albert H. Hall, "A Cloud on the New York State Tax Horizon," *NMR* 24, no. 11: 626; Harris, "Taxpayers Strike in Washington," *NMR* 22, no.1: 39.

55. Paige, "Governmental Research Association Notes," *NMR* 23, no. 11 (November 1934): 635.

56. Adams, *Secrets of the Tax Revolt*, 39; Harris, "Taxpayers Strike in Washington," 27; Jensen, "Legislative Proposals Last Year and This," 631–634.

57. Harris, "Taxpayers Strike in Washington," 27, 39; Sly, "The By-products of Tax Limitation in West Virginia," 612–614; Barrick, "Ohio Learns a Second Lesson," 617–618; Hall, "A Cloud on the New York State Tax Horizon," 630.

58. Robert S. Ford, "The Fifteen-Mill Limitation in Michigan," *NMR* 24, no. 12 (December 1935): 671.

59. Sly, "The By-products of Tax Limitation in West Virginia," 611–615; Barrick, "Ohio Learns a Second Lesson," 616–620.

60. Frederick L. Bird, "The Effect of Tax Rate Limits on Municipal Credit," *NMR* 24, no. 11 (November 1935): 607–610; Hall, "A Cloud on the New York State Tax Horizon," 626, 628, 630.

61. Ford, "The Fifteen-Mill Limitation in Michigan," 670; Editorial Comment, "Tax Limitation with a Vengeance," *NMR* 24, no. 10 (October 1935): 501; Walker, "Overhauling State Revenue Systems," 424–425; Smith, "Taxation and Government," *NMR* 24, no. 9 (September 1935): 488; Smith, "Taxation and Government," *NMR* 23, no. 12 (December 1933): 700–702.

62. Harris, "Taxpayers Strike in Washington," 40.

63. "Editorial Comment," *NMR* 24, no. 11 (November 1935): 605.

64. Simon E. Leland, "Probable Effect of Tax Limitation in Illinois," *NMR* 24, no. 11: 621, 655.

65. Jensen, "Legislative Proposals Last Year and This," 631–634.

66. Bird, "The Effect of Tax Rate Limits on Municipal Credit," 607, 610; "Editorial Comment," 605; *Padukah (KY) Sun-Democrat*, April 16, 1933, 4; Sly, "The By-products of Tax Limitation in West Virginia," 613–615.

67. Sly, "The By-products of Tax Limitation in West Virginia," 615.
68. Brinkley, *Voices of Protest*, 261.

CHAPTER 5

1. Beito, *Taxpayers in Revolt*, 40–44, 51–71, 81–86.
2. Ibid., 59–69, 72–75; *Champaign and Urbana (IL) Citizen*, June 24, 1932, 4, 8.
3. David Ray Papke, *The Pullman Case: The Clash of Labor and Capital in Industrial America* (Lawrence: University Press of Kansas, 1999), 14–29; Gerald G. Eggert, *Railroad Labor Disputes: The Beginning of Federal Strike Policy* (Ann Arbor: University of Michigan Press, 1967), 152–161; Melvin I. Urofsky, *Supreme Decisions: Great Constitutional Cases and Their Impact* (Boulder, CO: Westview Press, 2012), 159–168.
4. Papke, *The Pullman Case*, 29–100; Urofsky, *Supreme Decisions*, 168–174; Eggert, *Railroad Labor Disputes*, 161–175; Ray Ginger, *The Bending Cross: A Biography of Eugene Victor Debs* (Chicago: Haymarket Books, 2007), 108–151; Almont Lindsey, *The Pullman Strike: The Story of a Unique Experiment and of a Great Labor Upheaval* (Chicago: University of Chicago Press, 1942); *In re Debs*, 158 U.S. 564 (1895).
5. Forbath, *Law and the Shaping of the American Labor Movement*, 37–54, 169, App. A; Karen Orren, *Belated Feudalism: Labor, the Law, and Liberal Development in the United States* (Cambridge: Cambridge University Press, 1991), 112–116; *Lochner v. New York*, 198 U.S. 45 (1905); Urofsky, *Supreme Decisions*, 202–206.
6. Forbath, *Law and the Shaping of the American Labor Movement*, 1–2, 17, 38–42, 47, 53–62, 78, 94–97, 135, 168–171; Eggert, *Railroad Labor Disputes*, 175–177, 225, 231–235, 239.
7. *Altoona (PA) Tribune*, February 3, 1933, 4: *Paducah (KY) Sun-Democrat*, April 6, 1933, 4; *Des Moines (IA) Tribune*, March 16, 1933, 5.
8. Smith, "Taxation and Government," *NMR* 23, no. 5 (May 1934): 285.
9. Beito, *Taxpayers in Revolt*, 80–86, 100.
10. Ibid., 40–44.
11. Ibid., 51–59.
12. Ibid., 59–70, 177.
13. Ibid., 65–67, 98.
14. Ibid., 72–78.
15. Ibid., 72–79, 88–95.
16. Ibid., 96, 100.
17. Ibid., 22–23, 28–32.
18. Steed, "Adventures of a Tax Leaguer," November 11, 1933.
19. *Des Moines (IA) Tribune*, March 16, 1933, 5; *Lancaster (PA) New Era*, January 9, 1933, 3; *Morning Call* (Allentown, PA), January 9, 1933, 7; *Pittsburgh Post-Gazette*, January 10, 1933, 11; *The Record* (Hackensack, NJ), February 22, 1933, 13; *Grand Island (NE) Herald*, February 24, 1933, 1; *Oregon Tax Payer*, May 1, 1933, 8; *Statesman Journal* (Salem, OR), March 3, 1933, 1.
20. *Chattanooga (TN) News*, April 5, 1933, 5; *La Grande (OR) Observer*, July 14, 1933, 1; *Times* (San Mateo, CA), January 4, 1933, 4; *Salt Lake (UT) Tribune*, October 16, 1933, 6; *Salina (UT) Sun*, October 20, 1933, 1; *Ephraim (UT) Enterprise*, Decem-

ber 3, 1933, 1; *Indiana (PA) Gazette*, November 27, 1933, 2; *Evening Report* (Lebanon, PA), November 27, 1933, 7.

21. *NYT*, January 27, 1933, 7.
22. *NYT*, January 19, 1933, 36; February 2, 1933, 2.
23. *NYT*, February 24, 1933, 18. There is no indication in the *New York Times* or other contemporary sources as to how long the strike lasted or what was its end result.
24. *NYT*, June 10, 1933, 25.
25. *NYT*, March 1, 1933, 18; March 8, 1933, 14; March 11, 1933, 7; March 16, 1933, 3; March 21, 1933, 4, 7; April 27, 1933, 4; May 9, 1933, 13; May 10, 1933, 4; May 11, 1933, 4.
26. *NYT*, May 10, 1933, 4.
27. *Oregon Tax Payer*, May 1, 1933, 8; *Champaign and Urbana (IL) Citizen*, June 24, 1932, 4; *Ligonier (PA) Echo*, May 10, 1933, 2.
28. Traylor, "What Can Be Done about Taxes," 13–14.
29. *NYT*, October 11, 1933, 37.
30. "Mr. Taxpayer versus Mr. Taxspender," 359, 364.
31. John Maynard Keynes, *The General Theory of Employment, Interest and Money* (New York: Harcourt, 1936). For further discussion on the role of Keynesian economics in the Depression-era economy and New Deal policy, see Alan Brinkley, *The End of Reform: Deal Liberalism in Recession and War* (New York: Vintage Books, 1996), 65–66, 128–131, 134–135, 232–233, and Badger, *The New Deal*, 29–32, 114–117.
32. *NYT*, October 11, 1933, 37.
33. "Constructive Economy in State and Local Government," 4.
34. "Mr. Taxpayer versus Mr. Taxspender," 364.
35. *NMR* 22, no. 9 (September 1933): 406.
36. Frank Mann Stewart, *A Half Century of Municipal Reform: The History of the National Municipal League* (Berkeley: University of California Press, 1950), 11–22.
37. "The League's Business," *NMR* 22, no. 9 (September 1933): 406; "Constructive Economy in State and Local Government," 1–13; "Editorial Comment," *NMR* 22, no. 10 (October 1933): 490.
38. "Editorial Comment," *NMR* 22, no. 10 (October 1933): 490.
39. Wade S. Smith, "Taxation and Government," *NMR* 23, no. 2 (February 1934): 129–130.
40. Wade S. Smith, "Taxation and Government," *NMR* 23, no. 3 (March 1934): 185.
41. Wade S. Smith, "Taxation and Government," *NMR* 24, no. 6 (June 1935): 356.
42. Wade S. Smith, "Taxation and Government," *NMR* 23, no. 8 (August 1934): 446–447. See Beito, *Taxpayers in Revolt*, 101–139, for an extended discussion of the National Pay Your Taxes Campaign.
43. *Paducah (KY) Sun-Democrat*, August 13, 1934, 4.
44. Smith, "Taxation and Government," *NMR* 23, no. 9 (September 1934): 485.
45. Leuchtenburg, *Franklin D. Roosevelt and the New Deal*, 151; Badger, *The New Deal*, 120, 134–137, 300.
46. Herbert G. Gutman, *Work, Culture and Society in Industrializing America* (New York: Vintage Books, 1977), 295–296.
47. Beito, *Taxpayers in Revolt*, 29, 54–62.

48. Beito, *Taxpayers in Revolt*, xi–xiv, 19–20, 160–164; F. Alan Coombs, "The Impact of the New Deal on Wyoming Politics," in *The New Deal: The State and Local Levels*, 234; Hoan, *City Government*, 19–20, 158–159.

CHAPTER 6

1. *Middlesboro (KY) Daily News*, July 29, 1931, 4.
2. Eugene McQuillen, *The Law of Municipal Corporations*, 3rd ed. (St. Paul, MN: Thompson West, 2003), §52.02.
3. I endeavored to tabulate this data by extracting it from the Third, Fourth, and Fifth Decennial Digests of the American Digest System, *Municipal Corporations*, Keys 987–1000 (7), but found that many of the taxpayers' suits of which I am aware were not reported there and that, consequently, any such compilation would not prove accurate.
4. Third, Fourth, and Fifth Decennial Digests of the American Digest System, *Municipal Corporation*, Keys 987–1000 (7).
5. Note, "Taxpayers' Suits as a Means of Controlling the Expenditure of Public Funds," *Harvard Law Review* 50 (1937): 1276–1284.
6. *Wertz v. Shane*, 249 N.W. 661 (Iowa, 1933); Recent Cases, *Illinois Law Review* 28 (Chicago: Northwestern University Press, 1934): 1115–1116.
7. *Land, Log & Lumber Company v. McIntyre*, 100 Wis. 245, 254–255, 257, 75 N.W. 964, 967–968 (1898).
8. See the Second through the Tenth Decennial Digests of the American Digest System, *Municipal Corporations*, Key 987–1000 (7).
9. Lawrence M. Friedman, *A History of American Law*, 2nd ed. (New York: Simon & Schuster, 1985), 530–531.
10. See, for example, *Winn v. Shaw*, 87 Cal. 631, 25 P. 968 (1891); *City of Richmond v. Davis*, 103 Ind. 449, 3 N.E. 130 (1885).
11. *New Orleans M. & C.R. Co. v. Dunn*, 51 Ala. 128 (1874); *Poppleton v. Moores*, 67 Neb. 388, 93 N.W. 747 (1903).
12. *Jackson v. Norris*, 72 Ill. 364 (1874).
13. See, for example, *Miller v. Jackson Township of Boone County*, 178 Ind. 503, 99 N.E. 102 (1912).
14. *Steele v. Municipal Signal Co.*, 160 Mass. 36, 35 N.E. 105 (1893); *Baldwin v. Wilbraham*, 140 Mass. 459, 4 N.E. 829 (1886).
15. *Mooers v. Smedley*, 6 Johns Ch. 28, 29 (1822).
16. *Doolittle v. Broome County*, 18 N.Y. 155 (1858).
17. Ibid., 163.
18. *Craft v. Comm'rs Jackson County*, 5 Kan. 518 (1870); *Miller v. Grandy*, 13 Mich. 540 (1865).
19. *Land, Log & Lumber Company v. McIntyre*, 100 Wis. at 257, 75 N.W. at 968.
20. *Carman v. Woodruff*, 10 Ore. 133, 138 (1882).
21. Ibid., 135.
22. *Keen v. Waycross*, 101 Ga. 588, 592–593, 29 S.E. 42, 43–44 (1897).
23. *State v. Frear*, 148 Wis. 456, 500–501, 134 N.W. 673, 687 (1912). Other cases in which the courts liken the duties of public officials to those of directors in private

corporations and discuss the breach of trust principle include *Jackson v. Norris*, 72 Ill. 364 (1874) and *Sherburne v. City of Portsmouth*, 72 N.H. 539, 58 A. 38 (1904).

24. See Charles W. McCurdy, "Justice Field and the Jurisprudence of Government-Business Relations: Some Parameters of Laissez-Faire Constitutionalism, 1863–1897," *Journal of American History* 61, no. 4 (March 1975): 970–1005; Arnold M. Paul, "Legal Progressivism, the Courts, and the Crisis of the 1890s," *Business History Review* 33, no. 4 (1959): 495–509; Susan Sterett, *Public Pensions: Gender and Civic Service in the States, 1850 to 1937* (Ithaca, NY: Cornell University Press, 2003).

25. Jacobs, *Pocketbook Politics*, 1–5.

26. This is a recurring theme in American legal history, especially during the past two generations in which, for example, African Americans have initiated actions to enforce their civil rights, pro-choice advocates have turned to the courts to define and protect the reproductive rights of women, and, more recently, gay activists have sought and obtained judicial recognition of gay marriage.

27. Friedman, *A History of American Law*, 530–531. For example, in *Brown v. Reding*, 50 N.H. 336 (1870), the plaintiffs sought to restrain the county from purchasing certain articles of furniture for the county poor farm.

28. See, for example, *Jackson v. Norris, Land, Log & Lumber Company v. McIntyre*, and *Carman v. Woodruff*.

29. *Patten v. Chattanooga*, 108 Tenn. 197, 227, 65 S.W. 414, 422 (1901).

30. *Putnam v. Grand Rapids*, 58 Mich. 416, 419, 25 N.W. 330, 331 (1885).

31. Ibid.

32. James Willard Hurst, *Law and Economic Growth: The Legal History of the Lumber Industry in Wisconsin, 1836–1915* (Cambridge, MA: Harvard University Press, 1964), 523, 529.

33. Hurst, *Law and Economic Growth*, n. 41, 895; *Land, Log, & Lumber v. McIntyre*, 100 Wis. at 254, 75 N.W. at 967.

34. Hurst, *Law and Economic Growth*, 531–533.

35. *Baldwin v. Wilbraham*, 140 Mass. 459, 4. N.E. 829 (1886).

36. *Bunker v. Hutchinson*, 74 Kan. 651, 87 P. 884 (1906).

37. *Myers v. Gibson*, 147 Ind. 452, 46 N.E. 914 (1897).

38. *Altshul v. Ludwig*, 216 N.Y. 459, 464, 111 N.E. 216, 218 (1916).

39. Ibid., 216 N.Y. at 463, 465, 111 N.E. at 217–218; *Talcott v. City of Buffalo*, 125 N.Y. 280, 285–286, 26 N.E. 263, 264 (1891).

40. *Talcott v. City of Buffalo*, 125 N.Y. at 286, 26 N.E. at 264.

41. *Altshul v. Ludwig* and *Talcott v. City of Buffalo* both contain a good discussion of the convoluted legislative history of the 1872 and the 1881 statutes. The 1881 statute essentially conferred on New York taxpayers the same rights to relief for misconduct by local officials that courts of equity in most other states had developed for their citizens by the late nineteenth century.

42. Kerber, *No Constitutional Right to Be Ladies*, 81–123.

43. *Parker v. Concord*, 71 N.H. 468, 52 A. 1095 (1902); *Lindsey v. Allen*, 112 Tenn. 637, 657, 82 S.W. 171, 175 (1904); *Keen v. Waycross*, 101 Ga. 588, 593, 29 S.E. 42, 44 (1897); *State v. Frear*, 148 Wis. 456, 501, 134 N.W. 673, 687 (1912).

44. *Altshul v. Ludwig*, 216 N.Y. 459, 111 N.E. 216 (1916).

45. Horowitz, *The Transformation of American Law, 1780–1860*, xii, xvi, 1, 25, 27, 30.

Notes to Chapter 6 | *187*

46. Hurst, *Law and the Conditions of Freedom*, 5–7, 10, 32–33, 107.
47. Hall, *The Magic Mirror*, 7.
48. Friedman, *A History of American Law*, 530.
49. *Carman v. Woodruff*, 10 Ore. at 137.
50. Hurst, *Law and the Conditions of Freedom*, 5, 10, 32, 107.
51. Eugene McQuillen, *The Law of Municipal Corporations*, 2nd ed. (Chicago: Callaghan, 1937), §2740; John F. Dillon, *Commentaries on the Law of Municipal Corporations* (Boston: Little, Brown, 1911), §1588.
52. *Taxpayers' Association of Harris County v. Houston Independent School District*, 81 S.W. 2d 815, 816 (Texas Court of Civil Appeals, 1935).
53. Ibid., 815 S.W. 2d at 819–820.
54. *Taxpayers' Association of Harris County v. City of Houston*, 105 S.W. 2d 655 (Texas 1937).
55. *Mayor and City Council of Baltimore v. Employers' Assoc. of Maryland, Inc.*, 159 A. 267 (Md. 1932).
56. *Taxpayers League of Wayne County v. Benthack*, 285 N.W. 577 (Neb. 1939).
57. *Maclay v. Finegan*, 299 N.Y.S. 897 (N.Y. 1937); *The New York Edison Company, Inc. v. City of New York*, 198 N.E. 550 (N.Y. 1935); *Arkansas-Missouri Power Co. v. City of Kennett*, 78 F. 2d 911 (8th Circ. 1935).
58. *Taxpayers' League of Carbon County v. McPherson*, 54 P. 2d 897 (Wyo. 1936).
59. Ibid., 54 P. 2d at 901, 905.
60. Upham-Bornstein, "Citizens with a 'Just Cause,'" 117, 124–125.
61. *Berlin Taxpayers Association v. The Mayor and City Council of Berlin, and the Fidelity & Deposit Company of Maryland*, Coos County Superior Court, October term, 1933, 1.
62. Ibid., 9, 10.
63. Ibid.; Berlin City Reports, Journal no. 13, January 1932 to December 1934, May and June 1934; *Coos (NH) Guardian*, May 3, 1934, 1, 2; May 10, 1934, 2; May 17, 1934, 1, 2; May 24, 1934, 1; June 14, 1934, 1. The surety company had appealed the Superior Court's decision and, on June 28, 1934, obtained a ruling from the New Hampshire Supreme Court that the Berlin Taxpayers Association petition should be dismissed unless the taxpayers alleged the details of the fraud and proved the same at trial. *Berlin Taxpayers Association v. the Mayor and City Council of Berlin*, 87 N.H. 80, 173 A. 810 (1934). This ruling, however, did not derail the settlement agreement or the prosecution of Labrie.
64. *State v. John A. Labrie*, Coos County Superior Court, #1727 to #1738, October term, 1934; Upham-Bornstein, "Citizens with a 'Just Cause,'" 124–125.
65. *Hoskins v. Helton*, 67 S.W. 2d 975 (Ky. 1934).
66. *Kaiser v. City of Portage*, 225 N.W. 188 (Wis. 1929).
67. *Mayor and City Council of Baltimore v. Employers' Assoc. of Maryland, Inc.*, 159 A. 267 (Md. 1932).
68. *The New York Edison Company, Inc. v. City of New York*, 198 N.E. 550 (N.Y. 1935); *Arkansas-Missouri Power Co. v. City of Kennett*, 78 F. 2d 911 (8th Cir. 1935); *City of Allegan v. Consumers' Power Co.*, 71 F. 2d 477 (6th Cir. 1934).
69. Badger, *The New Deal*, 101–102, 177–178; Upham-Bornstein, "Citizens with a 'Just Cause,'" 131.

70. Henry Harvey Fuson, *History of Bell County Kentucky* (New York: Hobson Book Press, 1947), 1, 77–80, 298; *Taxpayers' League of Bell County v. Vanbeber*, 252 Ky. 282, 66 S.W. 2d 516 (1933).

71. *Middlesboro (KY) Daily News*, June 11, 1930, 6; March 27, 1931, 7.

72. Ibid., July 29, 1931, 4.

73. Ibid., March 27, 1931, 7.

74. *Taxpayers' League of Bell County v. Sun Publishing Company*, 256 Ky. 37, 38, 75 S.W. 2d 564 (1934); *Middlesboro (KY) Daily News*, March 27, 1931, 7.

75. *Middlesboro (KY) Daily News*, March 27, 1931, 7.

76. Ibid.

77. Ibid., June 3, 1931, 4.

78. For example, in September 1931, the members of the league's executive committee brought suit against the Pineville Board of Education seeking to set aside the purchase of an athletic field, and in January 1933, representatives of the league filed suit against the Middlesboro Board of Commissioners to recover excess salaries paid to the mayor and commissioners. *Middlesboro (KY) Daily News*, September 11, 1931, 2; January 17, 1933, 1, 6.

79. See *Hoskins v. Helton*, 252 Ky. 616, 67 S.W. 2d 975 (1934); *Taxpayers' League of Bell County v. Vanbeber*, 252 Ky. 282, 66 S.W. 2d 526 (1933); *Pursifull v. Taxpayers' League of Bell County*, 257 Ky. 202, 77 S.W. 2d 783 (1935); *Motch v. City of Middlesboro*, 242 Ky. 653, 47 S.W. 2d 56 (1932); *Allen v. Hollingsworth*, 246 Ky. 812, 56 S.W. 2d 530 (1933); *Middlesboro (KY) Daily News*, September 11, 1931, 2, reporting on *Vicars v. Pineville Board of Education*.

80. *Hoskins v. Helton*, 252 Ky. at 619, 67 S.W. 2d at 976–977; *Middlesboro (KY) Daily News*, July 15, 1931, 1, 4.

81. *Middlesboro (KY) Daily News*, October 18, 1930, 1; November 21, 1931, 1; *Motch v. City of Middlesboro*, 242 Ky. at 656, 47 S.W. 2d at 57.

82. *Allen v. Hollingsworth*, 56 S.W. 2d at 534, 531, 533; *Middlesboro (KY) Daily News*, January 17, 1933, 1, 6.

83. The court's opinion does not indicate how, if at all, the two Vanbebers were related, but it is not unreasonable to assume that they were related. *Taxpayers' League of Bell County v. Vanbeber*, 252 Ky. 282, 66 S.W. 2d 516 (1933).

84. *Pursifull v. Taxpayers' League of Bell County*, 257 Ky. 202, 77 S.W. 2d 783 (1935); *Middlesboro (KY) Daily News*, February 5, 1935, 1.

85. *Taxpayers' League of Bell County v. Sun Publishing Company*, 256 Ky. 37, 75 S.W. 2d 564 (1934). The league did not prevail in this defamation action: the court concluded that the newspaper's statements were not libelous.

86. *Middlesboro (KY) Daily News*, March 27, 1931, 7.

87. Hurst, *Law and the Conditions of Freedom*, 10, 17.

88. Marc Gallanter, "The Radiating Effects of the Courts," in *Empirical Theories about Courts*, edited by Keith O. Boyum and Lynn Mather (New York: Longman, 1983), 117–142.

89. Tocqueville, *Democracy in America*, Vol. 1, 330.

90. Tomlins, *Law, Labor and Ideology*, 16.

91. Horowitz, *The Transformation of American Law, 1870–1960*, 270–272.

CONCLUSION

1. *Lowell (MA) Sun*, October 8, 1931, 5.
2. George L. Leffler, "Ebb Tide in Taxation: A Depression Aftermath," *NMR* 22, no. 11 (November 1933): 541–543, 557.
3. Tharp, *Control of Local Finance*, 16–27, 76, 84.
4. Paige, "Governmental Research Association Notes," *NMR* 24, no. 3 (March 1935): 187; 24, no. 11 (November 1935): 654; 24, no. 7 (July 1935): 414; 24, no. 12 (December 1935): 712.
5. Elting, "The Tax Fight," 12, 37; Elting, "You CAN Cut Taxes," 10; Porter, "Taxpayers on the Warpath," 50–52, 162; Gaskill, "Caviar on Your Tax Bill," 116–119.
6. "Mr. Taxpayer versus Mr. Taxspender," 359, 361, 365; Hoan, *City Government*, 19–25, 158–159.
7. Bird, "The Effect of Tax Rate Limits on Municipal Credit," 607–610.
8. Smith, "Taxation and Government," *NMR* 23, no. 1 (January 1934), 39–40.
9. Sidney Demers, "A Plea for Research," *NMR* 24, no. 10 (October 1935): 523.
10. Thomas H. Reed, "Organizing to Save Our Communities," *NMR* 22, no. 7 (July 1933): 311.
11. Beito, *Taxpayers in Revolt*, 108–110, 133–134, 155.
12. "Retrenching in State and Local Expenditures," 1–2.
13. "Constructive Economy in State and Local Government," 4.
14. Jones, "Unrest in County Government," 472.
15. Barrows, "A Challenge to Reform," 223, 226, 230.
16. Beito, *Taxpayers in Revolt*, 141.
17. McMillan, "The Farmer Buys Less Government," 7; West Virginia Taxpayers' Association, *The Tax Burden in West Virginia*.
18. *St. Cloud (MN) Times*, September 17, 1934, 9.
19. Glickman, *Free Enterprise*, 6, 11–12, 14, 81.
20. Zelizer, "The Uneasy Relationship," 276, 280, 291; "Mr. Taxpayer versus Mr. Taxspender," 358, 361, 363.
21. Jacobs, *Pocketbook Politics*, 9.
22. "Editorial Comment," *NMR* 21, no. 11 (November 1933): 623.
23. Sugrue, "All Politics Is Local," 302; Elting, "The Tax Revolt," 12; Elting, "You CAN Cut Taxes," 10–11, 27.
24. "Mr. Taxpayer versus Mr. Taxspender," 364.
25. Clyde L. King, "Political Patronage Threatens Democracy," *NMR* 22, no. 10 (October 1933): 497.
26. Howard P. Jones, "Progress in County Government: A Bird's Eye View," *NMR* 23, no. 10 (October 1934): 502.
27. "Citizens Must Organize," *NMR* 24, no. 4 (April 1935): 195–196. The type of organization for which the National Municipal League advocated was a nonpartisan citizens' council, but the sentiments apply with equal force to other citizens' organizations such as taxpayers' associations.
28. *NMR* 24, no. 12 (December 1935): 663.
29. Paige, "Governmental Research Association Notes," *NMR* 26, no. 9 (September 1937): 455.

30. Paige, "Governmental Research Association Notes," *NMR* 24, no. 7 (July 1935): 410.

31. Simone Weil, *Gravity and Grace* (New York: Routledge, 2002), 156.

32. Hurst, *Law and the Conditions of Freedom*, 5.

33. Ibid., 7, 33.

34. Elting, "You CAN Cut Taxes," 10; "Taxpayers Organizations in the United States," *Tax Policy* 5 (September 1938): 1; "Taxpayers' Organizations: Supplement," *Tax Policy* 6 (March 1939): 1; Porter, "Taxpayers on the Warpath," 51, 52; Gaskill, "Caviar on Your Tax Bill," 116–119.

35. Beito, *Taxpayers in Revolt*, 158.

36. https://www.kerntaxpayers.org/; https://www.caltax.org/; http://www.iowataxpayers.org/; https://www.nevadataxpayers.org/; https://utahtaxpayers.org/; https://taxpayersci.org/; https://taxtopics.org (all accessed July 7, 2020).

37. https://www.statetaxes.net/florida; https://www.statetaxes.net/hawaii (accessed July 26, 2020).

38. http://www.ati-taxinfo.com/ (accessed July 13, 2020); http://capemaytaxpayers.com/; https://tpairc.org/; https://www.taxpayersleague.org/; https://oregonwatchdog.com/; http://www.ptcc.us/peta.htm (all accessed July 7, 2020).

39. Associated Press, "Grim Economy Dominates NH Town Meetings," *Caledonian (VT) Record*, March 9, 2009.

40. Garry Rayno, "Most NH Voters Keep Tight Hold on Purse Strings," *New Hampshire Union Leader*, March 12, 2009.

41. "County Assessors Get Set for Property Tax Protests," *Des Moines (IA) Register*, March 2, 2009, http://www.desmoinesregister.com/apps/pbcs.dll/article?AID=200... (accessed March 10, 2009).

42. "Officials Try to Soothe Tax Revolters," *Chapel Hill (NC) News*, March 8, 2009, http://chaphillnews.com/news/v-print/story/44376.html (accessed March 10, 2009); "Tax Fight in Hoboken," WABC-TV/DT, March 5, 2009, http://abclocal.go.com/wabc/story?section=news/local&id=6689475... (accessed March 10, 2009); Carly Baldwin, "Protest Outside Hoboken City Hall Reveals Anger, Frustration," Hoboken Now Blog, March 4, 2009, http://blog.nj.com/hobokennow_impact/2009/03/protest_outside_Hoboken... (accessed March 10, 2009).

43. Nate Schweber, "Property Owners Lash Double-Digit Tax Increase," *NYT*, March 1, 2009, http://www.nytimes.com/2009/03/03/nyregion/new-jersey/01westnynj.html (accessed March 10, 2009); "Another Rally Planned in West New York to Protest Soaring Property Taxes," *Jersey Journal*, March 6, 2009, http://www.nj.com/hudson/index.ssf/2009/03/another_rally_planned... (accessed March 10, 2009); Charles Hack, "Protesters Assail Hikes, Demand Spending Freeze," *Jersey Journal*, March 9, 2009, http://www.nh.com/printer/printer.ssf?/base/news-o/1236579970567... (accessed March 10, 2009).

44. The states are Arizona, California, Florida, Hawaii, Idaho, Illinois, Iowa, Louisiana, Massachusetts, Minnesota, Montana, Nevada, New Mexico, Rhode Island, Texas, Utah, Washington, and Wyoming. https://www.statetaxes.net/directory (accessed July 22, 2020).

45. https://www.statetaxes.net/hawaii; https://www.statetaxes.net/newmexico; https://www.statetaxes.net/arizona; https://www.states.net/florida; https://www.state

taxes.net/idaho; https://www.statetaxes.net/iowa; https://www.statetaxes.net/minnesota (all accessed July 26, 2020).

46. "San Diego County Taxpayers Association Creates Nonpartisan March 2020 Voter Guide," *KUSI News Room*, February 14, 2020; February 24, 2020, https://www.kusi.com/author/kusinewsroom/; "Civic Associations Urge Atlantic City Residents to Vote Against Change of Government," *Press of Atlantic City*, February 29, 2020, pressofatlanticcity.com; "Federal Court Dismisses Suit Against CalSavers Program for Second Time," *Pension & Investments*, March 11, 2020; "Brown County's 0.59% Sales Tax Conforms with Legislative Intent, Judge Rules," *Green Bay (NC) Press Gazette*, March 25, 2020, https/greenbaypressgazette.com; "BCTA to Appeal Tax Ruling," May 20, 2020, https://www.bctaxpayers.org (all accessed July 14, 2020); "Jarvis Appeals CalSavers Decision," April 7, 2020, https://www.asppa.org.news/jarvis-appeals-calsavers-decision (accessed April 9, 2021).

47. Michelmore, *Tax and Spend*, 6, 106, 128; Theda Skocpol and Vanessa Williamson, *The Tea Party and the Remaking of Republican Conservatism* (Oxford: Oxford University Press, 2012), 6–7. Grassroots populism also contributed to the Tea Party movement, but to a lesser extent. Skocpol and Williamson, *The Tea Party*, 12–13, 18.

48. Michelmore, *Tax and Spend*, 148 (arguing that in the mid-1980s the "defense of taxpayers' rights . . . became . . . the fundamental principle and overriding concern of American domestic and even foreign politics.")

49. There is a fair amount of imbrication among these groups. Many Tea Partiers, for instance, identify with the Christian Right and espouse free enterprise values.

50. Quoted in Glickman, *Free Enterprise*, 229.

51. Michelmore, *Tax and Spend*, 138.

52. Brownlee, *Federal Taxation in America*, 177–178; Michelmore, *Tax and Spend*, 133–134.

53. Brownlee, *Federal Taxation in America*, 185–186; Michelmore, *Tax and Spend*, 125, 137, 148.

54. Skocpol and Williamson, *The Tea Party*, 12–13, 18.

55. Ibid., 9, 46, 50, 66.

56. Ibid., 8, 27, 75.

57. "The State-Budget Train Crash," *Economist*, June 18, 2020, https://www.economist.com/united-states/2020/06/18/the-state-budget-train-crash (accessed June 18, 2020).

Selected Bibliography

This bibliography is not exhaustive. It lists the primary sources (other than newspapers, a few minor sources, and court case citations), secondary sources (other than legal treatises and short law review notes), and manuscript collections on which I have relied in preparing this manuscript.

MANUSCRIPT COLLECTIONS

Columbia University, Butler Library, New York, New York
  Citizens Union Papers, 1897–1964
New Hampshire Supreme Court, John W. King New Hampshire Law Library, Concord, New Hampshire
  Documents regarding *Berlin Taxpayers Association v. The Mayor and City Council of Berlin*, 87 N.H. 80 (1934)
New York Public Library, Humanities and Social Science Library, New York, New York
  Bard, Albert S. Papers, 1893–1962
  Kelly, Nicholas Papers, 1885–1965
  Turkel, Stanley, Collection of City Club Memorabilia, 1908–1997
  Welling, Richard Papers, 1881–1941
Tuck Library, New Hampshire Historical Society, Concord, New Hampshire
  Brown Company, Ledgers
  Farmer-Labor Party of New Hampshire Papers
University of California, Los Angeles, Charles E. Young Research Library, Department of Special Collections, UCLA/DSC
  Franklin Hichborn Papers

PRIMARY SOURCES

American Taxpayers' Quarterly 1, no. 1 (November 1931). New York: American Taxpayers' Inc.

Annual Reports of the Receipts and Expenditures of the City of Berlin, NH, 1930–1939. Berlin, NH: Berlin Publishing, 1930, 1932, 1936, 1938, 1939/Smith & Town, 1931, 1933–1935/Foley & Weber, 1937.

Barrows, Edward M. "A Challenge to Reform." *National Municipal Review* 22, no. 5 (May 1933): 223–226, 230.

Berlin, New Hampshire Centennial, 1829–1929. Berlin, NH: Smith & Town, 1929.

Coos Guardian. 1934. University of New Hampshire, Milne Special Collections.

Edmunds, Sterling E. *The Federal Octopus in 1933: A Survey of the Destruction of Constitutional Government and of Civil and Economic Liberty in the United States and the Rise of an All-Embracing Federal Bureaucratic Despotism*, 3rd ed. Charlottesville, VA: Michie, 1933.

Elting, John. "The Tax Fight." *Forbes*, February 15, 1939.

———. "You CAN Cut Taxes." *Forbes*, March 1, 1939.

Gaskill, Gordon. "Caviar on Your Tax Bill." *American Magazine* 131 (April 1941): 116–119.

Governmental Research Association. "The Search for Facts in Government." *Supplement to the National Municipal Review* 22, no. 6 (June 1933): 301–305.

Jones, F. Robertson. "Taxing Misfortune." Washington, DC: American Taxpayers League, 1933.

Jones, Howard P. "Unrest in County Government." *National Municipal Review* 21, no. 8 (August 1932): 469–472.

McMillan, Wheeler. "The Farmer Buys Less Government." *National Municipal Review* 22, no. 1 (January 1933): 7–8, 11.

"Mr. Taxpayer versus Mr. Taxspender." *National Municipal Review* 22, no. 8 (August 1933): 358–365.

National Municipal League, Committee on Citizens' Councils for Constructive Economy. "A Citizens' Council, Why and How?" New York, 1933.

National Municipal League. *National Municipal Review.* 1932–1937.

New York Civil Service Reform Association. *Purposes of the Civil Service Reform Association.* New York, 1881.

Porter, S. F. "Taxpayers on the Warpath." *American Magazine* 130 (October 1940): 50–52, 162.

Reed, Thomas H., ed. *Government in a Depression: Constructive Economy in State and Local Government.* Chicago: University of Chicago Press, 1933.

———. "Organizing to Save Our Communities." *National Municipal Review* 22, no. 7 (July 1933): 310.

Seasongood, Murray. "Getting Our Bearings." *National Municipal Review* 22, no. 12 (December 1933): 585–586.

Steed, Hal. "Adventures of a Tax Leaguer." *Saturday Evening Post* 206, no. 19 (November 4, 1933); no. 20 (November 11, 1933).

Teaneck Taxpayers' League. "Teaneck's Most Progressive 12 Years, 1929–1941," pamphlet. Teaneck Collection at Teaneck Public Library, Teaneck, NJ.

Tharp, Claude R. *Control of Local Finance through Taxpayers' Associations and Centralized Administrations.* Indianapolis, IN: M. Ford, 1933.

Thorpe, Merle. "In Behalf of the Delinquent Taxpayer—Present and Prospective." n.p., 1932.

Traylor, Melvin A. "What Can Be Done about Taxes" An Address by Melvin A. Traylor. University of North Carolina at Chapel Hill, North Carolina Collection, 1932.

Vandegrift, Rolland A. "The State Tax System of California," pamphlet. Reprinted from *The Tax Digest*, October 1927, Hichborn Papers, UCLA/DSC.

"Why a Farmer-Labor Party in New Hampshire?" leaflet. Berlin, NH: Ruemely Press, 1936.

SECONDARY SOURCES

Adams, James Ring. *Secrets of the Tax Revolt.* San Diego: Harcourt Brace Jovanovich, 1984.

Badger, Anthony J. *The New Deal: The Depression Years, 1933–1940.* Chicago: Ivan R. Dee, 1989.

Beckert, Sven. *The Monied Metropolis: New York City and the Consolidation of the American Bourgeoisie, 1850–1896.* New York: Cambridge University Press, 2001.

Beito, David T. *Taxpayers in Revolt: Tax Resistance during the Great Depression.* Chapel Hill: University of North Carolina Press, 1989.

Boyum, Keith O., and Lynn Mather, eds. *Empirical Theories about Courts.* New York: Longman, 1983.

Braeman, John, Robert Hamlett Bremner, and David Brody, eds. *The New Deal: The National Level.* Columbus: Ohio State University Press, 1975.

———. *The New Deal: The State and Local Levels.* Columbus: Ohio State University Press, 1975.

Braudel, Fernand. *The Structures of Everyday Life: The Limits of the Possible.* New York: Harper & Row, 1985.

Brinkley, Alan. *Voices of Protest: Huey Long, Father Coughlin, and the Great Depression.* New York: Vintage Books, 1983.

Brownlee, W. Elliot. *Federal Taxation in America: A History*, 3rd ed. New York: Cambridge University Press, 2016.

Capozzola, Christopher. *Uncle Sam Wants You: World War I and the Making of the Modern American Citizen.* New York: Oxford University Press, 2008.

Cerillo, Augustus Jr. "The Reform of Municipal Government in New York City: From Seth Low to John Purroy Mitchel." *New York Historical Society Quarterly* 57, no. 1 (1973): 51–71.

"The Collection of Real Property Taxes." *Law and Contemporary Problems* 3, no. 3 (June 1936): 335–461.

Connolly, James J. *An Elusive Unity: Urban Democracy and Machine Politics in Industrializing America.* Ithaca, NY: Cornell University Press, 2010.

Cornell, Saul. *The Other Founders: Anti-Federalism and the Dissenting Tradition in America.* Chapel Hill: University of North Carolina Press, 1999.

Einhorn, Robin L. *American Taxation, American Slavery.* Chicago: University of Chicago Press, 2006.

Ernst, Daniel R. *Lawyers against Labor: From Individual Rights to Corporate Liberalism*. Urbana: University of Illinois Press, 1995.

Ewick, Patricia, and Susan S. Silbey. *The Common Place of Law: Stories from Everyday Life*. Chicago: University of Chicago Press, 1998.

Feingold, Kenneth. *Experts and Politicians: Reform Challenges to Machine Politics in New York, Cleveland and Chicago*. Princeton, NJ: Princeton University Press, 1995.

Foner, Eric. *Reconstruction: America's Unfinished Revolution, 1863–1877*. New York: HarperCollins, 2005.

Forbath, William E. "Courts, Constitutions, and Labor Politics in England and America: A Study of the Constitutive Power of Law." *Law and Social Inquiry* 16, no. 1 (1991): 1–34.

———. *Law and the Shaping of the American Labor Movement*. Cambridge, MA: Harvard University Press, 1991.

Fox, Kenneth. *Better City Government: Innovation in American Urban Politics, 1850–1937*. Philadelphia: Temple University Press, 1977.

Friedman, Lawrence Meir. *A History of American Law*, 2nd ed. New York: Simon & Schuster, 1985.

Fuson, Henry Harvey. *History of Bell County, Kentucky*. New York: Hobson Book Press, 1947.

Ginger, Ray. *The Bending Cross: A Biography of Eugene Victor Debs*. Chicago: Haymarket Books, 2007.

Glaeser Edward L., and Claudia Goldin, eds. *Corruption and Reform: Lessons from America's Economic History*. Chicago: University of Chicago Press, 2006.

Glickman, Lawrence B. *Free Enterprise: An American History*. New Haven, CT: Yale University Press, 2019.

Goodwyn, Lawrence. *The Populist Moment: A Short History of the Agrarian Revolt in America*. Oxford: Oxford University Press, 1978.

Gordon, Colin. *New Deals: Business, Labor, and Politics in America, 1920–1935*. New York: Cambridge University Press, 1994.

Gutman, Herbert G. *Work, Culture and Society in Industrializing America*. New York: Vintage Books, 1977.

Hall, Kermit. *The Magic Mirror: Law in American History*. New York: Oxford University Press, 1989.

Hammack, David C. *Power and Society: Greater New York at the Turn of the Century*. New York: Russell Sage Foundation, 1982.

Harris, William C. *The Day of the Carpetbagger: Republican Reconstruction in Mississippi*. Baton Rouge: Louisiana State University Press, 1979.

Hartley, James E., Steven M. Sheffrin, and David Vasche. "Reform during Crisis: The Transformation of California's Fiscal System during the Great Depression." *Journal of Economic History* 56, no. 3 (September 1996): 657–678.

Harvard Law Review Association. "Taxpayers' Suits as a Means of Controlling the Expenditure of Public Funds." *Harvard Law Review* 50 (1937): 1276–1284.

Hicks, John D. *The Populist Revolt: A History of the Farmers' Alliance and the People's Party*. Lincoln: University of Nebraska Press, 1931.

Higgens-Evenson, R. Rudy. *The Price of Progress: Public Services, Taxation, and the American Corporate State, 1877 to 1929*. Baltimore: Johns Hopkins University Press, 2003.

Hoan, Daniel W. *City Government: The Record of the Milwaukee Experiment.* New York: Harcourt Brace, 1936.

Hofstadter, Richard. *The Age of Reform: From Bryan to F.D.R.* New York: Vintage, 1955.

Horowitz, Morton J. *The Transformation of American Law, 1780–1860.* New York: Oxford University Press, 1992.

———. *The Transformation of American Law, 1870–1960: Crisis of Legal Orthodoxy.* New York: Oxford University Press, 1992.

Hurst, James Willard. *Law and Economic Growth: The Legal History of the Lumber Industry in Wisconsin, 1836–1915.* Cambridge, MA: Belknap Press of Harvard University Press, 1964.

———. *Law and the Conditions of Freedom in the Nineteenth-Century United States.* Madison: University of Wisconsin Press, 1956.

Jacobs, Meg. *Pocketbook Politics: Economic Citizenship in Twentieth-Century America.* Princeton, NJ: Princeton University Press, 2005.

Jacobs, Meg, William J. Novak, and Julian E. Zelizer, eds. *The Democratic Experiment: New Directions in American Political History.* Princeton, NJ: Princeton University Press, 2003.

Kaufman, Jason. "Three Views of Associationalism in 19th-Century America: An Empirical Examination." *American Journal of Sociology* 104, no. 5 (March 1999): 1296–1345.

Kazin, Michael. *The Populist Persuasion: An American History.* Ithaca, NY: Cornell University Press, 1998.

Kerber, Linda K. *No Constitutional Right to Be Ladies: Women and the Obligations of Citizenship.* New York: Hill & Wang, 1998.

Keynes, John Maynard. *The General Theory of Employment, Interest and Money.* New York: Harcourt, 1936.

Kurland, Gerald. "The Amateur in Politics: The Citizens Union and the Greater New York Mayoral Campaign of 1897." *New York Historical Society Quarterly* 53, no. 4 (1969): 342–382.

Lee, Mordecai. *Bureaus of Efficiency: Reforming Local Government in the Progressive Era.* Milwaukee: Marquette University Press, 2008.

Leff, Mark Hugh. *The Limits of Symbolic Reform: The New Deal and Taxation, 1933–1939.* New York: Cambridge University Press, 1984.

Lemann, Nicholas. *Redemption: The Last Battle of the Civil War.* New York: Farrar, Straus and Giroux, 2006.

Leuchtenburg, William E. *Franklin D. Roosevelt and the New Deal.* New York: HarperCollins, 2009.

———, ed. *The New Deal: A Documentary History.* New York: Harper & Row, 1968.

Lindsey, Almont. *The Pullman Strike: The Story of a Unique Experiment and of a Great Labor Upheaval.* Chicago: University of Chicago Press, 1942.

MacMath, Robert C. Jr. *American Populism: A Social History, 1877–1898.* New York: Hill & Wang, 1993.

McAllister, Breck P. "Taxpayers' Remedies—Washington Property Taxes." *Washington Law Review and State Bar Journal* 13, no. 2 (1938): 91–130.

McCurdy, Charles W. "Justice Field and the Jurisprudence of Government-Business Relations: Some Parameters of Laissez-Faire Constitutionalism, 1863–1897." *Journal of American History* 61, no. 4 (1975): 970–1005.

Mehrotra, Ajay K. *Making the Modern American Fiscal State: Law, Politics and the Rise of Progressive Taxation*. New York: Cambridge University Press, 2013.

Michelmore, Molly C. *Tax and Spend: The Welfare State, Tax Politics, and the Limits of American Liberalism*. Philadelphia: University of Pennsylvania Press, 2012.

Moffitt, Benjamin. *The Global Rise of Populism: Performance, Political Style, and Representation*. Stanford, CA: Stanford University Press, 2016.

Muccigrosso, Robert. "The City Reform Club: A Study in Late Nineteenth-Century Reform." *New York Historical Society Quarterly* 52 (July 1968): 235–254.

Mudde, Cas. "The Populist Zeitgeist." *Government and Opposition* 39, no. 4 (2004): 541–563.

Mudde, Cas, and Cristobal Rovira Kaltwasser. *Populism: A Very Short Introduction*. Oxford: Oxford University Press, 2017.

Müller, Jan-Werner. *What Is Populism?* Philadelphia: University of Pennsylvania Press, 2016.

Munro, William. "Taxation Nears a Crisis." *Current History* 37 (1933): 652–662.

Onuf, Peter S. *Jefferson's Empire: The Language of American Nationhood*. Charlottesville: University Press of Virginia, 2000.

Orren, Karen. *Belated Feudalism: Labor, the Law, and Liberal Development in the United States*. Cambridge: Cambridge University Press, 1991.

Papke, David Ray. *The Pullman Case: The Clash of Labor and Capital in Industrial America*. Lawrence: University Press of Kansas, 1999.

Paul, Arnold M. "Legal Progressivism, the Courts and the Crisis of the 1890s." *Business History Review* 33, no. 4 (1959): 495–509.

Podolefsky, Ronnie L. "Illusion of Suffrage: Female Voting Rights and the Women's Poll Tax Repeal Movement after the Nineteenth Amendment." *Notre Dame Law Review* 73 (1998): 839–888.

Recchiuti, John Louis. *Civic Engagement: Social Science and Progressive-Era Reform in New York City*. Philadelphia: University of Pennsylvania Press, 2007.

Recent Cases. *Illinois Law Review* 28 (1934): 1115–1116.

Remini, Robert B. *Andrew Jackson and the Course of American Freedom, 1822–1832*. New York: Harper & Row, 1981.

Saloutos, Theodore, and John D. Hicks. *Twentieth Century Populism: Agricultural Discontent in the Middle West, 1900–1939*. Lincoln: University of Nebraska Press, 1951.

Salyer, Lucy E. "Captives of Law: Judicial Enforcement of the Chinese Exclusion Laws, 1891–1905." *Journal of American History* 76, no. 1 (1989): 91–117.

Schiesl, Martin J. *The Politics of Efficiency: Municipal Administration and Reform in America, 1880–1920*. Berkeley: University of California Press, 1977.

Schlesinger, Arthur M. Jr. *The Age of Jackson*. Boston: Little, Brown, 1945.

———. *The Age of Roosevelt: The Crisis of the Old Order, 1919–1933*. New York: Bookspan, 2002.

———. *The Age of Roosevelt: The Politics of Upheaval, 1935–1936*. Boston: Houghton Mifflin, 2003.

Sellers, Charles. *The Market Revolution: Jacksonian America, 1815–1846*. New York: Oxford University Press, 1991.

Simpson, Sidney Post. "Fifty Years of American Equity." *Harvard Law Review* 50, no. 2 (1936): 171–251.

Skocpol, Theda, and Vanessa Williamson. *The Tea Party and the Remaking of Republican Conservatism*. Oxford: Oxford University Press, 2012.

Sterett, Susan Marie. *Public Pensions: Gender and Civic Service in the States, 1850–1937*. Ithaca, NY: Cornell University Press, 2003.

Stewart, Frank Mann. *A Half Century of Municipal Reform: The History of the National Municipal League*. Berkeley: University of California Press, 1950.

Taggart, Paul. *Populism*. Buckingham, UK: Open University Press, 2000.

Teaford, Jon C. *The Unheralded Triumph: City Government in America, 1870–1900*. Baltimore: John Hopkins University Press, 1984.

Terkel, Studs. *Hard Times: An Oral History of the Great Depression*. New York: New Press, 2000.

Tocqueville, Alexis de. *Democracy in America*, Vols. 1 and 2. New York: Schocken Books, 1961.

Tomlins, Christopher L. *Law, Labor, and Ideology in the Early American Republic*. Cambridge: Cambridge University Press, 1993.

Upham-Bornstein, Linda. "'Citizens with a 'Just Cause'': The New Hampshire Farmer-Labor Party in Depression-Era Berlin." *Historical New Hampshire* 62, no. 2 (Fall 2008): 117–137.

———. "'Men of Families': The Intersection of Labor Conflict and Race in the Norfolk Dry Dock Affair, 1829–1831." *Labor: Studies in Working Class History* 4, no. 1 (Spring 2007): 65–97.

Urofsky, Melvin I. *A March of Liberty: From 1877 to the Present*. New York: Oxford University Press, 2002.

———. *Supreme Decisions: Great Constitutional Cases and Their Impact*. Boulder, CO: Westview Press, 2012.

Watson, Henry L. *Jacksonian Politics and Community Conflict*. Baton Rouge: Louisiana State University Press, 1981.

———. *Liberty and Power: The Politics of Jacksonian America*. New York: Hill & Wang, 1990.

Weil, Simone. *Gravity and Grace*. New York: Routledge, 2002.

Willrich, Michael. *City of Courts: Socializing Justice in Progressive Era Chicago*. Cambridge: Cambridge University Press, 2003.

Yearley, Clifton K. *The Money Machines: The Breakdown and Reform of Governmental and Party Finance in the North, 1860–1920*. Albany: State University of New York Press, 1970.

Index

American Taxpayers' Inc, 42
Anti-Federalism/Anti-Federalists, 83–86, 99
Antistatism, 15, 44; and modern tax resistance, 162; and New Deal opponents, 34–35, 50–51, 151, 173n111; and tax resistance, 7, 13, 46–47, 153; and tax strikes, 14, 122
ARET. *See* Association of Real Estate Taxpayers
Arizona, taxpayers' groups/tax resistance in, 39, 62–63, 103
Arizona Taxpayers' Association, 39, 62
Arkansas, taxpayers' groups/tax resistance in, 101
Asbury Park (NJ) Citizens and Taxpayers' Association, 93
Associationalism, 20–21, 155, 157, 168n7
Association of Omaha (NE) Taxpayers, 69, 147
Association of Real Estate Taxpayers (ARET) of Illinois, 35, 106–7, 110–12, 121–22, 151
Audubon (NJ) Taxpayers' Association, 93

Barrows, Edward M., 49; on proliferation of taxpayers' groups, 2, 35–37, 42; views on taxpayers' groups, 36, 42, 150
Bell County (KY) Taxpayers' Association, 15, 123–24, 140–43, 188n78
Bergeron, Arthur, 97–99
Berlin (NH) Farmer-Labor Party, 14, 51, 81–82, 95–99, 152
Berlin (NH) Taxpayers' Association, 51, 81–82, 95, 97, 139, 152, 157, 187n63

Big government, 6, 13, 15, 50–52, 150, 153
Brown Company, 97, 99

California, taxpayers' groups/tax resistance in, 13–14, 17–18, 39, 54–55, 62–63, 65–66, 69, 71, 73–77, 114, 159
California Taxpayers' Association, 13–14, 159; constructive economy programs, 54, 62–63, 65–66, 69, 73–77; objectives, 39, 54, 73–74; Riley Stewart Amendment, 75–76
Chicago tax strike, 14, 106–7, 110–13, 117, 121–22, 151
Citizenship: and associationalism, 20–21; and Reconstruction-era taxpayers' leagues in the South, 28; and taxpayers' groups, 12–13, 15, 18–21, 28, 48–49, 99, 123–24, 153–57; and taxpayers' lawsuits, 133
Connecticut, taxpayers' groups/tax resistance in, 37, 42–43, 65, 71, 95, 147
Constructive economy, 9–11, 13–14, 52, 55–56; and activities of Depression-era taxpayers' groups, 61–80, 149–51, 159–61
Coos County (NH) Workers Club, 81, 95
Coughlin, Father Charles, 11, 87–89, 105
Critical legal studies (CLS), 7
CTA. *See* California Taxpayers' Association

Delaware, taxpayers' groups/tax resistance in, 64–65, 100, 103, 147

Elting, John, 71–74, 79–80, 92, 94–95, 147, 154

Farm Credit Administration, 45, 47
Farm Holiday Association, 45
Fitchburg (MA) Taxpayers Association, 38, 66–67
Florida, taxpayers' groups/tax resistance in, 103
Free enterprise, 50–51, 151, 162–63

Gaskill, Gordon, 91, 148, 158
Georgia, taxpayers' groups/tax resistance in. *See* Taxpayers' League of Atlanta and Fulton County
Gilded Age, taxpayers' groups during, 21–24
Good government ideology: role in organized tax resistance, 5, 10–11, 13–14, 52, 56, 61, 77–78; Progressive-era origins and objectives of, 56–61, 69, 77–78, 104, 161
Government Research Association, 35, 59, 64
Great Depression, and taxpayers' association movement, 31–32, 40, 43–48
Greater Brooklyn Property Owners Association, 113, 121–22
Gulick, Luther, 6, 117–18, 149, 153

Hamilton County (TN) Taxpayers' Association, 64–65, 114
Hichborn, Franklin, 74–76
Hoan, Daniel W., 31, 51, 155; attitudes toward taxpayers' associations, 3, 148; on HOLC, 46; "Mr. Taxpayer versus Mr. Taxspender" radio play, 6, 117, 153; on tax strikes, 117–18, 122
Home Owners' Loan Corporation (HOLC), 46–48, 120
Hoover, Herbert: administration's relationship to taxpayers' association movement, 4, 13, 43–44; on New Deal, 51

Illinois, taxpayers' groups/tax resistance in, 14, 35, 103, 106–7, 110–13, 121–22, 147, 151
Indiana, taxpayers' groups/tax resistance in, 62–67, 71, 90, 93, 95, 100–101, 103, 114, 147–48, 159
Indiana Taxpayers' Association, 62–63, 90
Instrumentalism, 8, 11–12, 122, 125, 134–35, 144–45, 157–58
Iowa, taxpayers' groups/tax resistance in, 103, 113, 159
Iowa Taxpayers Association, 159

Jersey City Taxpayers' Association, 93–94, 115–16

Jones, Howard P.: on proliferation of taxpayers' groups, 2–3, 41–42; views on taxpayers' groups, 149–50, 156

Kansas, taxpayers' groups/tax resistance in, 63, 72
Kentucky, taxpayers' groups/tax resistance in, 15, 34–35, 55, 64, 66, 68, 90–91, 123–24, 140–43
Kentucky Tax Reduction Association, 35, 64, 68
Kern County (CA) Taxpayers Association, 159

Labor movement, 11, 52, 107–9, 120–22
Lake County (IN) Taxpayers' Association, 64–65, 67
Localism, 4–5, 7–8, 15, 154–55, 166n23, 167n24
Long, Huey, 11, 87–89, 105
Louisiana, taxpayers' groups/tax resistance in, 62, 65, 72
Lowell (MA) Taxpayers' Association, 34, 37–38

Maryland, taxpayers' groups/tax resistance in, 23, 103, 136
Massachusetts, taxpayers' groups/tax resistance in, 34, 37–39, 63–66, 69–72, 91–92, 103, 147–48, 158
Massachusetts Federation of Taxpayers, 69, 72, 92
Michigan, taxpayers' groups/tax resistance in, 100–101, 147
Middlesex County (MA) Taxpayers' Association, 34, 37–39
Minnesota, taxpayers' groups/tax resistance in, 37, 63–64, 66, 69, 72, 90–91, 95, 100–101, 103, 150–51, 156
Minnesota Taxpayers' Association, 37, 69, 72, 90–91
Missouri, taxpayers' groups/tax resistance in, 137
Modern tax resistance, 15, 160–63
Montana, taxpayers' groups/tax resistance in, 62, 69
Montana Taxpayers' Association, 62, 69
"Mr. Taxpayer versus Mr. Taxspender" radio play. *See* Hoan, Daniel W.
Municipal Research Bureaus, 59–60, 71–72, 148–49
Munro, William B., 73; and taxation crisis, 32

National Municipal League, 2, 6, 35, 60, 149, 152, 189n27; and Citizens Councils for

Constructive Economy, 49, 79; and manager plan of government, 69; and National Pay Your Taxes Campaign, 119–20; on tax limits, 102–03
National Pay Your Taxes Campaign, 119–20, 150
National Recovery Administration, 81, 96, 98–99
Nebraska, taxpayers' groups/tax resistance in, 69, 100–101, 103, 137, 147–48
Nebraska Federation of County Taxpayers' Leagues, 148
Nevada, taxpayers' groups/tax resistance in, 101, 159
Newark (NJ) Taxpayers' Association, 93, 116
New Bedford (MA) Taxpayers' Association, 64, 66
New Deal: attitudes of tax resisters toward, 46–48; and localism, 7, 167n24; opposition to, 50–51, 161, 173n111; and populist insurgents, 88–89; relationship to taxpayers' association movement, 4–5, 13, 43–48, 122
New Hampshire, taxpayers' groups/tax resistance in, 51, 81–82, 95–99, 138–39, 152
New Hampshire Farmer-Labor Party, 98
New Haven (CT) Taxpayers' Association, 37, 65, 147
New Jersey, taxpayers' groups/tax resistance in, 22, 37, 39, 41, 48–49, 62–63, 65–66, 69–70, 90–91, 93–94, 103, 114–16, 151–52
New Jersey Taxpayers' Association, 37, 39, 63–65, 69–70, 90–91, 115
New Mexico, taxpayers' groups/tax resistance in, 37, 62–63, 65, 70, 100–101, 120
New Mexico Taxpayers' Association, 62, 64, 70
New York, taxpayers' groups/tax resistance in, 17–18, 22–23, 66, 71, 92, 103, 113, 121–22, 137, 147–48
North Bergen (NJ) Taxpayers' and Civic Association, 114–15

Ohio, taxpayers' groups/tax resistance in, 65, 72, 100–103
Oklahoma, taxpayers' groups/tax resistance in, 100–01
Oregon, taxpayers' groups/tax resistance in, 114

Pennsylvania, taxpayers' groups/tax resistance in, 18, 22, 72, 92, 110, 113–14
Pennsylvania Economy League, 72
Philadelphia (PA) Taxpayers' Association, 92
Pierce County (WA) Taxation Bureau, 64

Populism, 11, 14, 52, 81–82, 179n2; in 1930s, 83–84, 87–89, 104–5; concepts of, 82–83; in early Republic, 83–86; in Jacksonian era, 84, 86; in late nineteenth century, 84, 86–87; and tax resistance in Berlin, New Hampshire, 81, 95–99
Populist (or People's) Party, 84, 86–87
Porter, Sylvia F., 73, 91–92, 147–48, 158, 177n61
Public Works Administration (PWA), 47–48, 70–71, 172n92

Real estate taxation, 4, 35
Reconstruction: and organized taxpayer violence, 27–28; taxpayers' groups/tax resistance during, 12, 19, 24–28, 31
Reconstruction Finance Corporation, 44, 97, 112
"Redeemer" politics, 12, 19, 24–25, 27–28
Reed, Thomas H., 3; and constructive economy, 55, 156; and National Pay Your Taxes Campaign, 119; on proliferation of taxpayers' groups, 35; on taxation crisis, 33; views on taxpayers' groups, 149
Rhode Island, taxpayers' groups/tax resistance in, 65–66
Riley-Stewart amendment, 76
Roosevelt, Franklin D.: agriculture policy, 45, 47; housing policy, 45–48; relief programs, 46; tax policy, 44, 47

Seasongood, Murray: on proliferation of taxpayers' group, 36; on taxation crisis, 33; views on taxpayers' groups, 149
Share Our Wealth Clubs, 87–88
Smith, Wade S., 119–20, 148
Social Security Act (1935): and taxpayers' groups influence on, 44–45, 47
South Bend (IN) Taxpayers' League, 148
Stark County (OH) Tax League, 65, 101
Stearns County (MN) Taxpayers' Association, 91
Steed, Hal, 1–3, 35, 49, 52, 61, 79, 94, 113, 150

Tax limitation measures, 10, 14, 38, 80, 89, 99–103, 158; efficacy of, 103, 151; negative impacts of, 15, 101–3; and populist heritage, 105; taxpayers' suit to enforce, 66, 151
Taxpayers and Rentpayers Association of West New York, New Jersey, 94, 115
Taxpayers' Association of Central Iowa, 159
Taxpayers Association of Vigo County (IN), 159

Taxpayers' Forum of Pennsylvania, 72
Taxpayers' groups, post-1945, 159–61
Taxpayers' lawsuits, 10–12, 14–15, 122, 151, 157; in Baltimore, 136; in Bell County Kentucky, 15, 123–24, 140–43; in Berlin, New Hampshire, 81, 138–39; in Chicago tax strike, 111–12; and citizenship, 123–24, 133; conceptual basis for, 129–30; evaluation of, 125–27, 133–35, 143–44; evolution of, 125–35; in Houston, 135–36, 140; and instrumentalism, 134–35, 144–45; judicial limitations on, 130–31; legislative authorization for, 132; in Missouri, 137; in Nebraska, 137; in New York, 137; objectives of, 14–15, 52, 80, 124–25, 127, 130, 135, 140, 142; in Wyoming, 137–38
Taxpayers' League of Atlanta and Fulton County (GA), 1–2, 9, 35, 49, 52, 94, 113, 150–51
Taxpayers' League of Letcher County (KY), 34, 55, 64, 91
Taxpayers' League of St. Louis County (MN), 64, 66, 69, 151, 156
Taxpayers' Research Association of Fort Wayne (IN), 67, 71
Taxpayers' Research League of Delaware, 64–65, 147
Tax Policy League, 3, 42, 158
Tax strikes, 10–11, 14–15, 52, 80, 105, 106–22, 151; Chicago tax strike, 14, 106–7, 110–13, 117, 121–22, 151; contrasted with labor strikes, 120–21; evaluation of, 120–22; opposition to, 111–13, 116–21; rationales for, 116–17
Teaneck (NJ) Taxpayers' League, 39, 48–49, 90
Tea Party movement, 15, 161–63
Tennessee, taxpayers' groups/tax resistance in, 25–26, 37, 62–69, 71, 114, 130
Tennessee Taxpayers' Association, 37, 62, 64–69

Texas, taxpayers' groups/tax resistance in, 72, 103, 135–36, 140
Tharp, Claude: survey of taxpayers' groups, 37–39, 42, 61–63, 74, 79, 89, 147; on taxation crisis, 33
Thorpe, Merle, 34–35, 48, 50–51, 150
Townsend, Francis E., 11, 87–89
Traylor, Melvin A., 32–33, 112, 117

Upson, Lent D.: and good government reform, 56; on proliferation of taxpayers' groups, 36; on taxation crisis, 33
Utah, taxpayers' groups/tax resistance in, 62, 64, 103, 114, 159
Utah Taxpayers' Association, 64, 159

Virginia, taxpayers' groups/tax resistance in, 72, 95
Voluntarism, 107, 109, 122

Washington, taxpayers' groups/tax resistance in, 64, 73, 91–92, 100–01
Washington State Taxpayers' Association, 73, 91–92
Westchester County (NY) Taxpayers' Association, 148
Western Taxpayers' Associations, 42, 89
West Virginia, taxpayers' groups/tax resistance in, 71, 100–02, 150
West Virginia Taxpayers' Association, 150
Wisconsin, taxpayers' groups/tax resistance in, 18, 64–66, 113, 147, 156
Wisconsin Taxpayers' Alliance, 64–66, 156
Women: and Depression-era taxpayers' groups, 40–41, 43, 171n70; New Jersey Women's Taxpayer's Association, 41
Worcester (MA)Taxpayers' Association, 37, 70–71, 91, 147
Wyoming, taxpayers' groups/tax resistance in, 137–38

Linda Upham-Bornstein is Senior Teaching Lecturer in History at Plymouth State University.